the French Baker

the French Baker

JEAN MICHEL RAYNAUD

MURDOCH BOOKS

This book is dedicated to my beautiful family,
without whom there would be nothing.

Contents

From then to eternity

It took some perspective for me

to fully understand how I became involved in the food industry and how I developed my passion for baking and pâtisserie. Certainly, it wasn't until I had moved away from the country that I was brought up in that I began to realise how deeply food is entrenched in French culture and how it infuses every aspect of one's life.

Surprisingly, perhaps, my family was never overly enthusiastic about food, unlike some of my friends' families. As a child I don't recall my parents ever cooking elaborate dishes, they rarely drank wine except on occasions such as Christmas or perhaps a birthday, and we hardly ever ate bread with our food or drank *café au lait* — hardly the typical French family at all. Nowadays, however, the story is a little different — my mother has discovered her inner masterchef and my father can be often found in the kitchen slicing tomatoes or foraging in the garden for herbs. But when my sister and I were growing up, food was regarded almost as an afterthought, a necessity more than anything else. Even today my father likes to remind me that one of the biggest shocks of his life was when I told him I was leaving school to become a pastry chef. Although he has always been supportive of my decision, it was such an unexpected announcement that I don't think he has ever fully recovered!

Food in general, and baking in particular, brings people together — it's part of the glue that binds societies. Although sharing a meal or celebrating an occasion with family and friends is undoubtedly part of the fabric of every culture the world over, in France food is regarded as one of the main pillars of the *art de vivre* (the art of living), alongside music, fine arts or philosophy.

Gastronomy in France has imbued every aspect of society; it has been ritualised, romanticised, politicised and even institutionalised, having been listed by UNESCO as an Intangible Cultural Heritage of Humanity. It is seen not as a mere necessity or as an accompaniment for a special occasion, but as an integral part of how French people define themselves. In every French city and every village you will find not only a shop that specialises in fine pâtisseries and confectioneries, a bakery for your breads and *viennoiserie* but also most likely a chocolate shop, a specialised confectionery boutique, a *traiteur* (delicatessen), a fruit and vegetable market, a cheese shop … the list goes on.

For as long as I can remember, I have always liked sweet things, not so much for their taste but for what they represented. Desserts and sweet food were, and still are, intimately linked with nearly every happy occasion in my life: a candle-lit cake for a birthday surrounded by all my friends and family; a *brioche des rois* studded with dried fruit for Christmas; or simply waking up on a Saturday morning with the smell of croissants baking in the oven and the sound of an old Jimi Hendrix record playing, and dragging myself to the terrace for breakfast with my mother, dad and sister.

The sheer smell of some cakes and desserts also takes me back to my kitchen at home, standing up on a wooden stool while I helped my mother make a pound cake and then, of course, the inevitable fight with my sister as to who was going to lick the bowl clean; or of sitting in my grandmother's kitchen, listening to her stories while she fried her delicious *bugnes*. These are just a few of the many hundreds of seemingly inconsequential moments that make up a childhood, lying dormant in the deepest confines of one's memory, ready to be unearthed in an instant by even the simplest taste or smell.

I remember clearly when I first began to understand the incredible emotive power of food. Every year my mother took my sister and me to the best pâtisserie in Marseille, to celebrate St Michel's day, our patron saint. On this day only, we were allowed to eat as many cakes and pastries, chocolates and ice creams as we wanted. This yearly treat was such an exciting time for me and, looking back on it now, I can see that this was actually where my baking journey began. One year, as we were sitting at a small table drinking out of fancy little tea cups, surrounded by dazzling displays of colourful cakes and biscuits, and knowing that I could literally eat the whole shop if I wanted to, I was prompted to ask my mother if I could spend my days off school doing some work experience in the kitchen. My mother talked to the chef and, amazingly, they both agreed, a decision that seemed so inconsequential at the time but was to change my life forever.

By 4 am the following Wednesday I was sitting nervously on the edge of my bed, showered and dressed, my head spinning with a mixture of fear and excitement. I will never forget that day. It was a bitterly cold morning as my mother and I stepped inside the shop and walked down the narrow, dusty wooden stairs. I remember the warm, sweet smell that wafted up to greet us, then stepping into a kitchen filled with gigantic blocks of butter and ridiculously large bags of flours, the tables covered with trays of shiny, translucent candied fruits and jars of golden honey. It was a total sensory overload — a sensation that is so deeply ingrained in my memory that even today I get nervous every time I walk into a new kitchen.

What I recall most about those mornings were all those burly chefs hard at work, lifting heavy sacks of flour and carrying back-breaking loads of butter, then moving seamlessly into subtle and precise movements, as they piped delicate ornaments on cakes or carefully cut croissants with their enormous knives. I soon realised how much work was needed, day in, day out, to produce these incredibly intricate and technical products, eaten without so much as a thought about the effort it took to make them. All those baguettes that I ate every day, the brioches, lemon tarts … so much effort for seemingly so little recognition or financial reward.

What I began to understand, over time, was that the real reward of working so hard to make something so complex look so simple, highlights the fact that baking and cooking fulfil those basic needs we all have — the need to create, contribute, share and love. For me, this encapsulates the essence of baking: using your own hands to make something out of simple, honest ingredients, something prepared not for sustenance or financial gain, but purely for the purpose of bringing warmth and happiness, however small, to another person's life.

The recipes that I have chosen to include in this book hold a lot of meaning for me. Some are more traditional than others, some are simple and others a bit more intricate, but all of them are achievable in your own kitchen. Being a good baker sometimes requires a basic understanding of chemistry, so I have tried to provide you with all the technical information you might need as well, not only to help you to make these recipes but also to give you the confidence to experiment and create and to motivate you to further your journey into the amazing and rewarding world of baking. I truly hope that this book will inspire you to give baking a chance. Everyone relates to food based on their own experiences but, for me, of all the tastes only sweet crosses the cultural, gender or generational gap by reaching directly into our deepest childhood memories, so that even the simplest of cakes or desserts made using the smallest amount of skill will always be received as the grandest of gestures.

Jean Michel Raynaud

Essential ingredients

Essential ingredients

Baking is as much about science as it is creativity. As such, this book is designed to equip you with strong baking foundations upon which you should feel free to add your own creative or personal stamp — this is, after all, how most traditional recipes came about to begin with. I've tried not to confuse you with too many technical terms or guidelines, as this book isn't meant to turn you into a professional pâtissier but rather to give you the basic tools to successfully bake delicious cakes and pastries at home.

The following two sections cover most of the essential ingredients and tools you'll need as a baker, but it certainly doesn't end here. There are limitless resources at your fingertips and I'd encourage you to read further, especially on subjects such as baking bread and working with chocolate, to further hone your cooking skills. As an apprentice I was told that you can get 80 per cent of the quality with 20 per cent of the skills, but you will need the other 80 per cent of the skills to achieve the remaining 20 per cent of the quality!

Flour

While most grains can be ground into a type of flour, in this book plain (all-purpose) flour always refers to wheat flour.

Flour is mostly graded following three criteria: the amount of mineral or ash (which is made mostly of bran), the protein (gluten) content and the humidity level, all of which vary according to the type of wheat and how it is processed. Systems for grading flour vary wildly across the globe, ranging from the different numerical classifications employed in France, Italy and Germany, which relates to the amount of bran in the flour (see below), to those used in the United Kingdom, America and Australia, where flour tends to be graded using words to describe the amount of protein (gluten) or the best application for the flour ('bread flour' or 'cake flour', for example).

Bran content: This is often classified using numbers, with larger numbers indicating a higher bran content:
'00' flour in Italy and T45 in France;
'0' flour in Italy and T55 in France;
'1' flour in Italy and T65 and above in France.

Which flour should I use?

Most of the recipes in this book will work well with a generic type of plain (all-purpose) flour, however I do recommend you try to find a flour suited for making bread. For best results, a good rule of thumb to follow when choosing which flour to use is as follows:

～ For all cake batters and short doughs, it's preferable to use a very refined, low-bran, low-protein plain (all-purpose) flour. While you need some gluten for 'short' mixes such as shortbread and sponges to provide structure, too much gluten will have a detrimental effect on their texture by making them tougher and less palatable. This flour is sold under many labels: pastry or cake flour, or soft flour.

～ For all yeasted pastry and breads, use a plain (all-purpose) flour, preferably with a high gluten content. Gluten is a critical ingredient in the manufacture of yeasted pastry and breads as it gives the dough its strength and elasticity (*corps*), which traps the air and carbon dioxide (CO_2) created by the yeasts during the proving process. This is typically sold as strong, baker's or bread flour.

～ For sourdough bread, I recommend using a less-refined, preferably organic plain (all-purpose) flour with a high gluten content. A higher bran content is important when baking sourdough because the higher mineral content helps the natural yeast to develop faster, improving both the texture and taste of the bread. This type of flour is best sourced from health food stores or, even better, from artisanal bakeries, who will usually be happy to sell you a small quantity of flour. This flour is also sold as hard or strong flour, baker's or bread flour.

Maize cornflour

Maize cornflour (cornstarch), also known as maizena, maize flour and maize starch, is made by grinding corn kernels and then separating the flour from its proteins and all other components. It is a very fine, tasteless powder and does not contain gluten. It is used to thicken sauces and as a replacement for some of the plain flour in shortbread dough, to reduce the gluten content, thus keeping the dough crumbly and short. You can find maize cornflour in major supermarkets, health food stores or specialist food stores.

Wheaten cornflour To confuse the issue, some brands of cornflour (cornstarch) sold in supermarkets in Australia are actually made from wheat, not corn (check the label carefully). Personally, I see no reason why you should use this type and I always recommend that you use true maize cornflour made from maize (corn). While wheaten cornflour looks very similar to maize cornflour, there are two distinct differences:

～ Firstly, as wheaten cornflour is ground from wheat and contains gluten, it will add a certain amount of elasticity to your sauces and custards. It can't be used as a flour substitute in shortcrust doughs.

～ Secondly, as a thickener, wheat starch absorbs less water than cornflour, so you will need to adjust the recipe by adding a little less liquid or a little more wheat starch.

Yeast

Yeast is a natural living organism that metabolises starch sugars into carbon dioxide gas and ethanol during the proving stages of dough-making. The dough rises thanks to the proliferation of carbon dioxide bubbles, which are trapped in the dough by the gluten, and is the underlying reason behind using flour with a high protein (gluten) content for baking breads and leavened pastries.

Fresh yeast

Fresh compressed yeast is packaged as a block of soft, moist living yeast cells. It is the preferred ingredient used by professional bakers for its leavening capacity, but has a short life-span, making it rather wasteful for the home baker. As a rule of thumb, to convert fresh yeast to instant dry yeast, use half the amount. For example, 14 g (½ oz) fresh yeast equals 7 g (¼ oz) instant dry yeast.

Instant dried yeast

This processed yeast is originally made from the same living culture as fresh yeast, but has been dried and transformed into small granules that can be added directly to your dough, very much as you would fresh yeast. It has a much longer life-span than fresh yeast, so is perfect for the home baker. All the recipes in this book use instant dried yeast for this reason.

Bicarbonate of soda and baking powder

These leavening (rising) agents release gases much faster than conventional yeasts and do not rely as much as yeasts do on the elasticity of the mixes created by the protein in the flour. Consequently, they are really useful when baking goods such as sponges, pound cakes or even certain types of shortbreads when the taste of fresh yeast is undesirable and the gluten content is low.

Bicarbonate of soda

Bicarbonate of soda (baking soda) is a potent leavening agent that creates rapid carbon dioxide bubbles when exposed to an acid, such as chocolate, brown sugar or lemon. A word of advice: this should be used in very small quantities and always measure it carefully. Too much will give a soapy taste to your products.

Baking powder

This is primarily bicarbonate of soda (baking soda) that has already been mixed with an acid, usually cream of tartar and cut with cornflour (cornstarch). It can be added to wet mixes that have little or no other acids and still produce carbon dioxide. Due to the fact that the active ingredient (bicarbonate of soda) has been diluted, the ratio of baking powder used in baking is always higher than bicarbonate of soda.

Sugar

Both sugar beet and sugar cane produce identical complex sugars (sucrose), composed of two simple sugars: dextrose, commonly called glucose; and fructose, the main ingredient in invert sugar (trimoline). Both these ingredients are used in professional baking. Technically speaking, they are hygroscopic (they absorb moisture from the air), which helps slow down the crystallisation of sugars in creams and caramels and prolongs the softness of sponges and cakes. The types of sugar most commonly used in this book include:

Caster sugar

Refined from both sugar cane and sugar beet, caster (superfine) sugar is highly processed pure sucrose and comes in the form of fine, clear crystals that dissolve easily in liquid. This makes it preferable to coarser regular white sugar for baking, especially when making meringue.

Raw sugar

Raw (demerara) sugar is a less refined form of sugar extracted from sugar cane. It is minimally processed and still contains some of its molasses (around 3.5 per cent), which gives it a more complex flavour and a light brown colour. As the crystals are relatively large, raw sugar doesn't dissolve as readily as caster (superfine) sugar, so it is used mainly to add depth of flavour and a little extra texture to biscuits and crumbles.

Brown sugar

Brown sugar is much less refined than both caster (superfine) sugar and raw (demerara) sugar. The heavy texture and brown colour is due to its very high molasses content (around 10 per cent). I'm not a big fan of this type of sugar because its strong flavour tends to easily overshadow other flavours.

Pure icing sugar

Pure icing (confectioners') sugar is a very fine white powdered sugar made of 100 per cent sucrose; it is simply the result of finely crushing caster (superfine) sugar. Most often, you will come across icing (confectioners') sugar mixture, which is essentially the same product but has a small amount of starch added to prevent the sugar from absorbing humidity from the air and forming hard lumps. I prefer to use pure icing sugar over the mixture and just pass it through a fine mesh sieve to remove any lumps. You can also whizz it up in a food processor before using it.

Pearl sugar

Pearl sugar (also called hail sugar or nibbed sugar) is often used to decorate and to add crunch and sweetness to biscuits and pastries, such as *chouquettes*. This highly refined form of sugar is compacted and then crushed into small balls, which can withstand high heat without melting.

Salt

A pinch of salt goes a long way in cooking and is critical for developing flavour, balance and stability. Baking is no exception. There is a multitude of different salts on the market these days, ranging in colour from pink to grey, and in price from the cheapest table salt to high-end 'gourmet' salts. So what salt should you use and when?

Sea salt or rock salt?

Let's put this to rest once and for all. Salt is a mineral called sodium chloride. Irrespective of whether it has been harvested directly from the sea or dissolved from rock sediments created over hundreds of millions of years ago, sodium chloride remains sodium chloride. In both cases, it would have come from the sea at one time or another. There is, however, a very distinct difference in how the salt is processed, resulting in several types of salt crystals, each used for different purposes.

Cooking salts

Fine salt

Fine salt (table salt) is made of very small, cubic crystals created by rapid vacuum evaporation of the brine from rock salt or sea water. Unlike salt flakes, these crystals of salt are tightly packed together and are hard to melt and cannot be used as textural elements, as this type of salt always tastes too 'salty'. Fine table salt, however, is perfect for use in doughs, creams, sauces and stocks, or to dry meat and pickle vegetables.

Finishing salts

Salt flakes

Salt flakes are created by gentle evaporation of the brine. Unlike fine table salt, they are made of larger pyramid-like flakes that melt easily, so are ideal as a condiment, or sprinkled on caramels, chocolate or candied fruits. Due to the larger size of their crystals and their ability to dissolve quickly in the mouth, salt flakes provide a less salty taste than fine salt.

Fleur de sel

Originating from Guérande, on the west coast of France, this is considered the Rolls Royce of salts. This type of salt is made of large crystals and is ideal for adding both texture and a subtle hint of saltiness to your caramels or fruit. The salt crystals only form under specific climatic conditions and are harvested by hand, making it a labour-intensive, finite resource and, as such, is quite expensive.

Butter

One of the fundamental ingredients in French cookery, butter is especially important in pâtisserie and baking. Like many things, not all butter is created equal and varies significantly in both quality and taste, and therefore price. Here are a few important things to consider when buying butter for baking.

Salt or no salt?

Historically, salt was added to butter as a preservative before the advent of refrigeration. Today it is mainly used in savoury cooking, for the manufacture of acidic creams such as a hollandaise or *beurre blanc*, or to spread on toast to add another layer of taste. In baking, however, a lot of recipes do not require salt, so it is far better to add salt to recipes that need seasoning rather than using salted butter.

How much fat is too much fat?

Believe it or not, there is such a thing in French baking as too much of a good thing! Today butters from around the world contain between 80 and 85 per cent fat. Typically, European butter contains a slightly higher fat content (hence less water) and is better suited for use in flaky pastries such as croissant and puff. Butter with a lower fat content (and therefore higher water content), such as those found in New Zealand, Australia and America, emulsify better so are more suitable than European butters when making emulsified bases such as curds, ganaches and creamed cake batters.

Cultured or not cultured?

Cultured butter was traditionally made from fermented raw cream, but today it is usually made by adding a culture and lactic acid to the pasteurised cream before the churning process, then letting the butter age in storage. This process provides an added depth of flavour compared to regular butter and has a more yeasty or 'buttery' flavour. It's ideal for balancing the tartness or bitterness of creams such as salted caramel, lemon curds, or ganaches made with a high cocoa content. For any other creams, especially those made with subtle flavours or sweeter chocolate such as milk or white chocolate, I recommend you use a standard, off-the-shelf unsalted butter.

Cream

Buttermilk fat is less dense than buttermilk, so it rises to the top of the milk and forms a thick layer, which is skimmed off before the milk is homogenised. The different types of cream refer to the amount of butterfat they contain and, as a general guide, they are broken into three groups.

Types of cream

Light cream

Also known as single cream or pouring cream, this contains 18–25 per cent fat. Personally, I never use this cream. It is too thin to use on fruit or for pouring directly on a tart or dessert, and does not contain enough fat to contribute to the texture and feel of any baked goods.

Whipping cream

This cream contains 35 per cent fat. It is the most common cream used in baking, and is the only cream I ever use in cooking. It has the perfect ratio of fat to liquid and adds a wonderful creaminess to your ganache, curds or cake batters. It is the only cream you can use to whip into a smooth and fluffy crème Chantilly. Confusingly, some 35 per cent fat creams contain gelatine and are labelled 'thickened cream', so make sure you check the label.

Thick cream

Also known as double cream, heavy or thick dollop, this type contains 48 per cent fat and over. While some bakers occasionally use this cream, I only ever use it as a serving accompaniment. I often add a small amount of alcohol to mitigate its richness; for example, a small amount of Calvados mixed with a generous dollop of thick cream, to serve on a warm tarte tatin.

However, this system of categorising creams is often confusing for the cook because the fat content varies from country to country and even from brand to brand. The best way to choose the right cream for your needs is to go by the fat content on the label and not by the type of cream listed on the label.

Eggs

I always choose free-range eggs over caged eggs for obvious reasons, but surprisingly enough, when it comes to baking, there are no noticeable differences between the two. The type of egg you choose is entirely up to you, and will be a decision based more on economical and ethical reasons than anything else.

While eggs come in a variety of sizes, ranging from medium (40–50 g/$1^{1}/2$–$1^{3}/4$ oz), large (50–60 g/$1^{3}/4$–$2^{1}/4$ oz) to extra-large (60–70 g/$2^{1}/4$–$2^{1}/2$ oz), with some weighing almost 80 g ($2^{3}/4$ oz), all the eggs used in this book are 55 g (2 oz), which is a baking industry standard size.

Here are a few useful tips:

~ When baking with small quantities of eggs, break the eggs into a bowl and whisk them lightly with a fork so that you end up with an even distribution of egg yolk and white.

~ When making meringue, always make sure your bowl is spotlessly clean before adding the whites — use a piece of paper towel moistened with a little vinegar to wipe the bowl clean — and make sure your whites do not contain any traces of egg yolk. Egg yolk contains about 60 per cent fat and will prevent your egg whites from whisking to their fullest potential.

~ Use eggs at room temperature. This is very important when making meringue because cold egg whites are less elastic, and so are less able to retain air. In recipes using whole eggs, the warmth of the air temperature softens the fat in the yolk and makes it easier to emulsify with other liquids.

~ Sometimes a recipe will call for an exact weight of egg whites rather than a number, so you will need to separate the eggs into a bowl and weigh them. As a guide, a 55 g (2 oz) egg can be broken down into three parts: 30 g (1 oz) for the white, 20 g ($3/4$ oz) for the yolk and 5 g ($^{1}/8$ oz) for the shell.

Egg wash

Used to add colour and shine to pastries and breads, most egg washes are simply made of lightly whisked eggs and a pinch of salt. Sometimes a dash of milk, cream or water is added to thin the egg wash. There are a few key factors that will determine how fast and deep the colour develops.

The ratio of albumen (egg white) to egg yolk: While both the egg white and yolk contain proteins that brown during baking, it is the fat in the yolk that contributes most to a shinier and darker finish.

The sugar content of the batter or dough: There are two browning reactions that happen during baking: caramelisation (browning of the sugar, or sucrose, in the batter) and the Maillard reaction (the browning of the proteins and carbohydrates). Put simply, the more sugar in your pastry, the more it is going to colour during baking.

Oven temperature: If your oven is too hot, the top will brown before the dough inside is cooked, so colouration is not always a reliable sign that your pastries and breads are done.

Here are a few tips to help you decide what type of egg wash to use:

~ When baking pastries or breads that have a high sugar content, such as shortbread and brioche, make an egg wash using whole eggs and a pinch of salt. This prevents the top from browning too quickly and too much before the dough is cooked through.

~ When baking doughs that have a low sugar content, such as puff pastry or *pâte brisée*, add more yolks to the egg wash to achieve good colour in the time it takes the pastry to cook.

Chocolate

Most of the chocolate we eat today comes from three types of cocoa bean (or cacao bean) — Forastero, Criollo and Trinitario — which all vary immensely in richness, flavour and taste, as well as yield and availability. Forastero is the most widely available; it has a blander flavour and a cheaper price. Criollo has a very strong taste and is the rarest and therefore the most expensive cocoa bean. Trinitario, a hybrid crop, has a more refined flavour and is preferred by smaller, more specialised chocolate manufacturers.

The chocolate manufacturing processes

Before ending up as the product we love so much, cocoa beans must undertake a lengthy series of processes, all critical to the finished flavour and texture of the chocolate.

Fermentation: The fruits are harvested, then split to remove the beans and pulp, which are then left to ferment naturally over several days. This process is critical for the bean to develop its key flavours and nuances and reduces its inherent bitterness.

Drying and roasting: The fermented beans and pulp are then separated and the beans are dried to prevent mould growth. The beans are roasted to refine the flavours and further reduce the acidity.

Grinding and conching: Once the beans have been roasted, the nibs are separated from the husks, ground and liquefied into a thick paste called cocoa mass or liquor. This paste is then further refined into two components: cocoa butter (the flavour carrier) and cocoa solids (the flavour). At this stage, cocoa butter, cocoa solids, sugar and a small amount soy lecithin are mixed in various ratios, depending on the manufacturer's preference, to manufacture dark chocolate. Milk solids are added to make milk chocolate. These ingredients are then put through a process called conching, where they are ground together, sometimes over days, to further refine the texture and flavour of the final product.

Tempering: This process involves heating and then cooling the chocolate, to avoid the formation of large, irregular fat crystals, typically exemplified by a white, mould-like coating and grainy texture.

Types of chocolate

Dark chocolate

Most chocolate sold today has a percentage reference clearly printed on the packaging, typically ranging from 55–80 per cent. This percentage refers to the amount of cocoa (or cocoa mass) the chocolate contains. For example, a 60 per cent chocolate will be made of 60 per cent cocoa mass with the remaining 40 per cent representing the sugar content and a small amount of emulsifying soy lecithin. Consequently, the flavour of the chocolate will become increasingly pronounced with the increase in percentage (and the consequent reduction in sweetness).

Milk chocolate

This is made by adding milk solids (milk powder) to a conventional dark chocolate. They come in a variety of percentages, some sweeter than others. I always recommend using a high percentage cocoa content, around 40–45 per cent, which, by definition, contains less sugar and consequently retains more of the original cocoa characteristics.

White chocolate

The elephant in the room, white chocolate does not contain any cocoa solids. It is a concoction of milk solids (milk powder), cocoa butter and sugar. It should be used sparingly as it tends to be overly sweet (it contains up to 60 per cent sugar) and can quickly overpower other subtle flavours.

Cocoa powder

This is made by extracting cocoa butter from the cocoa mass by hydraulic pressing. It is then pulverised into a powder. In its pure form, cocoa powder is unsweetened and bitter and this is the cocoa I use in all my recipes. Dutch cocoa is unsweetened cocoa that has been treated to neutralise its inherent acidity. However, because you sometimes need the acid in the cocoa to help activate bicarbonate of soda and give a lift to cakes and biscuits, I prefer to use regular cocoa powder. Sweetened cocoa powder is typically used for hot chocolate and is too sweet to cook with.

Which chocolate should I choose?

As a cook, it's easy to fall into the trap of buying high percentage chocolate because it is perceived as being better — but it's all about balance. The type of chocolate you use will have a critical impact on how your creams emulsify and set. Using a chocolate with a higher cocoa percentage than recommended in the recipe will harden your creams too much and most likely destabilise (split) the emulsion due to the increase in cocoa fat. Conversely, using a chocolate with a lower ratio of cocoa than recommended will give you a softer finished product.

The amount of sugar the chocolate contains is another key consideration, as it's important to find the right balance of sweetness and flavour. For example, if you're cooking with chocolate that contains a high percentage cocoa (and thus low in sugar), you will need to neutralise the inherent bitterness with a touch of chilli, strong spices, salt or pepper. A sweet chocolate, on the other hand, will benefit from the addition of a tart or acidic taste such as lime, pineapple or Greek yoghurt.

Tools of the trade

Tools of the trade

People have been baking for thousands of years with little more than a pot, a cutting device and some fire. While it's tempting to buy lots of beautiful bits and pieces, many of these end up in the bottom of a drawer gathering dust, or break easily and end up in the bin. Rather than buying lots of equipment, I think it's much better to invest in a few basic good-quality pieces. To achieve good results you don't necessarily need all the bells and whistles, and you can always improvise — a simple bottle makes a perfect rolling pin and a pair of hands can knead bread dough to perfection.

Ovens

There are several different types of ovens available, but I will focus on the ones you are likely to use in a domestic kitchen.

Convection (fan-forced) ovens

This is the most common domestic oven and all the recipes in this book use this type. Convection ovens work by rotating the ambient heat generated by the heating element, ensuring a better heat distribution. It also increases the overall oven temperature in the oven compared to a static (non-fan-forced) oven.

Static ovens

These ovens use radiant heat via elements situated inside the cooking chamber and rely upon natural convection to distribute the heat. As such, they are more likely to have an irregular cooking pattern and are prone to hot spots (see tips, below). When using a static oven, increase the recommended temperature for the recipes in this book by 10°C (18°F).

Refractory ovens

Most often powered by wood-fire or electricity, these ovens work by ambient heat, where the heating element warms a thick layer of bricks or baking stones situated on the bottom of the oven. The heat is then refracted from the top by another layer of bricks or stone. Personally, I think this is the only type of oven suitable for baking sourdough breads and because most home cooks don't have access to this type of oven, I did not include any recipes for sourdough bread in this book. If, however, you're lucky enough to have a backyard wood-fired oven, all of the bread recipes in this book will cook perfectly in it.

Important tips :

Cool it: Keep in mind that the oven in your kitchen is a fraction of the size we use in commercial baking and, as such, the heating element will be closer to your goods. While I have tried to adjust the recommended cooking temperatures to accommodate this, your oven will almost always be hotter than what the dial indicates. To be safe, begin baking at 10°C (18°F) less than recommended; you will have fewer problems cooking with a slightly cooler oven than a hotter one.

Never cook with radiant heat … insulate: We have all experienced this before: when you sit in front of a radiant heater you soon start to fry, but take one step away and you freeze — such is the wonder of radiant heat! Likewise, if the heating element inside your oven is visible, you will need to insulate it to disperse the heat. To do this, place a baking tray between the element and your goods during baking. This will help dissipate the radiant heat, making it more regular and 'softer'.

Hot spots: Most ovens, from the domestic kitchen to the largest factory oven, will have hot spots. These are areas where the heat is more prominent than others. In order to work out where that is and fix it, heat your oven to its maximum temperature, sprinkle an even layer of flour over your baking tray, then place the tray in the middle of the oven. Close the door and wait for the flour to brown — watching very carefully to make sure that it doesn't catch alight. If you notice that some areas are darker than others, simply cut a 20 cm (8 in) square of foil, fold it into quarters, then place it on your insulating tray (the one between the heating element and your baked goods) on the spot where the flour browned the most.

You will find that unless you bake in a refractory oven, the bottom of your pastries are almost always going to be cooked less than they are on the top, so I recommend using the thinnest baking tray you can find.

Thermometers

I recommended a digital probe thermometer scaled to 200°C (400°F), as it allows you to get an instant, easy and accurate reading. This is especially useful when doing sugar work and tempering chocolate, and also for checking the internal temperature of cakes, creams, meat and fish. Traditional lead thermometers are fine, although they are infinitely more fragile and can be difficult to read.

Kitchen scales

'What is heavier, a kilo of lead or a kilo of feathers?'

The most critical piece of equipment for a baker or pastry chef is an accurate digital scale. Unlike other areas of cooking, where you can add a splash of this and a handful of that and end up with something delicious, the success of baking relies entirely on following the recipe carefully and precisely measuring each ingredient.

For decades, professionals have avoided the volumetric system (cups) to measure ingredients, not only for the sake of accuracy, but mainly to simplify production. Each ingredient has its own specific density. For instance, a cup of water doesn't weigh the same as a cup of oil, and similarly flour is lighter than sugar, but a kilogram of anything will always weigh a kilogram, irrespective of how much volume there is. As such, what matters is the weight of ingredients in your recipe, never the volume.

I recommend a good digital scale that weighs to the single gram as opposed to those that weigh in 5 g ($^1/_8$ oz) increments. This will make all the difference when it comes to measuring out small quantities of ingredients such as yeast, baking powder and salt. You don't have to spend a small fortune either, as most digital scales are quite affordable.

A golden rule to follow :

I recommend that you have all your ingredients ready and weighed before you start baking. This is important for two reasons. Firstly, some ingredients react with another; for instance, if you pour sugar on egg yolks without stirring immediately, the sugar will absorb water from the yolk and create a protein lump (this is called 'burning the eggs'). Secondly, if your ingredients are not weighed before you begin, you might find yourself burning a toffee while weighing out your cream, or overwhipping your egg whites while measuring your sugar when making meringue.

Electric mixers

While it will be one of the most expensive pieces of equipment in your kitchen, a good stand mixer with a strong motor will last you a lifetime and will save you a lot of time and effort. When choosing a mixer, stick to the basics: all you need are the three attachments (whisk, paddle and hook) and variable speed buttons. If you don't have a dough hook or you think the motor isn't quite up to the challenge of working a bread dough, knead the dough by hand, the old-fashioned way.

Food processors

Food processors are not exactly essential for baking, but will certainly make your life a lot easier. They're great for emulsifying creams and custards, crushing nuts, slicing fruits and vegetables or even mixing small amounts of dough, such as shortbread. My personal recommendation is to look for a processor with double blades. They're a lot more efficient, provide a more consistent finish and generate a lot less friction and therefore heat, which is especially important when crushing nuts, as too much heat will turn them into a paste.

Immersion or stick blenders

An immersion or stick blender is an important tool in a bakers' arsenal. It does a great job of emulsifying the fat and liquid in creams and sauces, from chocolate ganache to *beurre blanc* or mayonnaise. Unlike a whisk, which introduces air into the mixture, an immersion blender binds the fat and the liquid together (making an emulsion), thus improving the texture and reducing the fatty sensation on the palate.

Knives and spatulas

Chefs are notoriously protective of their knives and spatulas, not just because they're so costly but also because they're almost like an extension of our hands. The more we become used to their weight or shape, the more precise and fast we become when using them, and the less likely we are to cut ourselves. While this applies to a lesser extent to amateur bakers, I would always advise you to invest in quality tools (or put it on your Christmas wish list), as they will last longer and perform better over many years than poorer quality tools. My suggestion for buying knives, spatulas and, indeed, any kitchen tool is to go to a good kitchenware shop, touch and hold them in your hands until you find one that feels comfortable.

Ideally, you should have three types of knives and one spatula:

Chef's knife

This knife is used for everything, from cutting croissants to cutting zest into julienne, and comes in a wide range of sizes. While entirely subjective, I think excessively long or heavy knives are difficult to handle and not very useful in baking. I recommend a heavy-handled knife with a 25 cm (10 in) blade. Paradoxically, the bigger the knife, the less likely you are to injure yourself.

Paring knife

This knife is used for more precise tasks, such as coring or peeling fruit and vegetables. It is a multi-purpose knife, very similar to a chef's knife but with a smaller blade of around 10 cm (4 in).

Serrated knife

Also known as a bread knife, the blade is typically 15–20 cm (6–8 in) in length, very sharp and designed to cut through soft breads and brioches.

Steel spatula

These are used to fill or decorate cakes. Choosing the length of spatula, its weight and flexibility is entirely a matter of personal preference.

Piping bags and nozzles

A piping bag is one of my favourite tools in the kitchen. I use it for simple tasks such as piping and filling choux puffs, to very tricky decorating and writing techniques. For the recipes in this book, you will only require one small (4 mm/^{1}/8 in) plain nozzle and one large (1 cm/^{1}/2 in) nozzle and a small piping bag. They are cheap and readily available online or from a cake decorating store.

Tins and rings

You don't need one of every shape and size on the planet. If you don't have exactly the right tin, use the closest size you have — generally 1 cm (^{1}/2 in) larger or smaller won't make much difference.

A few basic tins that you will need are a 20 cm (8 in) and 25 cm (10 in) round cake tins, a 25 cm (10 in) tart tin with removable base (or tart ring) and a 25 cm (10 in) loaf (bar) tin. As long as the volume of the tin is roughly the same as what the recipe calls for, you can also use square or rectangular cake tins instead of round tins. Tart rings (also called ring moulds) are often used by pâtissiers for aesthetic reasons but are interchangeable with fluted tart tins with removable bases. If you are using a tart ring, place the ring on a piece of baking paper, line with the pastry, then slide a thin baking tray underneath.

Silicone mats

While completely interchangeable with baking paper, silicone mats are a worthwhile, if not necessary, investment because they're reusable and virtually indestructible. When buying a mat, make sure it matches the size of your baking trays, as they can't be trimmed to fit.

Biscuits secs

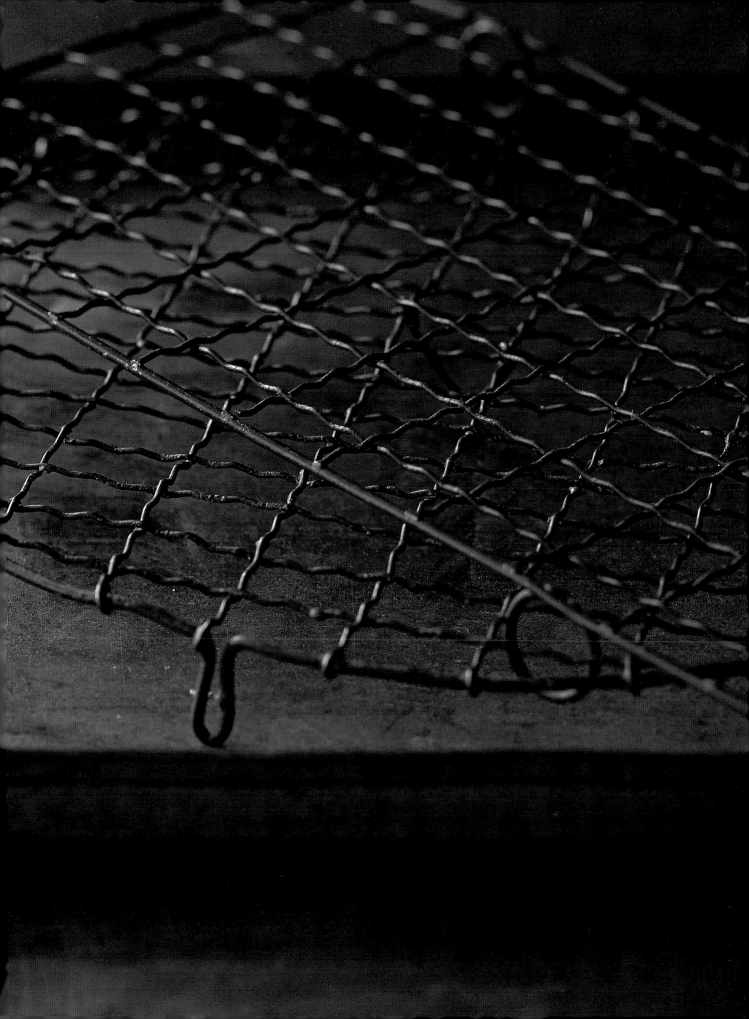

'Poetry is the synthesis of hyacinths and biscuits.'

CARL SANDBURG

Biscuits secs

(Biscuits)

I don't know why we love biscuits as much as we do. Maybe it's the fact that most cultures have been baking biscuits in one form or another for hundreds of years, ingraining them into our collective consciousness. Or maybe it's their size — things just look better and cuter when they are small. In any case, everyone has most likely gazed longingly at the huge assortment of colourful and delicious-looking biscuits that adorn the shelves of their local bakery and, almost certainly, each of us is guilty of shaking the biscuit tin at home, hoping to find the last remaining biscuit, only to end up scavenging a few crumbs.

I decided to feature biscuits as the first chapter in this book because they are amazingly simple to make and are therefore ideal to hone your baking skills, or to introduce your kids to the joys of baking. The great thing about baking biscuits is that once you understand the basics of making a simple dough, you can substitute ingredients based on your own preferences, or have fun experimenting with flavours by adding a hint of spice or some nuts or dried fruits if you like. Who knows, you may just stumble upon the next classic biscuit recipe!

Tuiles aux amandes (Almond tuiles) ~ page 34 with *Tuiles dentelle à l'orange et à la cannelle (Orange and cinnamon lace tuiles)* ~ page 35

I wanted to include this typically Provençal biscuit in this book because, for me, it lies at the core of what I love most about baking — its ability to unlock memories long thought forgotten. It amazes me how the simple act of biting into a small, seemingly inconsequential biscuit can transport me, but for a brief moment, straight back to my childhood, to a warm and happy place.

Many years ago when I was young and living in Marseille, I had a friend Thierry whose mother was an excellent baker, particularly famed for her *croquants aux amandes*. Every time we visited, we raided the kitchen cupboard in a desperate search for the biscuit tin. Her *croquants* were fragrant but not overbearing, crunchy (which, by the way, is the direct translation of *croquant*) yet soft, and there never seemed to be enough of them. For many years I begged Thierry to ask her for the recipe, but she would never part with it. Then, on my last day in France, as we were all waiting in the airport lounge before my trip to Australia, Thierry slipped something into my pocket. It was a sealed envelope, stamped 'State Secret'. I smiled gratefully at him and got on the plane.

Croquants aux amandes

(Almond biscotti)

Makes about 50

250 g (9 oz) plain (all-purpose) flour
250 g (9 oz) caster (superfine) sugar
250 g (9 oz) almond meal
3 eggs, lightly beaten, plus 1 extra, to glaze
2 teaspoons natural vanilla extract
2 teaspoons orange blossom water
200 g (7 oz) raw almonds, roasted
100 g (3 1/2 oz) pistachios

～ Preheat the oven to 170°C (340°F). Line two large baking trays with baking paper.

～ Combine the flour, sugar and almond meal in a bowl, then transfer to a work surface and make a well in the centre. Pour the eggs, vanilla and orange blossom water into the well and, using your fingertips, start to bring the dry ingredients into the eggs and begin mixing. Continue to incorporate more and more of the flour mixture, then add the almonds and pistachios and mix until all the ingredients have formed a supple dough.

～ Divide the dough into five pieces, then roll each piece into a cylinder about 5–6 cm (2–2 1/2 in) in diameter and place on one of the lined trays. Lightly beat the extra egg in a small bowl, then brush the egg over the top of the dough cylinders.

～ Bake the cylinders for 20 minutes, then remove from the oven and cool slightly. When cool enough to handle, use a large chef's knife to cut the cylinders into 2–3 cm (3/4–1 1/4 in) thick slices. Place the biscuits on the lined trays in a single layer and bake on the bottom shelf of the oven for 15 minutes, or until light golden brown. Transfer to a wire rack to cool.

～ *Croquants* are delicious eaten with a cup of tea or coffee, or as a small treat for kids with a glass of milk. Store them in an airtight container for up to 1 month. As with all other biscuits, if they start to soften a little, simply dry them in a 100°C (210°F) oven for 10 minutes.

It has been quite a journey for these humble biscuits. Originally called *casse-dents* or 'teeth-breakers', these were baked twice so they would last for a long time, to cater for the demands of sailors on long journeys at sea. Nowadays, they have been refined into a more palatable biscuit, and are commonly found in most Mediterranean cities under the name *croquant* or biscotti.

Tuiles

This circular, concave biscuit is meant to resemble the shape of a roof tile (which, incidentally, is the literal translation of the word 'tuile'), usually found in the southern region of France. There are hundreds (I assume) of variations of the original almond tuile, ranging from brandy snaps to fruit-based lace tuiles, all characterised by their distinctive curve and crunchy texture.

Tuiles aux amandes

(Almond tuiles)

Makes 20–25

note : All ingredients must be at room temperature. Start this recipe a day ahead.

75 g (2³/₄ oz) unsalted butter
125 g (4¹/₂ oz) egg whites (about 4)
200 g (7 oz) caster (superfine) sugar
¹/₄ teaspoon natural vanilla extract
50 g (1³/₄ oz) plain (all-purpose) flour
200 g (7 oz) flaked almonds

~ Put the butter in a small saucepan over very low heat. Stir occasionally until melted, then remove from the heat and leave to cool for 5 minutes.

~ Put the egg whites, sugar and vanilla in a large bowl. Using a hand-held whisk, whisk the mixture until the egg whites begin to foam. Combine the flour and almonds in a small bowl, then use a spatula to fold them into the egg whites. Stir in the butter until well combined. Do not let the butter cool down too much, or it will harden upon contact with the cooler egg white mixture. Spoon the mixture into a small bowl, cover with plastic wrap and refrigerate overnight.

~ Preheat the oven to 180°C (350°F). Line two large baking trays with baking paper or a silicone mat.

~ Stir the chilled mixture until smooth, then drop ²/₃ tablespoons of mixture onto one of the lined trays, spacing them about 10 cm (4 in) apart. Lightly dip a fork in water and use the back of the fork to spread the mixture into thin 6 cm (2¹/₂ in) rounds. Bake the tuiles for 5–7 minutes, or until they begin to brown around the edges. Don't wait for them to brown completely, or they will become too brittle to shape. Remove the tray from the oven.

~ Working quickly, use a spatula to carefully lift the tuiles off the tray, then lay them over a rolling pin or small bottle. You should be able to shape four or five at a time on the rolling pin. Leave until completely cool. Prepare and bake the next batch of tuiles, alternating the trays so the tray you are using has had time to cool down. Almond tuiles are best eaten freshly baked, but can be kept for a few days in an airtight container.

tip

You don't need to use all the mixture at once. Use half and bake some biscuits for afternoon tea, then store the rest of the mixture in an airtight container in the fridge for up to 2 weeks.

Tuiles dentelle à l'orange et à la cannelle

(Orange and cinnamon lace tuiles)

Makes about 20

note : All dry ingredients must be at room temperature.

40 g (1½ oz) unsalted butter
2½ tablespoons strained orange juice
140 g (5 oz) pure icing (confectioners') sugar, sifted
2 tablespoons plain (all-purpose) flour
small pinch of ground cinnamon
finely grated zest of ½ orange

~ Put the butter in a small saucepan over very low heat. Stir occasionally until melted, then remove from the heat and leave to cool for 5 minutes. When cool, add the orange juice and stir to combine.

~ Put the icing sugar, flour and cinnamon in a large bowl and whisk together well. Pour the butter and orange mixture into the flour mixture, add the orange zest, then use a wooden spoon to combine well. Spoon the mixture into a small bowl, cover with plastic wrap and refrigerate for at least 2 hours.

~ Preheat the oven to 190°C (375°F). Line two large baking trays with baking paper or a silicone mat.

~ Stir the chilled mixture until smooth, then drop ½ tablespoons of mixture onto one of the lined trays, spacing them about 10 cm (4 in) apart. Bake the tuiles for 5 minutes, or until light golden brown. Remove from the oven and leave on the tray to cool for 2–3 minutes, or until you can lift them off the tray with a spatula. Do not attempt to handle them too early, because the soft caramel may stick to your skin and cause very deep burns.

~ Working quickly, use a spatula to carefully lift the tuiles off the tray, then lay them over a rolling pin or small bottle. You should be able to shape four or five at a time on the rolling pin. Leave until completely cool. Prepare and bake the next batch of tuiles, alternating the trays so the tray you are using has had time to cool down. Lace tuiles are best eaten freshly baked, but can be kept for a few days in an airtight container.

Serve these delicate and elegant lace tuiles as an accompaniment to a simple fruit salad or ice cream to add texture, or as a sophisticated nibble for your next Champagne cocktail. They are versatile too; create your own version by simply swapping the orange juice with any other juices, such as grapefruit juice, pineapple or guava.

It's often thought (and often debated) that the florentine biscuit came from France, and while they have been a staple in almost every French bakery since the Renaissance, their name provides an obvious clue as to where they actually originated. I love these biscuits for their bright contrasting colours and the perfect balance between the bitterness of the dark chocolate and the sweetness of the caramelised almonds and candied fruits. Enjoy them with a cup of strong coffee or an Earl Grey tea.

Florentines

Makes about 20

180 g (6¼ oz) flaked almonds
30 g (1 oz) almond meal
30 g (1 oz) candied orange peel
30 g (1 oz) glacé cherries, coarsely chopped
30 g (1 oz) plain (all-purpose) flour
100 g (3½ oz) unsalted butter
150 g (5½ oz) caster (superfine) sugar
50 g (1¾ oz) honey
40 g (1½ oz) whipping cream (35% fat)
500 g (1 lb 2 oz) dark chocolate (70% cocoa solids), chopped

⌒ Preheat the oven to 170°C (340°F). Line three baking trays with baking paper or a silicone mat.

⌒ Put the almonds, almond meal, orange peel, glacé cherries and flour in a bowl and combine well. Put the butter, sugar, honey and cream in a heavy-based saucepan over high heat and stir continuously until it comes to the boil. Reduce the heat to medium, then continue stirring until the mixture reaches 115°C (240°F) on a sugar thermometer. Remove the pan from the heat, add the dry ingredients and combine well.

⌒ Using two tablespoons (one to pick up the mixture and the other to push it off), drop tablespoons of hot mixture onto the lined trays, spacing them about 5 cm (2 in) apart. You will have to work fast, as the mixture will harden quickly as it cools down. When each tray is full, place a sheet of baking paper over the top and use the palm of your hand to gently flatten the florentines to a 1 cm (½ in) thickness. They need to be the same thickness so they cook evenly.

⌒ Remove the top piece of baking paper, then place the trays in the oven and bake for 10–15 minutes, or until golden brown. Watch them like a hawk — burnt florentines aren't very pleasant! Remove from the oven and, if desired, use a lightly greased round biscuit cutter to even out the shape. Leave on the trays until cool.

⌒ To coat the florentines, slowly melt the chocolate in a bain-marie (see tips), then remove the bowl from the heat and set aside until the chocolate is cool. Working with one biscuit at a time, dip the flat side of the florentine in the chocolate. If you feel creative, use a comb or a fork to create the distinctive wavy pattern on the chocolate. Place the florentines, chocolate side up, on a tray lined with baking paper and refrigerate for about 10 minutes, or until set. Store in an airtight container at room temperature.

tips

A bain-marie is a water bath used to gently cook ingredients such as eggs or chocolate. To prepare a bain-marie, place a heatproof bowl over a saucepan filled with water, making sure the bottom of the bowl does not touch the water. Bring the water to a simmer over medium heat. This ensures that the ingredients in the bowl will heat up very gradually and that the cooking temperature never exceeds 80°C (175°F).

It's important to note that dark chocolate tends to melt easier than milk chocolate, which contains less cocoa butter and therefore tends to burn a lot quicker. If you are melting milk chocolate, take your time, leave the heat on low and stir often with a spatula until melted.

The first thing you will notice about these macarons is that they seemingly bear little resemblance to the macarons you are probably more familiar with — the *macaron Gerbert*, a very popular biscuit that comes in hundreds of different colours, flavours and fillings. We bake over 20,000 of these every week, but they are technical and time-consuming to make and probably outside the scope of this book.

The *macaron de Nancy* is a very traditional biscuit; in fact, it is the ancestor of the famed *macaron Gerbert*. Macarons first arrived in France in the sixteenth century with Catherine de Medici's Italian pastry chefs, but really gained notoriety during the French Revolution when two nuns, Sister Marguerite and Sister Marie-Elisabeth, began manufacturing them from a town called Nancy. At this point they were single almond biscuits, with a chewy centre and brittle, crunchy shell. It was not until the nineteenth century that Pierre Desfontaines, a cousin of a founding member of the Pâtisserie Ladurée, created the *macaron Gerbert* by softening up the mixture with a meringue and sticking two shells together with a flavoured filling.

The recipe for *macarons de Nancy* is incredibly simple and remains one of the most popular biscuits sold in bakeries throughout France.

Macarons de Nancy
(Traditional Nancy macarons)

Makes about 40

250 g (9 oz) almond meal

320 g (11$\frac{1}{4}$ oz) caster (superfine) sugar

100 g (3$\frac{1}{2}$ oz) egg whites (about 3–4)

$\frac{1}{4}$ teaspoon bitter almond essence, or to taste

100 g (3$\frac{1}{2}$ oz) pure icing (confectioners') sugar

tip

When baking Nancy macarons, do not stress too much about the baking time. Remove the macarons after the recommended cooking time, leave to cool a little, then taste one to see if it is cooked to your liking — it should be soft and chewy on the inside with a crispy shell. If you find your macarons are too soft, simply return them to a low oven to dry out for a little longer.

~ Preheat the oven to 180°C (350°F). Lightly grease two baking trays, then line with baking paper.

~ Combine the almond meal and caster sugar in a bowl. Add the egg whites and almond essence in one addition and stir with a wooden spoon for 2–3 minutes, or until a very stiff paste forms. The mixture will begin to soften as the water in the egg whites starts to dissolve the sugar.

~ Spoon the mixture into a piping bag fitted with a 1 cm ($\frac{1}{2}$ in) plain nozzle and pipe 5 cm (2 in) rounds onto the lined trays, spacing them 3–4 cm (1$\frac{1}{4}$–1$\frac{1}{2}$ in) apart. Using a pastry brush lightly dipped in cold water, brush over the top of each macaron, then sprinkle a generous amount of icing sugar over the top. Use the brush to wet the tops again until all the icing sugar has dissolved.

~ Bake for 15 minutes, or until just beginning to colour. Do not let the macarons caramelise too much, as they need to be fairly soft. Remove from the oven and leave to cool on the trays, then carefully remove from the baking paper. If your macarons stick to the paper, simply wet the underside of the baking paper with a pastry brush or a very wet cloth. After a few minutes, you will be able to remove your precious little biscuits from the paper. Store in an airtight container at room temperature for up to 7 days.

These little biscuits follow straight after the macaron recipe, because I wanted to clarify the point that macarons and macaroons are actually two distinctly different things, however similar their names might be when translated in English. Both the traditional Nancy macaron and the more famous Gerbert macaron are made with almond meal, while macaroons are made with coconut.

The coconut macaroon is not actually a French creation, but a typically Anglo-Saxon one, said to have originated from Scotland in the 1930s. They quickly spread to Germany and the Netherlands, then to North America and Australia before finding their well-deserved spot on the shelves of almost every bakery in France. They are amazingly simple to bake, packed full of fibre and, more importantly, they are just delectable.

Congolais à l'orgeat
(Coconut macaroons with orgeat syrup)

Makes about 20

150 g (5 1/2 oz) shredded coconut
1/8 teaspoon fine salt
60 g (2 1/4 oz) egg whites (about 2)
2 teaspoons honey
150 g (5 1/2 oz) caster (superfine) sugar
1/2 teaspoon natural vanilla extract
2 tablespoons orgeat syrup

~ Preheat the oven to 180°C (350°F). Line a baking tray with baking paper or a silicone mat.

~ Put the coconut and salt in a large heatproof bowl. Put the egg whites, honey, sugar, vanilla and orgeat syrup in a saucepan and whisk continuously over low heat just until the mixture feels tepid to the touch (about 45°C/115°F). Pour the sugar mixture onto the coconut and mix with a spatula until well combined.

~ Take small handfuls of the mixture and roll into 3–4 cm (1 1/4–1 1/2 in) balls, then place on the lined tray. Unlike tuiles or florentines, macaroons will not spread during baking so you can place them close together, but not touching. Bake for 10 minutes, or until the coconut shreds on top of the macaroons begin to brown.

~ Remove from the oven and transfer to a wire rack to cool. If your macaroons stick to the baking paper, simply wet the underside of the paper with a pastry brush or a very wet cloth. After a few minutes, you will be able to remove the macaroons from the paper. Macaroons are best eaten fresh, but will keep in an airtight container at room temperature for up to 4 days.

Orgeat syrup is available in large supermarkets or specialist delicatessens and is often sold as almond syrup. It is made by blending almonds, bitter almonds, sugar and a small amount of orange blossom water. The syrup can be mixed with water as a refreshing drink, mixed with alcoholic beverages to make cocktails such as Mauresque and Mai Tai, or with fruit juices such as orange and banana or mango and peach. Forget the Hanging Gardens of Babylon, my seventh wonder of the world is a small patch of grass in Provence in summer, where I can lay in a long chair wearing a straw hat, listening to cicadas and sipping on a cold orange, banana and orgeat cocktail.

Let's face it; everyone loves a soft, crumbly and buttery shortbread. What makes these so special is that they can be cut to any shape and size, filled with jam of any flavour and, more importantly, making a batch of shortbread on a Sunday afternoon is a great activity the whole family can enjoy together. Traditionally, *sablés à la confiture* are made with two round biscuits sandwiched together with strawberry jam, with three holes revealing the shiny red spheres from behind a veil of icing sugar. Frankly, I am at a loss to explain the technical reason as to why they taste so good, but they just do.

Sablés à la confiture

(Jam shortbreads)

Makes about 12 sandwiched shortbreads

600 g (1 lb 5 oz) Pâte Sablée (pages 80–3)
pure icing (confectioners') sugar, for dusting
250 g (9 oz) strawberry jam

tip

Unlike *pâte sucrée*, which has the tendency to toughen with excessive mixing, *pâte sablée* can be rolled over and over again and still remain very short and tasty. This makes it an ideal pastry for kids to play with, as they can make fun biscuit shapes then reroll the dough scraps and continue cutting. Feel free to keep any dough offcuts in the fridge or freezer, covered in plastic wrap, to reuse at a later stage.

～ Preheat the oven to 170°C (340°F). Line three baking trays with baking paper or a silicone mat.

～ Divide the pastry in half, then cover one half in plastic wrap and place in the fridge. Don't attempt to roll out all the dough at once, as it's too difficult to achieve an even thickness when rolling out a large amount. Roll out the dough on a piece of baking paper until about 5 mm (1/4 in) thick, making sure you dust the paper and rolling pin with a little bit of flour so the dough doesn't stick. Using an 8 cm (3 1/4 in) round cutter, cut out as many discs as you can (you will need an even number of discs). If the dough is sticking to the paper, place in the fridge for 15 minutes to firm up a little. Repeat with the remaining dough.

～ Place the discs on the lined trays. Using a 2 cm (3/4 in) round cutter, stamp out three small holes from half the discs (leave the other half uncut, as these will form the base). Bake for 15 minutes, or until light golden. Remove from the oven, leave on the trays to cool a little, then carefully turn the shortbread bases upside down. When completely cool, dust a generous amount of icing sugar over the top of the shortbread discs with holes.

～ Put the jam and 1 tablespoon water in a small saucepan and stir over medium heat until soft and well combined. Remove from the heat. Spread about 1 tablespoon hot jam onto the upside-down shortbread bases, then gently cover with the sugared tops. Store in an airtight container at room temperature.

Writing a book on baking and not including a recipe for chocolate biscuits would be almost sacrilegious, regardless of whether they are typically French or not. Personally, I like my chocolate biscuits crunchy on the outside with a soft, chewy centre and, of course, with pistachios. I have developed a reputation for overdoing the pistachios a bit, but I really can't imagine a world without this amazing nut. Whether just for their colour — sprinkled on a plate to create a beautiful contrast with red cherries or chocolate — or for their texture or subtle sweetness, I have used pistachios for over thirty years, across every possible range of products, from breads to brioches and cakes. In this recipe, the pistachios add an additional layer of texture and a stunning contrast of colour but, of course, if you don't love them like I do, replace them with any other type of nut, such as macadamias, walnuts or peanuts.

Biscuits au chocolat, aux amandes et aux pistaches

(Chocolate, almond and pistachio biscuits)

Makes about 45

note : All ingredients must be at room temperature.

125 g (4^1/$_2$ oz) blanched almonds
120 g (4^1/$_4$ oz) pistachios
220 g (7^3/$_4$ oz) dark chocolate (60–70% cocoa solids), chopped
150 g (5^1/$_2$ oz) unsalted butter, chopped
225 g (8 oz) plain (all-purpose) flour
^{1}/$_2$ teaspoon fine salt
5 g (^{1}/$_8$ oz) baking powder
220 g (7^3/$_4$ oz) caster (superfine) sugar
75 g (2^3/$_4$ oz) eggs (lightly beat 2 eggs together, then measure)

Preheat the oven to 175°C (345°F). Put the almonds on a baking tray and roast for about 10 minutes, or until golden. Remove from the oven and cool. Put the almonds and pistachios in a food processor and process until coarsely chopped, then set aside.

Melt the chocolate and butter in a bain-marie (see tips, page 37). When melted, remove the bowl from the heat and cool to room temperature.

Line two baking trays with baking paper or a silicone mat.

Sift the flour, salt and baking powder into a bowl and set aside. Put the sugar and eggs in a large bowl. Using a hand-held whisk, whisk the sugar and eggs until thick and pale, then add the cooled chocolate mixture and fold in well with a wooden spoon. Make sure your eggs are at room temperature, as cold eggs may cause your chocolate to crystallise and form hard lumps. Fold in the sifted flour mixture, then add the crushed nuts and combine well.

Shape level tablespoons of the mixture into balls and place onto the lined trays, spacing them about 5 cm (2 in) apart (see tips), then flatten the balls with the palm of your hand to about 5 cm (2 in) in diameter. Bake for about 10 minutes, or until you can see well-defined cracks all the way to the centre of the biscuit. Cool on a wire rack, then store in an airtight container for up to 7 days.

tips

It's important that the dough balls are all about the same size, so they cook evenly. I like to weigh each dough ball to make sure they are all the same size.

This dough freezes well. Roll any left-over dough into a long cylinder about 5 cm (2 in) in diameter, cover in plastic wrap and freeze. To use, thaw the cylinder to room temperature and then cut into 3 cm (1¼ in) thick slices and bake as you would fresh dough.

Bugnes are typically from Lyon but every region has their own adaptation and names. In Provence they are called *merveilles* or *oreillettes* — they are similar to *bugnes* but made without the baking powder and are typically flavoured with orange blossom. In Nice they are called *ganses Niçoises*, and are made with olive oil instead of butter.

I have very clear and happy memories of when I was a small boy, sitting on the side of the kitchen table, watching my mother and grandmother making *bugnes*. I loved the whole process, from the initial discussion over who was going to do what, to the actual moment when they started cutting, rolling and then baking the dough. By late afternoon, when all the work was done, the whole family would regroup and chat about their day over some freshly baked *bugnes* and a glass or two of rosé. Making those biscuits embodied everything that I love about baking. It was the catalyst that brought everyone together, naturally and effortlessly.

For this recipe, I always use the traditional method that my grandmother taught me. The little extra bit of love and care given to the dough by mixing the ingredients by hand somehow always makes these biscuits taste even better.

Bugnes
(French vanilla crostoli)

Makes 50–60

5 eggs
1 tablespoon natural vanilla extract or vanilla bean paste
3 tablespoons rum
500 g (1 lb 2 oz) plain (all-purpose) flour
100 g (3 1/2 oz) maize cornflour (cornstarch)
1 tablespoon caster (superfine) sugar
2 teaspoons baking powder
1 teaspoon fine salt
finely grated zest of 1 lemon
250 g (9 oz) unsalted butter, at room temperature, chopped
vegetable oil, for deep-frying
pure icing (confectioners') sugar, for dusting

technical tip

The characteristic bubbles on these biscuits, very much like those found on Sicilian cannoli, are created by the addition of alcohol directly into the dough. The alcohol is trapped under a thin layer of dough, but evaporates almost instantly on contact with the hot oil, creating the lunar landscape on your biscuit. The baking powder takes longer to release carbon dioxide, which consequently becomes trapped by the dough as it cooks, lightening up the whole biscuit.

~ Using a fork, lightly beat the eggs, vanilla and rum in a small bowl. Put the flour, cornflour, sugar, baking powder, salt and lemon zest in a mound on your work surface and make a well in the centre. Rub the butter into the dry ingredients by pushing the butter and flour mixture together with the palm of your hand until all the butter is fully incorporated into the dry ingredients. This process, called *sablage*, is designed to keep the dough short by insulating the gluten in the flour with the fat (this prevents it from toughening up once the eggs are added).

~ Add the egg mixture, a little at a time, and incorporate the flour until the dough comes together. (Alternatively, you can follow the same process using an electric mixer fitted with a dough hook attachment.) Flatten the dough into a disc, then cover in plastic wrap and refrigerate for at least 2 hours.

~ Roll out the dough on a lightly floured work surface until about 2 mm (1/16 in) thick. You can use a pasta machine to roll it out, if you prefer. Using a paring knife, cut the dough into rectangles about 5 cm (2 in) wide and 12 cm (4 1/2 in) long, then make a 3 cm (1 1/4 in) cut lengthways through the middle and fold one end of the rectangle through the incision. Place on baking trays lined with baking paper, cover with a cloth and set aside for 10 minutes.

~ Heat the oil in a deep-fryer or large, heavy-based saucepan to 190°C (375°F). Working in batches, cook the *bugnes* for 2 minutes on each side, or until golden. Remove and drain on paper towel. When cool, dust with icing sugar. Store in an airtight container for up to 7 days.

Let's close this chapter with a specialty from Marseille. *Navettes* are a typical Provençal biscuit usually served in Marseille at *La Chandeleur* (Candlemas) — a religious celebration held in February — instead of the traditional crêpes served everywhere else in France. They are small and oblong in shape, with pointed ends and a deep cut down their length, and are meant to resemble a small regional fishing boat called a *pointu*, meaning 'pointed'. *Navettes* are deliciously crunchy and infused with subtle hints of olive oil and orange blossom, and rank, along with the *croquant*, as one of my favourite biscuits.

Navettes à l'eau de fleur d'oranger

(Orange blossom navettes)

Makes 32

500 g (1 lb 2 oz) plain (all-purpose) flour
250 g (9 oz) caster (superfine) sugar
1/2 teaspoon fine salt
2 eggs, lightly beaten
120 ml (4 fl oz) olive oil
finely grated zest of 1 orange
1 tablespoon orange blossom water
2 eggs, extra

⌒ Combine the flour, sugar and salt in a bowl and make a well in the centre. Add the lightly beaten eggs, olive oil, orange zest and orange blossom water. Use your hands to mix everything together for 5 minutes, or until smooth. Cover with a cloth and set aside at room temperature for 1 hour. Any short doughs, such as shortbreads made with flour and a liquid (eggs), must be left to rest for at least an hour to allow the gluten strands (wheat protein) to relax and shorten. Failing to do this will inevitably lead to a tough and unpleasant texture.

⌒ Line two baking trays with baking paper or a silicone mat. Divide the dough into four portions, then roll each portion into a cylinder about 4 cm (1 1/2 in) in diameter. Using a small sharp knife, cut each cylinder into eight pieces. Shape each piece into a 10 cm (4 in) long roll, then pinch the ends slightly to give them a tapered shape. Place on the lined trays, spacing them about 5 cm (2 in) apart.

⌒ Using a sharp paring knife, make a deep incision lengthways down the middle of each roll. Put the extra eggs in a small bowl and whisk with a fork until well combined. Lightly brush the tops of the rolls with the egg wash, then place in the fridge to rest for 1 hour.

⌒ Preheat the oven to 180°C (350°F). Cooking one tray at a time, bake on the bottom shelf of the oven for 15–20 minutes, or until the bases are slightly brown and the tops are dark blonde. If your biscuits are browning too quickly, cover loosely with a piece of foil and continue baking. Cool on the trays, then store in an airtight container for up to 2 weeks.

A lot of traditional recipes from the Mediterranean basin use olive oil instead of butter, because oil tends to be more resilient in hot climates than dairy products. Butter remained the preserve of regions with cooler climates until the invention of refrigeration, a fact that has had a huge influence on regional specialties the world over.

Gâteaux et desserts

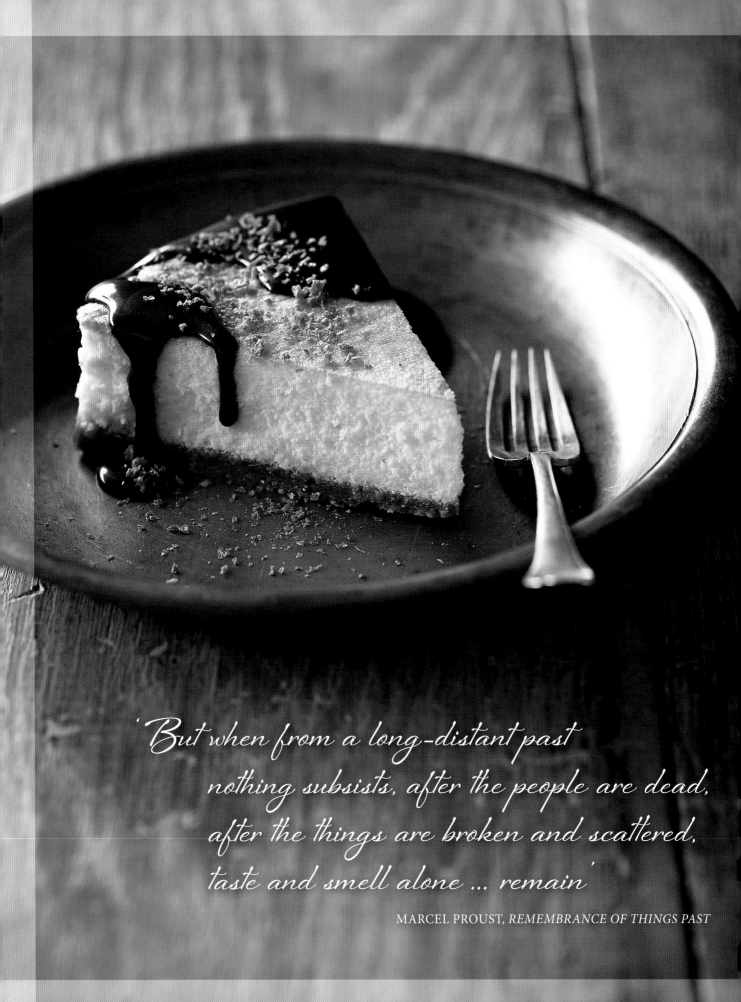

'But when from a long-distant past
nothing subsists, after the people are dead,
after the things are broken and scattered,
taste and smell alone ... remain'

MARCEL PROUST, *REMEMBRANCE OF THINGS PAST*

Gâteaux et desserts

(Cakes and desserts)

Baking conjures up different things for different people. For some, it is all about breads — artisan bakers who, like magicians, transform a handful of ingredients into a seemingly endless array of wondrous golden brown rolls and loaves — and for others it's more to do with delicious cakes, fine pâtisserie and fancy desserts. For me, baking is more about the emotions and connections I have when I'm cooking — the simple, everyday pastries, breads and cakes that my mother or grandmother cooked, just as their own mothers and grandmothers had done. When I'm in my own kitchen, my hands and face dusty with flour, I am so often reconnected with scenes from my childhood, long ago now, of happy times spent sitting at a wooden table in a kitchen filled with the wonderful aroma of cakes baking in the oven, while my mother chatted and bustled about, and my dad and sister licked the left-over batter from the bowls and spoons.

All the cakes and desserts included in this chapter have left an impression on me, whether it's because they rekindled a long-lost moment in time, or for the simple fact that they are just delectable. The one thing they do have in common, however, is that these are delicious and almost failproof recipes that you can achieve at home using simple, readily available ingredients. ℘

Gâteau au fromage, sauce mandarine-chocolat
(Baked cheesecake with mandarin-chocolate sauce) ~ page 54

Unlike the traditional Moroccan *meskouta* (orange and almond cake), made with flour and oil and served soaked in orange juice and cinnamon syrup, this particular cake does not contain any flour, oils or butter, so if you are gluten intolerant or counting your kilojoules, then this is for you!

I like to serve this cake with blood orange segments, some candied lemon slices and a sprinkle of chopped almonds. These flavours work so beautifully together and it's a visual treat too, with the colours popping off the plate.

Gâteau marocain

(*Flourless Moroccan orange and almond cake*)

Serves 12–14

note : This recipe makes two cakes, so feel free to halve the recipe if you prefer.

2 oranges
600 g (1 lb 5 oz) almond meal
15 g ($^1/_2$ oz) baking powder
430 g (15$^1/_4$ oz) caster (superfine) sugar
6 eggs

To decorate

2 blood oranges, segmented
50 g (1$^3/_4$ oz) raw almonds, roasted and coarsely chopped
candied lemon slices (page 69)
edible small flowers, such as violas

tips

You can replace the oranges with any other citrus fruit — try lime, lemon, pink grapefruit or mandarin. If using lime or lemon, increase the sugar to 600 g (1 lb 5 oz) to balance the tartness.

To achieve the professional shiny finish you see on the top of cakes in pâtisseries (and used for many of the cakes in this chapter, such as this one), boil 100 g (3$^1/_2$ oz) apricot jam with 2 tablespoons water for 1 minute and brush the glaze over the cake and fruit. If you find your glaze is too thin, boil it for an additional minute or so.

⌐ Put the oranges in a saucepan and cover with cold water. Cover with a lid and bring to the boil over medium heat, then reduce the heat and simmer for 45 minutes, or until the oranges begin to crack open. Drain the oranges and set aside until cool, then break them open and remove the seeds. Place the unpeeled fruit in a food processor and purée until smooth.

⌐ Preheat the oven to 170°C (340°F). Lightly grease and flour two 8 x 25 cm (3$^1/_4$ x 10 in) loaf (bar) tins.

⌐ Put the almond meal and baking powder in a large bowl, combine well and set aside. Using an electric mixer fitted with a whisk attachment, whisk the sugar and eggs on high speed for 10 minutes, or until light and fluffy. Add the orange purée and stir with a wooden spoon until well combined, then pour the mixture onto the almond meal mixture and gently fold in until combined.

⌐ Pour the mixture into the prepared tins until three-quarters full. The overall volume of mixture will vary slightly depending on how enthusiastically you mixed the batter, so only fill the tins three-quarters full and bake any left-over batter in a greased coffee cup or ramekin. Bake on the bottom shelf of the oven for about 35 minutes, or until a skewer inserted into the cake comes out clean. Remove from the oven and leave to cool before refrigerating in the tins for at least 1 hour.

⌐ To unmould, place the cakes in a 200°C (400°F) oven for 5 minutes, then invert onto a serving plate. Decorate the cakes with the blood orange segments, chopped almonds, some slices of candied lemon and edible flowers. If you like, make a glaze (see tips) to brush over the cake before adding the flowers. This cake will remain soft for 7 days if wrapped and stored in the fridge.

Cheesecakes have been around since the discovery of cheese, which itself dates back over 8000 years ago, and every region and country has adopted their own special techniques and preferences. The French version of cheesecake differs from many versions in that it is made with a small amount of meringue and is traditionally served with a chocolate sauce, curd or fruit coulis. In this recipe I have added some yoghurt to bring a subtle touch of sourness, which helps to offset some of the sweetness of the chocolate, and the mandarin works wonders at balancing the richness of the cheese. All in all, this is a sophisticated and delicate dessert that wouldn't feel out of place served anywhere, from a quick snack for breakfast (yes, really!) to a *petit four* served at a fancy cocktail party.

Gâteau au fromage, sauce mandarine-chocolat

(Baked cheesecake with mandarin-chocolate sauce)

Serves 8–10

200 g (7 oz) Pâte Sablée (pages 80–3)
460 g (1 lb) cream cheese or neufchâtel cheese
200 g (7 oz) Greek-style yoghurt
20 g (³/₄ oz) maize cornflour (cornstarch)
220 g (7³/₄ oz) caster (superfine) sugar
¹/₂ teaspoon fine salt
3 eggs
3 egg yolks
2 tablespoons strained mandarin juice
60 ml (2 fl oz) whipping cream (35% fat)
2 tablespoons full-cream milk
finely grated zest of 2 mandarins
2 egg whites

Mandarin-chocolate sauce

300 ml (10¹/₂ fl oz) strained mandarin juice
180 g (6¹/₄ oz) dark chocolate (65% cocoa solids), chopped
180 g (6¹/₄ oz) milk chocolate, chopped
2 tablespoons honey
finely grated zest of 1 mandarin
60 g (2¹/₄ oz) unsalted butter, at room temperature

To decorate

dried citrus zest (optional) (see tips)

‿ Preheat the oven to 180°C (350°F). Lightly grease a 25 cm (10 in) round cake tin and line the base and side with baking paper. Line a baking tray with baking paper.

‿ Roll out the pastry on a lightly floured work surface until 3–4 mm ($^{1}/_{8}$ in) thick, dusting with a little extra flour if necessary to stop the dough sticking. Using the cake tin as a template, cut out a circle of dough, then place on the lined tray and bake for 15 minutes, or until the pastry begins to turn golden brown. Remove from the oven and set aside to cool. Trim around the cold shortbread base with a sharp paring knife and then carefully drop it down onto the base of the prepared cake tin.

‿ Using an electric mixer fitted with a paddle attachment, beat the cream cheese, yoghurt, cornflour, 110 g ($3^{3}/_{4}$ oz) of the sugar and the salt on low speed until well combined. Scrape down the side of the bowl, then add the eggs, egg yolks and mandarin juice and beat until smooth. Scrape down the side of the bowl, then add the cream, milk and mandarin zest. Increase the speed to medium and beat until smooth and creamy.

‿ Transfer the cream cheese mixture to a large bowl. Wash the bowl of the electric mixer thoroughly to remove any traces of fat, then using the whisk attachment, whisk the egg whites and remaining 110 g ($3^{3}/_{4}$ oz) of sugar on the highest speed until the meringue is thick and shiny. Reduce the speed to low and continue whisking for 1–2 minutes, then gently fold the meringue into the cream cheese mixture with a spatula. Take care when handling the egg whites at this point, or you will push the air out of them and end up with a dense cheesecake — simply use a circular folding motion until combined.

‿ Reduce the oven temperature to 100°C (210°F). Pour the filling into the tin, on top of the pastry base, and bake for 60–80 minutes, or until the cake is firm and stops wobbling. Remove from the oven and cool to room temperature, then refrigerate for at least 30 minutes before removing from the tin. To do this, cover the top of the cheesecake with a piece of baking paper, then place a flat tray on top. Flip everything over, remove the tin, then flip the cheesecake onto a serving plate.

‿ Meanwhile, to make the mandarin-chocolate sauce, put the mandarin juice in a small saucepan and bring to the boil over high heat. Put the dark and milk chocolates, honey and mandarin zest in a heatproof bowl, then, whisking continuously, gradually pour the hot juice into the bowl (add the liquid in two or three batches, so the chocolate doesn't overheat). Whisk until smooth, then set aside until cooled to about 40°C (105°F), or until tepid to the touch. Add the butter, then use a stick blender to process until smooth and well combined.

‿ Just before serving, gently heat the sauce in a bain-marie until warm (see tips, page 37), or alternatively heat it in a microwave for a few seconds, but take care that it doesn't reach anywhere near boiling point or the chocolate will burn. To serve, drizzle the mandarin-chocolate sauce over the cheesecake and sprinkle with some dried citrus zest, if using.

tips

Cheesecakes should be served at room temperature, as this allows the fat to melt quicker in the mouth, dramatically improving both the texture and flavour.

To make dried zest for decoration, use a microplane or a grater to finely grate the zest of 4 mandarins, oranges, lemons or limes. Bring 500 ml (17 fl oz) water and 1 teaspoon salt to the boil in a small saucepan over high heat, then add the grated zest. Blanch for 3–4 minutes, then strain through a fine sieve and pat dry with paper towel. Spread onto a tray lined with baking paper and bake in a 80°C (175°F) oven for 1 hour, or until completely dry. Cool, then store in an airtight container for up to 1 month.

While most of my comments about the recipes in this book seem to indicate that flavour and taste are my most pressing concerns (probably because they are), remember that a lot of ingredients used in baking are high in saturated fat. I don't mean to warn you off saturated fats; rather, I want to point out that biscuits and cakes are meant not to feed you, but simply to liven your day a little, eaten as a small treat after a meal or with a cup of tea or coffee for afternoon tea. In my opinion, it is far better to reduce your portion size instead of compromising on the taste of your cakes by using substandard ingredients such as margarine or low-fat dairy products.

It would be unusual to find a book on French baking that didn't include a madeleine in its list of recipes. I remember as a child how I drooled over those little scalloped butter cakes as I looked at them longingly through the window of my local pâtisserie, never having quite enough money to afford to buy one on my daily trip to school. While this provided my first lesson in financial management, it also made me realise that the more you long for something the more delicious it tastes!

Reassuringly, everyone else seems to have the same affinity as I do for these small eighteenth-century cakes. Most famously, Marcel Proust in his much-heralded novel *Remembrance of Things Past* describes beautifully his first taste of a madeleine: 'No sooner had the warm liquid mixed with the crumbs touched my palate than a shiver ran through me and I stopped, intent upon the extraordinary thing that was happening to me.'

Madeleines

Makes about 24

note : For this recipe I strongly recommend using a metal madeleine tray rather than a silicone mould, as the metal transfers the heat a lot faster and will help create the characteristic ball-shaped top.

120 g (4¼ oz) unsalted butter
135 g (4¾ oz) plain (all-purpose) flour
4 g (⅛ oz) baking powder
3 eggs
160 g (5¾ oz) caster (superfine) sugar
1 teaspoon finely grated lemon zest
3 teaspoons vegetable oil

tip

While a typical madeleine always comes in an oval, scalloped shape, the batter in this recipe is the hero and not the shape. Feel free to use individual cake tins in other shapes, providing they are no deeper than about 5 cm (2 in). If you do use a madeleine tray, note that they are available in small and large sizes. Alternatively, real scallop shells can work, but they need to be greased with butter and floured before use.

~ Melt the butter in a small saucepan over low heat, then remove from the heat and leave to cool until tepid.

~ Sift together the flour and baking powder. Using an electric mixer fitted with a whisk attachment, beat the eggs, sugar and lemon zest until light and fluffy. Gently fold in the melted butter and the oil, then fold in the flour mixture. Transfer to a bowl, cover with plastic wrap and refrigerate for at least 3 hours, or overnight for a better result.

~ Preheat the oven to 220°C (430°F). Grease and lightly flour a madeleine tray. I generally use one with holes that measure about 7.5 x 5 cm (3 x 2 in) (see tip). Fill the holes three-quarters full with batter. Reduce the oven temperature to 190°C (375°F), then place the tray on the bottom shelf of the oven and bake for 8 minutes. Remove the cakes from the tray while still warm. When the tray is cool, wipe clean, then grease and lightly flour the tray again and repeat with the remaining batter. Madeleines are best eaten the day they are baked, preferably straight out of the oven.

Although better known as almond friands, these popular little cakes are actually called *financiers*, so-named because of their gold ingot shape. Interestingly, it is thought that the *financier* was inspired by a small cake called *visitandine*, named after the Catholic nuns who invented them. The nuns painted with tempura paint, which they made from egg yolks, and the recipe was the perfect solution for what to do with all the left-over egg whites. However, the cake's distinctive ingot shape and current name was the work of a chef called Lasne, who had a shop in the financial district of Paris, and baked them in this shape as a gimmick to entice the local traders.

While the *financier* continues to be baked as a small rectangle in France, it is now sold in all shapes and enhanced by a multitude of flavours. This version is my favourite; the tartness of the raspberries provides the perfect foil for the richness of the cake, and the coconut brings a little bit of texture. I consider them as the muffin's sophisticated cousin — richer, softer and with a more refined texture. Try them once and you will never look back!

Financiers aux framboises et à la noix de coco

(Raspberry and coconut friands)

Makes 20

note : All dry ingredients must be at room temperature. Start this recipe a day ahead.

200 g (7 oz) almond meal
300 g (10^{1}/$_{2}$ oz) pure icing (confectioners') sugar
150 g (5^{1}/$_{2}$ oz) plain (all-purpose) flour
250 g (9 oz) egg whites (about 8–9)
200 g (7 oz) unsalted butter
250 g (9 oz) raspberries, fresh or frozen whole
100 g (3^{1}/$_{2}$ oz) flaked coconut

~ Put the almond meal, icing sugar and flour in a bowl and combine well. Using a hand-held whisk, lightly whisk the egg whites until foamy; do not whisk the egg whites too much or your cakes will collapse during baking. Fold the egg whites into the almond meal mixture until just combined. Remember that any batter containing flour (and therefore gluten) will toughen up with excessive mixing, so don't be tempted to prepare this using an electric mixer.

~ Put the butter in a small saucepan and bring to the boil over high heat. Remove from the heat as soon as you notice the butter has started to brown — this is *beurre noisette*. Mixing continuously, pour the hot butter through a sieve into your batter and mix until combined well (see tips). Transfer to a small bowl, cover with plastic wrap and refrigerate overnight.

~ Preheat the oven to 200°C (400°F). Lightly grease and flour 20 financier moulds or use 125 ml (4 fl oz) friand or brioche tins. For the best results, use steel or aluminium moulds, and while the shape is entirely up to you, this recipe is designed to be baked in individual cake moulds.

~ Divide the batter among the prepared moulds. Place a few raspberries and sprinkle some coconut over the top of each one. Bake for 15–20 minutes, or until a skewer inserted into the centre of a cake comes out clean. Place on a wire rack to cool a little, then remove from the moulds. Like most cakes, these are best eaten the day they are baked.

tips

To avoid lumps forming in the batter when you add the hot butter, it's important that your ingredients (almonds, sugar, flour and eggs) are at room temperature before you start.

Although raspberries provide a good balance of tartness in these cakes, feel free to use other acidic fruit such as passionfruit, blackcurrants or even chopped granny smith apples.

I came up with this recipe in the early years of my apprenticeship at Pâtisserie Pasquet, in Marseille, long before I was aware of the existence of fudges, and while I was very pleased with my effort, the head chef was rather underwhelmed. He said it was too dense to be a good cake and too soft to be a biscuit and described it as unsophisticated, but I was quietly proud of my concoction. It may have been a rough diamond, but it had a wonderfully soft, buttery flesh enhanced by the texture of the walnuts, and just the right amount of sweetness. It ended up being one of our best-selling 'sort of cakes'.

Fondant au chocolat et aux noix

(Chocolate and walnut butter fudge cake)

Serves 12–14

9 egg yolks
135 g (4³/4 oz) raw (demerara) sugar
75 g (2³/4 oz) honey
345 g (12 oz) caster (superfine) sugar
180 g (6¹/4 oz) milk chocolate (35–40% cocoa solids), chopped
450 g (1 lb) unsalted butter, at room temperature, chopped
4 egg whites
250 g (9 oz) walnuts, coarsely chopped
finely grated zest of 1 lemon
180 g (6¹/4 oz) plain (all-purpose) flour

Caramel

70 ml (2¹/4 fl oz) whipping cream (35% fat)
140 g (5 oz) caster (superfine) sugar
100 g (3¹/2 oz) unsalted butter, chopped

To decorate

slivered pistachios
walnuts, roasted and roughly chopped
pure icing (confectioners') sugar, unsifted

~ To make the caramel, put the cream in a saucepan over medium heat and bring to just below the boil. Remove from the heat and set aside. Put the sugar and 2 tablespoons water in a medium heavy-based saucepan (see tip). Cook over medium heat, without stirring, until the sugar caramelises to golden brown. Stirring continuously, carefully pour in the warm cream (be extremely careful when you do this, as there will be a lot of very hot steam). Stir for 1 minute, then remove from the heat. Add the butter and stir until well combined. Using a stick blender, emulsify the caramel until smooth and shiny. Cool to room temperature.

~ Using an electric mixer fitted with a whisk attachment, beat the egg yolks, raw sugar, honey and 135 g (4³/4 oz) of caster sugar on high speed for 2–3 minutes, or until light and creamy. Transfer the mixture to a medium bowl.

~ Meanwhile, melt the chocolate in a bain-marie (see tips, page 37). Remove from the heat, add the butter and stir with a wooden spoon until smooth and well combined, then set aside.

~ Preheat the oven to 140°C (285°F). Lightly grease two 8 x 25 cm (3¹/4 x 10 in) loaf (bar) tins and line the base and sides with baking paper.

~ Put the egg whites in the clean bowl of the electric mixer fitted with the whisk attachment and whisk on the highest speed until soft peaks form. Be careful not to overwhisk the egg whites or they will split (see tip, page 71). Reduce the speed to low, then gradually add the remaining 210 g (7¹/2 oz) of caster sugar and continue mixing on low speed for 2 minutes, or until the meringue is thick and glossy. Using a rubber spatula, fold the chocolate and butter mixture, walnuts and lemon zest into the meringue until just combined. Fold in the egg yolk mixture, then the flour until well combined.

~ Divide the mixture between the prepared tins and bake for 40 minutes, or just until a skewer inserted into the centre of a cake comes out clean. Remove from the oven and set aside in the tin for 1 hour. Invert the tins onto separate serving plates, then pour half the soft caramel over the top of each loaf. Sprinkle with the pistachios, walnuts and icing sugar. This cake is delicious served cold with a scoop of mascarpone and a glass of fortified wine.

tip

When cooking caramel, it is best to use a medium-sized pan, even though you are only using a small amount of sugar and water. This allows the steam to escape when the cooler liquid is added to the warm caramel. As the sugar starts to caramelise, use a pastry brush dipped in cold water to clean off any sugar crystals on the side of the pan.

You might be surprised to see a muffin recipe in this book. They are not something you'd see very often in a French bakery, but I have included them here because they are incredibly quick and easy to make and almost failproof — the perfect recipe for budding bakers. Muffins can be amazingly versatile and I love experimenting with new flavours and textures. This banana and caramel version is one of my favourites, but feel free to use this recipe as a base and let your imagination run wild. You could try something adventurous, such as apricot and verbena, or bitter chocolate with coffee and cardamom, or if you prefer something a little more conservative, try raspberries and coconut.

Muffins caramel-banane
(Banana and caramel muffins)

Makes 24

3 medium bananas
juice of 1 lemon
200 g (7 oz) unsalted butter
200 g (7 oz) caster (superfine) sugar

Batter
660 g (1 lb 7 oz) plain (all-purpose) flour
540 g (1 lb 3 oz) caster (superfine) sugar
2 1/2 teaspoons fine salt
18 g (3/4 oz) baking powder
4 eggs
540 ml (18 1/4 fl oz) full-cream milk
330 ml (11 1/4 fl oz) vegetable oil

technical tip

Lemon juice is added to the sliced bananas to stop them from browning (oxidising). This is caused by a chemical process called 'enzymatic browning', where the enzymes in the fruit react to the presence of oxygen. This process can be slowed down by reducing the pH level of the fruit by adding an acid. In baking we usually use citrus fruit (they have a high content of ascorbic and citric acid), not only to slow oxidation but because their tart flavour works very well at reducing the perceived taste of sweetness. In savoury cooking or when an acidic taste is undesirable, soak the sliced fruit or vegetable in cold water to reduce their exposure to oxygen.

~ Cut the bananas into 1 cm (1/2 in) thick slices and place in a bowl. Add the lemon juice, toss to coat well, then set aside (see tip).

~ Put the butter and sugar in a large frying pan over high heat and cook until melted. Strain the bananas over a bowl and reserve the lemon juice, then place the banana slices in a single layer in the pan with the melted butter and sugar. Reduce the heat to medium and cook for 2–3 minutes, or until the sugar caramelises. Turn the bananas in the caramel until both sides are golden, then remove from the pan and place in a bowl. Add the reserved lemon juice to the caramel and combine well, then transfer to a heatproof bowl. Cover the two bowls containing the bananas and caramel, then refrigerate for 1 hour, or until cold.

~ Preheat the oven to 170°C (340°F). Line two 12-hole standard muffin tins with paper cases or squares of baking paper.

~ To make the batter, use an electric mixer fitted with a paddle attachment on low speed to combine the flour, sugar, salt and baking powder. Lightly beat the eggs, milk and oil in a bowl until well combined. With the motor running, gradually add the egg mixture to the dry mixture, scraping down the side of the bowl and the paddles as you go. Don't add too much liquid at once or you will end up with lumps. Cover the bowl with plastic wrap and refrigerate for at least 1 hour before using.

~ Half-fill the paper cases with the batter. Add a few slices of banana and a teaspoon of caramel to each, then top up with enough batter to come about 1 cm (1/2 in) from the top of the cases. Top with a few more slices of banana and another teaspoon of caramel, then bake for 40 minutes, or until a skewer comes out clean when inserted into the centre of a muffin. Leave to cool in the tin for 5 minutes, then remove to a wire rack.

If you have been experimenting with baking croissants, brioches or breads and you now have more than you know what to do with, the *diplomate* is the answer to your dilemma. Every day, every baker around the planet faces the problem of deciding how many *viennoiserie* they need to produce: not enough and the customers will get upset, too many and the wastage costs will soon amount to a small fortune. Now that we aren't allowed to give away our left-over stock because of overzealous regulations, the only choice left is to find an ingenious method to recycle them. Over the course of my career I have seen it all, from the surprisingly tasty rum balls, often made with left-over cake or pastries, to cutting almond meal with shredded croissants and, of course, the deliciously rustic and earthy bread and butter pudding.

Diplomate

(Bread and butter pudding)

Serves 6

500 g (1 lb 2 oz) day-old croissants and/or brioches
200 g (7 oz) sultanas (golden raisins)
1.5 litres (52 fl oz) full-cream milk
150 g (5^1/$_2$ oz) unsalted butter
2 vanilla beans, halved lengthways

12 eggs
250 g (9 oz) caster (superfine) sugar
50 ml (1^3/$_4$ fl oz) rum
200 g (7 oz) apricot jam, for glazing

Preheat the oven to 170°C (340°F). Lightly grease a 12 x 25 cm (4^1/$_2$ x 10 in) rectangular cake tin, then line the base and sides with baking paper.

Slice the croissants (and/or brioches) into 1 cm (^{1}/$_2$ in) thick slices and arrange a layer of pastries snugly over the base of the prepared tin. To achieve a better visual impact, lay the pastries so the light side (the inside of the pastry) is facing down. Sprinkle some of the sultanas over the top, then continue stacking and layering the remaining pastries and sultanas.

Put the milk, butter and vanilla beans in a saucepan over medium heat. As soon as the surface begins to shimmer, remove from the heat, cover with a lid and set aside. Using an electric mixer fitted with a whisk attachment, beat the eggs and sugar together until a creamy, pale yellow batter forms, then whisk in the rum. Remove the vanilla beans from the hot milk and reserve. Whisking continuously on low speed, gradually add the hot milk to the egg mixture — don't pour too fast or the sudden rise in temperature might cook the eggs and curdle your custard. Scrape the seeds out of the vanilla beans into the custard and whisk until evenly dispersed.

Pour the custard over the croissants until the mixture reaches the top of the tin. Set aside for a few minutes, then use your fingertips to punch holes through the pastries, to allow the custard to soak into them. Continue pouring in the custard in small additions until the pastries feel soft.

Bake for 45 minutes, or until a paring knife inserted into the pudding comes out clean. Remove from the oven, set aside to cool for 30 minutes, then cover and refrigerate for 2 hours. Remove from the fridge and use a serrated knife to remove any burnt or dried-up pastry from the top. To do this, run the knife straight over the edges of the tin, from one side all the way to the other. Place a serving plate over the tin and flip the pudding over, then remove the tin and baking paper.

To make a glaze, put the jam and 2 tablespoons water in a small saucepan and stir over medium heat until melted and smooth. Brush the glaze over the pudding. Serve warm with fresh berries and yoghurt or thick (double/heavy) cream. As with many custard cakes and puddings, this can be kept for up to 1 week in the fridge and tastes delicious served either cold or warmed in a 180°C (350°F) oven for 5 minutes.

To fully appreciate this cake, you need to take it back to its original setting in the Ardèche area, in the Rhône-Alpes region. This region is famed for its local produce, green pastures and rich cuisine — think quenelles, *gratin dauphinois*, cheese fondue, frog legs, polenta rabbit stew, *rissoles savoyardes* (puff pastry turnovers with a pear filling) and, of course, wines and cheeses. From Paul Bocuse to the Troisgros brothers, it is home to some of the most acclaimed Michelin-starred restaurants and is, without a doubt, the gastronomic capital of France.

As it happens, the whole maternal side of my family originates and still lives in this amazing region. Every time I return to France to visit my aunt and uncle in a beautiful medieval village called Crémieu, I am invariably treated to a banquet of some of the best traditional French food and wines imaginable, from the most outrageously rich gratins to an array of incredibly subtle cheeses.

Now, back to our chestnut and caramel cake. Yes, it is a decadent cake with its buttery, earthy, slightly chewy crumb and bitter chocolate glaze, but it is possibly one of the best desserts to enjoy with friends and family as you sit around a dining table in front of a fire on a long, cold winter's night, solving all of the world's problems.

Ardéchois à la crème de marrons et ganache au caramel salé

(Chestnut cake with salted caramel ganache)

Serves 10

500 g (1 lb 2 oz) tinned sweetened chestnut cream
  (crème de marrons), at room temperature
100 g (3¹/₂ oz) unsalted butter, at room temperature
4 eggs
2 egg yolks
40 ml (1¹/₄ fl oz) rum
3 tablespoons honey
100 g (3¹/₂ oz) plain (all-purpose) flour, sifted
1 teaspoon baking powder
100 g (3¹/₂ oz) candied chestnuts (marrons glacés), coarsely chopped
80 g (2³/₄ oz) raw almonds, coarsely chopped

Salted caramel ganache

80 ml (2³/₄ fl oz) whipping cream (35% fat)
80 g (2³/₄ oz) caster (superfine) sugar
100 g (3¹/₂ oz) dark chocolate (75% minimum cocoa
  solids), chopped
generous pinch of fleur de sel or other salt flakes

tip

It is important that you use chocolate with a high percentage of cocoa (less sugar) to reduce the sweetness of the salted caramel ganache. The salt will balance the bitterness of both the burnt caramel and chocolate.

~ Preheat the oven to 170°C (340°F). Lightly grease a 25 cm (10 in) round cake tin.

~ Using an electric mixer fitted with a paddle attachment, beat the chestnut cream and butter on medium speed for 3–4 minutes, or until smooth and creamy. Both the chestnut cream and butter must be at room temperature, or the butter will harden and won't emulsify properly with the chestnut cream. Add the eggs and egg yolks, one at a time, allowing each addition to be incorporated before adding the next. Add the rum and honey, then increase the speed to high and beat for another 5 minutes, or until light and fluffy. Remove the bowl from the machine, then fold in the sifted flour, baking powder, candied chestnuts and almonds until just combined. Don't be tempted to mix the batter too much once the flour has been added, or the water in the mixture will develop the gluten in the flour, resulting in a cake with a tough, elastic crumb.

~ Pour the mixture into the prepared cake tin. Bake on the bottom shelf of the oven for 40 minutes, or until a skewer inserted into the centre of the cake comes out clean. Remove from the oven and allow to cool before removing from the tin.

~ To make the salted caramel ganache, put the cream in a small saucepan and bring to the boil over medium heat. Remove from the heat and set aside. Put the sugar in a heavy-based saucepan and cook over medium heat, stirring continuously with a wooden spoon. When the sugar begins to caramelise, reduce the heat to low and continue cooking until the caramel begins to foam and smoke. At this stage, increase the heat to high, then slowly pour the warm cream onto the caramel. Be very careful when you do this, as the difference in temperature will create a lot of hot steam, so keep your hands as far away as you can from the caramel. Once well combined, remove from the heat.

~ Put the chocolate in a small heatproof bowl. Pour the hot caramel over the chocolate, stirring continuously, and combine well. Using a hand-held stick blender, process until smooth and shiny, then stir in the salt.

~ Place the cake on a flat serving plate and pour the chocolate ganache over the top, starting from the middle and making your way to the side. If you like, decorate with chocolate curls or candied chestnuts. This cake is delicious with a glass of Champagne or sweet wine.

Quatre-quarts (literally meaning 'four-quarters') is the French version of a pound cake, traditionally made by mixing the same amount of the four main ingredients: flour, eggs, sugar and butter. The *quatre-quarts*, along with many other classic desserts, such as Paris–Brest, éclairs and macarons, have enjoyed a resurgence in popularity over the last decade and can now be found in the best cake shops around the globe. While *quatre-quarts* remain rustic in appearance, they are now customised with an almost infinite array of added flavours and textures.

Quatre-quarts à la poire et aux dates

(Date and pear pound cakes)

Serves 10–12

200 g (7 oz) pitted dates, finely chopped
100 g (3¹/2 oz) sultanas (golden raisins)
300 g (10¹/2 oz) unsalted butter, at room temperature
300 g (10¹/2 oz) caster (superfine) sugar
110 g (3³/4 oz) Greek-style yoghurt
2 tablespoons honey
7 eggs
400 g (14 oz) plain (all-purpose) flour
10 g (¹/4 oz) baking powder
100 ml (3¹/2 fl oz) rum

Poached pear

1 pear, preferably williams (bartlett) or beurre bosc
350 g (12 oz) caster (superfine) sugar
2 teaspoons ground cinnamon
2 vanilla beans, halved lengthways

To decorate

slivered pistachios
flaked almonds
chopped glacé cherries

﹏ Put the dates and sultanas in a bowl, cover with warm water and soak for 1 hour.

﹏ Meanwhile, to make the poached pear, peel the pear and set aside. Put the sugar, cinnamon, vanilla beans and 1 litre (35 fl oz) water in a saucepan and bring to the boil over medium heat. Add the pear and simmer for 15 minutes, or until tender but still firm to the bite. To check if the pear is cooked, insert a paring knife into the fruit; the flesh should be soft for about 1 cm (¹/2 in) and then firm to the core. Remove from the heat and leave the pear in the syrup until cool. Drain the pear, reserving the syrup. Pat dry with paper towel, then halve and core the pear and cut into 1 cm (¹/2 in) pieces.

﹏ Preheat the oven to 160°C (320°F). Lightly grease and flour three 8 x 15 cm (3¹/4 x 6 in) cake tins or use two 18 cm (7 in) round tins if you prefer.

﹏ Using an electric mixer fitted with a paddle attachment, beat the butter, sugar, yoghurt and honey until light and fluffy. Reduce the speed to low, then add the eggs one at a time and beat until well combined. Sift the flour and baking powder together, then add to the batter in one go. Drain the dates and sultanas; add the drained fruit and the rum to the batter and beat on low speed until just combined.

﹏ Half-fill the prepared tins with the batter, arrange three-quarters of the pears over the top, then top with the remaining batter. Bake for 10 minutes, then open the oven door and, using a lightly oiled knife, cut a line lengthways down the top of each cake — this will control the cracking into a nice, straight line. Bake for another 1 hour, or until a skewer inserted into the centre of a cake comes out clean.

﹏ Remove the cakes from the oven, brush a generous amount of the poaching syrup over the top, then turn the hot cakes out of the tins onto a wire rack to cool. When cool, decorate with the remaining pears, the pistachios, almonds and glacé cherries.

Osmosis is a process whereby a light solvent (in this case, water and essences) naturally moves through a semipermeable membrane into a solvent with a higher density (the thick sugar syrup) until each solvent reaches the same density. In the instance of our candied lemons, the osmosis movement pushes the oil and water out of the lemon through the pectin membrane of the skin, and is replaced by the thicker syrup (reverse osmosis). When candying whole fruit, this process is repeated several times with syrup of ever-increasing density (more sugar).

Gâteau à l'huile, yoghurt cake, *quatre-quarts* ... there are dozens of variations of what are commonly known as pound cakes, all with their own origins and characteristics. This version has grown exponentially in popularity largely due to increased concerns about obesity and cardiovascular disease. With no butter, and therefore no cholesterol, this cake — long ignored by bakers anywhere north of the Mediterranean basin — seems to have become a perfect 'guilt-free' indulgence.

Gâteau à l'huile d'olive, au citron confit et à la lavande

(Olive oil cake with candied lemons and lavender)

Serves 8

note : Start this recipe a day ahead.

200 g (7 oz) plain (all-purpose) flour
1 teaspoon baking powder
150 g (5^1/$_2$ oz) caster (superfine) sugar
^{1}/$_2$ teaspoon fine salt
2 eggs
100 ml (3^1/$_2$ fl oz) full-cream milk
100 ml (3^1/$_2$ fl oz) virgin olive oil
50 ml (1^3/$_4$ fl oz) Limoncello or Grand Marnier
lavender essence, to taste

Candied lemons

500 g (1 lb 2 oz) caster (superfine) sugar
2 vanilla beans, halved lengthways
3 lemons, cut into 3 mm (^{1}/$_8$ in) slices

Using an electric mixer fitted with a paddle attachment, combine the flour, baking powder, sugar and salt on low speed. Lightly beat the eggs, milk, olive oil and alcohol in a bowl until combined. With the motor running, gradually add the egg mixture to the dry mixture, scraping down the side of the bowl as you go. Once combined, increase the speed to high and beat for another 2–3 minutes, or until emulsified. Cover the bowl with plastic wrap and refrigerate for 2 hours.

Meanwhile, to make the candied lemons, put 500 ml (17 fl oz) water, the sugar and vanilla beans in a saucepan and bring to the boil over medium heat. Add the sliced lemons, then reduce the heat to low and simmer for 10 minutes, or until the lemon skin is translucent and soft. Remove from the heat, transfer to a heatproof bowl and cover immediately with plastic wrap. Set aside until cool, then refrigerate overnight.

Preheat the oven to 170°C (340°F). Lightly grease and flour a 25 cm (10 in) round or a 10 x 25 cm (4 x 10 in) rectangular cake tin. Drain the lemon slices, reserving the syrup and vanilla beans. Arrange some of the candied lemon slices in a regular pattern to cover the base of the prepared tin. Coarsely chop the remaining lemons.

Remove the batter from the fridge and stir in 80 g (2^3/$_4$ oz) of the chopped lemons and a few drops of lavender essence, to taste. The amount will vary depending on the type of essence you have but you need to be sparing with essences in general; they are meant to add a gentle floral touch — too much will ruin the cake.

Pour the batter over the lemon slices, then bake for 30 minutes, or until a skewer inserted into the cake comes out clean. Remove the tin from the oven and pour 100 ml (3^1/$_2$ fl oz) of reserved lemon syrup over the top of the cake. Refrigerate immediately for at least 3 hours. To unmould, place the cake in a 200°C (400°F) oven for 5 minutes, then invert onto a serving plate. The cake is best eaten freshly baked, although it tastes delicious reheated the day after.

This wouldn't be a true French cookbook if it didn't include at least one soufflé recipe. This is quite a wonderful and impressive-looking dessert and I clearly remember how dazzled I was when I first laid eyes on this fluffy, wondrous concoction. My parents took my sister and me to the Negresco, one of the most iconic and luxurious hotels on the Côte d'Azur. It was the mid-seventies and soufflés and bombe Alaska reigned supreme. I remember sitting in my velvet-covered chair, under a huge crystal candelabra, when the waiter gently rested a soufflé in front of me. I was literally stunned; it was so high and fluffy — I'd never seen anything like it.

Even now that I understand the chemistry behind it all, making a soufflé remains a truly magnificent juggling act, needing just the right balance between starch and eggs to trap the steam necessary for it to rise and set, and just the right temperature so the eggs don't coagulate too fast. But don't be nervous; the method is actually very simple and almost failproof if you follow the recipe carefully.

Soufflé à la Chartreuse et coulis de fraises poivrées

(Chartreuse soufflé with peppered strawberry coulis)

Serves 2

melted unsalted butter, for greasing
caster (superfine) sugar, for dusting
2 egg whites
100 g (3½ oz) caster (superfine) sugar

Custard base

250 ml (9 fl oz) full-cream milk
1 vanilla bean, halved lengthways, seeds scraped
55 g (2 oz) caster (superfine) sugar
3 egg yolks
25 g (1 oz) plain (all-purpose) flour
15 ml (½ fl oz) Chartreuse liqueur

Strawberry coulis

50 g (1¾ oz) caster (superfine) sugar
150 g (5½ oz) strawberries, hulled and chopped
½ teaspoon finely grated lemon zest
⅛ teaspoon freshly ground black pepper

~ Using a pastry brush, lightly grease two 250 ml (9 fl oz) ramekins or ovenproof coffee cups with melted butter, making sure that the brush strokes go vertically, from the bottom to the top of the dish, to help the soufflé to rise. Spoon a little sugar into each ramekin, turning the dish around so that the sugar coats the entire surface. Tip the ramekins upside down and tap them to remove any excess sugar. Place the ramekins on a baking tray and set aside at room temperature.

~ To make the custard base, put the milk, vanilla bean and seeds in a saucepan and bring to the boil, then remove from the heat, pour into a bowl and set aside to cool for 1–2 minutes.

~ Meanwhile, put the sugar and 2 egg yolks in a bowl. Using a hand-held whisk, whisk the sugar and egg yolks for 2–3 minutes, or until light and creamy, then whisk in the flour until smooth. Whisking continuously, gradually add the warm milk and whisk until well combined. Pour the mixture into a saucepan and whisk continuously over medium heat until the mixture comes to the boil and is thick and smooth. Remove from the heat and whisk in the liqueur, then set aside for 5 minutes to cool a little before whisking in the final egg yolk (don't add it too soon or it will curdle). Cover the bowl with a damp cloth and set aside.

~ To make the strawberry coulis, put the sugar and 100 ml (3½ fl oz) water in a small saucepan and bring to the boil over high heat. Add the chopped strawberries, lemon zest and pepper, then reduce the heat to low and simmer for 2 minutes. Remove from the heat and transfer to a small bowl and while still hot, cover with plastic wrap and set aside to cool. Using a stick blender or food processor, purée the coulis until smooth, then transfer to a squeeze bottle or pouring jug. Refrigerate until needed.

~ Preheat the oven to 180°C (350°F). Place the egg whites in a spotlessly clean bowl. Using a hand-held whisk (I strongly recommend you whisk the egg whites by hand to avoid splitting the eggs — see tip), whisk the egg whites until foamy and soft, then gradually add the sugar and whisk until the meringue forms stiff peaks. The simplest way to check if the meringue is ready is to flip the bowl upside down. If the meringue doesn't drop on your head, it is ready! A better way to check this is to use the whisk to lift up a small amount of meringue; if it creates a stiff peak, it is ready.

~ Using a large spatula, fold the meringue into the cooled custard in three or four batches. A folding motion means that you gently rotate your spatula from the bottom to the top of the mix. Never whack the spatula from side to side or the mixture will release all the air and won't rise during baking.

~ Fill the sugar-dusted ramekins all the way to the top, making sure that no mixture touches the rim, as this exposed mixture will cook instantly and stop the soufflé from rising evenly. Bake for 10–12 minutes, or until the tops are golden. Don't be tempted to open the oven door during baking, as you need to build up steam inside the oven for your soufflé to rise properly. As soon as they are cooked, remove from the oven and poke a 2 cm (¾ in) hole through the top. Pour 1 tablespoon of coulis into each hole and serve immediately.

technical tip

The pressure point when making a soufflé is the meringue. If you underwhip the eggs, the soufflé will not rise; overwhip them and you will end up with a grainy and wet mess. To get it right you must first understand that a meringue rises by the act of pushing air into the elastic egg protein (albumen). As you whisk, the protein molecules weave together, trapping more and more bubbles of air, creating a shiny elastic foam. However, those molecules can only stretch so far. Overmixing will cause the eggs to 'split' or, technically speaking, the protein strands will separate and lose their ability to retain their water, in which case your meringue will become grainy and watery and will collapse during baking. Although this seems a little paradoxical, the golden rule is simple: when in doubt, always underwhip your meringue.

If you have ever been to France and browsed the dairy section of any supermarket, you would have noticed the huge range of rice-based puddings and desserts. Like many of the recipes in this book, rice puddings and cakes were part of my staple diet as a child. They are the ideal pick-me-up for kids (or adults for that matter) on the run.

Gâteaux de riz au caramel et à la fleur d'oranger

(Caramel and orange blossom rice cakes)

Serves 10

note : Start this recipe a day ahead.

20 g (³/4 oz) fine salt
180 g (6¹/4 oz) arborio rice
500 ml (17 fl oz) full-cream milk
250 ml (9 fl oz) whipping cream (35% fat)
2 vanilla beans, halved lengthways

150 g (5¹/2 oz) sultanas (golden raisins)
1 egg
320 g (11¹/4 oz) caster (superfine) sugar
1 tablespoon orange blossom water

~ Lightly grease ten 185 ml (6 fl oz) ramekins and place them on a baking tray. Alternatively, use a 2 litre (70 fl oz) tall cake tin or kugelhopf mould (because you are lining the base with caramel, don't use a springform tin).

~ Bring 1 litre (35 fl oz) water and the salt to the boil in a saucepan over high heat. Add the rice and cook for 4 minutes, then drain and rinse under cold running water. This process is designed to rid the rice of most of its starch.

~ Put the cold rice, milk, cream, vanilla beans and sultanas in a saucepan and simmer over low heat, stirring occasionally, for 20 minutes, or until the liquid has been absorbed. Towards the end of cooking, you will need to stir the rice continuously to prevent the mixture catching on the base of the pan. Meanwhile, using an electric mixer fitted with a whisk attachment, whisk the egg and 120 g (4¹/4 oz) of the sugar until thick and pale. When the rice is ready, add the egg mixture to the rice and combine well. Stir in the orange blossom water and set aside.

~ Preheat the oven to 170°C (340°F). To make the caramel, put 80 ml (2³/4 fl oz) water in a saucepan, then add the remaining 200 g (7 oz) of sugar. Cook over high heat until the sugar begins to caramelise around the edges, then reduce the heat to low and cook until golden. While the caramel is cooking, use a pastry brush dipped in cold water to clean off any sugar crystals on the side of the pan. Working quickly and carefully, pour the caramel evenly over the base of the ramekins.

~ Scrape the seeds out of the vanilla beans into the rice mixture, then discard the beans. Fill the caramel-lined ramekins with the rice mixture all the way to the top. Cover with foil and bake for 15–20 minutes, or until the rice is cooked through and doesn't wobble when you gently shake one of the ramekins. Remove the rice cakes from the oven and leave to cool, then refrigerate overnight.

tip
Sugar loses sweetness during the caramelisation process, but it gains bitterness. For this recipe, I prefer a light golden or a blonde (pale and lightly cooked) caramel, because the mixture for the rice cake has a low sugar content and will benefit from a sweeter caramel.

~ The following day, place the ramekins in a 200°C (400°F) oven for 3 minutes. Run the blade of a paring knife around the inside of each ramekin, then invert the rice puddings onto serving plates. It is important that you reheat the ramekins in a very hot oven — dipping them in boiling water will not be hot enough to soften the caramel at the base of the puddings.

Tartes et tourtes

'If you wish to make an apple pie from scratch,
you must first invent the universe.'

CARL SAGAN

Tartes et tourtes

(Tarts and pies)

Tarts are one of those staples of pâtisserie that have remained almost unchanged since they were first documented at the beginning of the Middle Ages. They are usually circular, made out of shortcrust or puff pastry, and are either sweet treats layered with fruit, filled with creams and sweet curds, or savoury, with fillings such as meats and vegetables. In this chapter, I have also included a few *tourtes* (pies), which are basically the same as a tart but covered with a thin layer of pastry. Again, there are sweet versions, such as the apple pie, or savoury, such as the classic meat pie.

When I was a child, tarts seemed to be the one thing that I was fascinated with. Whenever I walked past a pâtisserie, I was always so completely dazzled by the seemingly endless range of tarts and pies in the window display, in all shapes and sizes, colours and textures. The reason I was so enthralled with them was probably because I could almost understand how they were made. It was all there, right in front of me: the thinly sliced apples, the caramelised creams, the shiny glazed fruit — what I saw I could almost taste, unlike the *petits gâteaux* or *entremets* (multi-layered desserts), which were such elaborate works of art that I felt I had no hope of ever re-creating them.

I have included a lot of recipes in this chapter because tarts and pies are a perfect canvas to explore your creativity, improvise or use left-over ingredients. These are some of my favourite tarts and pies, but feel free to stamp your own style on any of these recipes and replace any of the fruits and creams based on your location, season or mood.

Tarte ganache aux framboises fraiches
(Chocolate ganache tart with fresh raspberries) ~ page 108

Pâtes

(Pastries)

Before the invention of puff pastries, Danishes or croissants, bakers and cooks had long been using sweet and savoury shortcrust pastries to prepare their dishes. These doughs, whether they are *pâtes sablées*, *brisées* or *sucrées*, are all made using three or four common ingredients: flour, fat, salt, sometimes with a liquid in the form of eggs or water, and, in the case of the sweet shortcrust and shortbread pastries, an addition of sugar. Typically, the type of shortcrust you require will dictate the technique applied to these ingredients. From the very short, buttery *pâte sablée* used for *petits fours* to the *pâte à pâté* (literally meaning 'shortcrust for pâté', or terrine), there is a bewildering array of pastry variations to cater for every need. I have chosen three basic pastries for the recipes in this book.

In French pastry cooking, we make a distinction between two types of shortcrust pastries: *pâte sablée* (similar technically to *pâte brisée*, which is used in savoury pastries) and *pâte sucrée*.

1. Pâte sablée (shortbread pastry):

Pâte sablée is a very short and buttery biscuit or shortbread pastry that is made by a method called *sablage*, meaning that you first need to mix the butter into the flour before introducing any liquids (if you choose to do so). This process 'greases' the gluten (protein) in the flour and stops it from absorbing any liquids you might add. This in turn stops the strands of gluten from lengthening, resulting in a very crumbly (short) pastry. However, a true *pâte sablée* (made of butter, sugar, salt and flour) is a challenge to roll for anything more than one or two tarts at a time, so in commercial kitchens it's mainly used in the manufacture of *petits fours secs* (biscuits).

You are probably unlikely to want to make hundreds of tarts at one time, so I recommend using this pastry for most of the tarts and pies in this chapter. To make the dough a little more pliable and easier to handle, I have added an egg yolk to the basic recipe. This pastry is much more delicate and flavoursome than *pâte sucrée* and is incredibly simple to make.

2. Pâte brisée (savoury shortcrust pastry):

This is actually very similar to a *pâte sablée* in its methodology, except that it is made without any sugar and contains a lot more liquids. The method of 'sanding' (*sablage*) the fat and flour together will ensure that your dough remains brittle, or short, and will reduce the risk of shrinkage, while the addition of liquid will add the necessary elasticity to make it easy to roll. Bakers tend to favour this type of pastry when baking tarts or pies filled with soft or liquid ingredients such as quiches because, unlike flaked doughs such as puff pastry, which relies on its dried-up layers of pastry for texture, a shortcrust will cook well regardless of the viscosity of its filling.

3. Pâte sucrée (sweet shortcrust pastry):

Made using almost the same ingredients as *pâte sablée*, this pastry is more elastic, and therefore ideal for the large-scale manufacture of tart and sweet pie bases. While it is a lot easier to handle, it tends to be crunchier and tougher than a *pâte sablée*. The difference between the two pastries lies not in their ingredients, although the ratio is slightly different, but in the technique used. For *pâte sucrée*, you need to cream the butter and sugar, then add the liquid (eggs), and finish off by adding the flour directly into the wet mixture. Because the gluten in the flour is directly exposed to a liquid, it will develop its characteristic elasticity and subsequent different texture.

Pâte sablée

(Shortbread pastry)

This crumbly, delicate pastry is the foundation for most of the sweet tarts in this chapter. It can be a little hard to handle, so if you are new to making pastry, I suggest you add the egg yolk.

Makes 600 g (1 lb 5 oz)

note : To make chocolate *pâte sablée*, substitute 60 g (2$^{1}/_{4}$ oz) of the flour with unsweetened cocoa powder.

300 g (10$^{1}/_{2}$ oz) plain (all-purpose) flour
1$^{1}/_{4}$ teaspoons fine salt
200 g (7 oz) cold unsalted butter, chopped
100 g (3$^{1}/_{2}$ oz) caster (superfine) sugar
1 egg yolk (optional)

By mixer

Using an electric mixer fitted with a dough hook attachment, combine the flour, salt and butter on low speed for 2–3 minutes, or until the lumps of butter are evenly dispersed and the mixture resembles coarse breadcrumbs (sablage).

Stop the mixer, scrape down the side of the bowl, then add the sugar and the egg yolk, if using, and mix until well combined. Transfer the pastry to the work surface and shape it into a ball. Cover in plastic wrap and refrigerate for at least 2 hours.

When you are ready to use it, transfer the cold pastry to an electric mixer fitted with a dough hook attachment and mix on low speed for 2–3 minutes, or until the pastry reaches a consistent, firm texture.

By hand

Put the flour and salt in a mound on your work surface and make a well in the middle. Place the butter in the well (*photo 1*) and mix the butter into the flour by rubbing your hands together (*2, 3*) until the mixture resembles coarse breadcrumbs (*sablage*).

Shape the mixture into a mound again (*4*) and make a well in the middle. Add the sugar (*5*), then the egg yolk (*6*) and use your fingertips and the heel of your hand (*7, 8*) to incorporate them into the flour without kneading the dough (*fraisage*). Note that kneading will develop the gluten and toughen the pastry.

Shape into a disc (*9*), cover in plastic wrap and refrigerate for at least 2 hours.

cooking tips :

⌣ Never want to forget this recipe again? Weigh any amount of butter, divide it by two to work out the amount of sugar, then combine the weight of the butter and sugar to work out the weight of the flour.

⌣ To make deliciously buttery Scottish shortbread, simply substitute 10 per cent of the flour in the recipe above with maize cornflour (cornstarch) and do not add the egg yolk. This will make your dough incredibly short, but amazingly buttery and brittle.

1

Pâte sablée

2

3

4

5

6

7

8

9

Pâte sablée

Pâte brisée

(Savoury shortcrust pastry)

This savoury pastry is very similar to *pâte sablée*, except it is made without sugar and contains more liquids (egg yolks and water). The method for making this pastry by hand is the same as for *pâte sablée*.

Makes 900 g (2 lb)

500 g (1 lb 2 oz) plain (all-purpose) flour
1¼ teaspoons fine salt
½ teaspoon finely ground black pepper
250 g (9 oz) cold unsalted butter, chopped
2 egg yolks
100 ml (3½ fl oz) cold water

By mixer

Using an electric mixer fitted with a dough hook attachment, combine the flour, salt, pepper and butter *(photo 1)* on low speed for 2–3 minutes, or until the lumps are evenly dispersed and the mixture resembles coarse breadcrumbs *(sablage)*.

Stop the mixer, scrape down the side of the bowl, then add the egg yolks and cold water *(2)* and mix until well combined *(3)*.

Transfer the pastry to the work surface and shape it into a flattened disc *(4)*. Cover in plastic wrap and refrigerate for at least 2 hours.

When you are ready to use it, transfer the cold pastry to an electric mixer fitted with a dough hook attachment and mix on low speed for 2–3 minutes, or until the pastry reaches a consistent, firm texture.

cooking tips :

⌐ This dough, as for all short doughs, should not be worked too much, as this develops the gluten in the flour and not only increases shrinkage but also gives you a tough finished product. Most savoury tart shells will be filled with a liquid, so any shrinkage will increase the risk that the liquid will spill over the edge of the shell and run underneath the pastry, making it soggy. To prevent this, cook your savoury shortcrust pastry with a little excess dough folded over the top of the tin. This ensures the filling won't spill over the top if the pastry shell shrinks during baking. As soon as the tart comes out of the oven, run a knife around the top of the tin to trim the excess cooked pastry.

⌐ You can personalise your tart or pie by adding some finely chopped basil leaves or a small handful of blanched, chopped baby spinach to the dough. This not only gives an additional layer of flavour to your tart but also gives the pastry shell a lovely green hue. You can also add ½ teaspoon of your favourite spice — whatever best suits the filling or topping you are using. Add the herbs and spices at the same time as when you add the egg yolks and cold water.

1

2

3

4

Pâte brisée

Pâte sucrée

(Sweet shortcrust pastry)

The recipe I have given below is actually a *pâte sucrée légère*, (light sweet shortcrust pastry)
because it contains baking powder, which gives the dough a more brittle and more delicate texture.
For a traditional version of *pâte sucrée*, simply omit the baking powder.

Makes 850 g (1 lb 14 oz)

270 g (9¹/₂ oz) caster (superfine) sugar
240 g (8¹/₂ oz) unsalted butter, at room temperature
1 egg
2 egg yolks
300 g (10¹/₂ oz) plain (all-purpose) flour
75 g (2³/₄ oz) almond meal
1 teaspoon fine salt
1 teaspoon baking powder (optional)

By mixer

Using an electric mixer fitted with a paddle attachment, beat the sugar and butter on low speed for 2 minutes, or until just combined. Be careful not to cream the mixture.

Add the egg and egg yolks and beat on low speed for another 3–5 minutes, regularly scraping down the side of the bowl. Don't worry if the mixture looks as if it has split — the eggs don't have to be fully incorporated into the mixture. Stop the mixer and replace the paddle attachment with a dough hook. Add the dry ingredients and mix on low speed until just combined.

Remove the pastry from the bowl and shape it into a disc (the thinner the disc of dough, the quicker it will firm up), cover in plastic wrap and refrigerate for at least 2 hours.

By hand

Put the sugar in a mound on your work surface and make a well in the middle. Add the butter *(photo 1)*, then, using the heel of your hand, press the sugar into the butter *(2)* until smooth and well combined. Shape the mixture into a small mound and make another well in the middle. Add the egg and egg yolks *(3)* and use your fingertips to combine well *(4, 5)*. Use a pastry scraper or flat spatula to help scrape the butter off the work surface. Avoid using your hands to do this, as it will soften the butter too much.

Put the flour, almond meal, salt and baking powder, if using, in a bowl and combine well. Shape the butter and egg mixture into a thin disc, put the flour mixture on top *(6)* and use the *fraisage* method with the heel of your hand to press the two together *(7)*. Lift the pastry off the work surface with a pastry scraper *(8)*, turn it over and press together again (don't ever knead a shortcrust pastry or it will become tough and unpalatable). Shape into a disc *(9)*, cover in plastic wrap and refrigerate for at least 2 hours.

freezing doughs :

~ Most of the tarts in this chapter require only half the quantity of dough, but I have suggested these quantities because it is easier for the mixer to mix well. The left-over dough freezes very well, and can be used for another tart. Cover in plastic wrap and freeze for up to 3 months.

If you are going to freeze any left-over dough for future use, add a 500 mg Vitamin C tablet for each 500 g (1 lb 2 oz) of flour. Crush the tablet and dissolve it in the eggs when making the dough. While this tip is more relevant for yeasted doughs or a wet dough such as puff pastry, it will help prolong the life span of the gluten and reduce the rate of oxidation (formation of brown spots) in the flour (for more on freezing doughs, see page 149).

1

2

3

4

Pâte sucrée

5

6

7

8

9

Pâte sucrée

Rolling, lining and blind baking

Once you've invested time and love making your pastry, you want to make sure you treat it with the same delicate hand when rolling it out and lining the tart shell.

Rolling the pastry

While most pastry tends to shrink a little during baking, you can help reduce this by working the pastry as little as possible when rolling it out. Overworking the pastry develops the gluten in the flour and this not only increases the chances of shrinkage, it also toughens it. Always roll pastry on a lightly floured work surface from the centre outwards, rotating the pastry 45 degrees at regular intervals rather than rolling the pin back and forth.

If it is warm in your kitchen and the dough becomes too soft to work with and sticks to the work surface, roll the pastry out between two pieces of baking paper, then refrigerate it briefly until it firms up a little.

Lining the tin

To transfer the pastry to the tin, place your rolling pin on the bottom end of the pastry and loosely roll the pastry around the pin. Carefully unroll the pastry into the tin. If you have rolled out your pastry between pieces of baking paper, remove the top sheet, then carefully invert the pastry over the tart tin (make sure you centre the pastry over the tin when you do this, because it's difficult to move it once in the tin), then peel off the paper.

Once the pastry is in the tin, quickly lift up the excess pastry hanging over the side, so it doesn't break over the sharp edge of the tin. Dust lightly with flour *(photo 1)*. To trim the pastry, carefully run a small sharp knife around the rim of the tin and cut away the excess pastry *(2)*.

Alternatively, if you are using a liquid filling, such as a filling for quiche, leave the edge of the pastry slightly overhanging

the side of the tin to allow for any shrinkage. If the pastry shrinks, you run the risk of the filling seeping over the edge of the pastry and underneath the base, which will make it soggy. As soon as the cooked tart is removed from the oven, trim around the edge of the tin using a small sharp knife. Cutting the pastry after cooking does look a bit less tidy than if you had cut it beforehand, but it ensures you won't have a soggy base.

Refrigerate the pastry-lined tin for 30 minutes before baking. This helps the gluten in the flour to 'relax' and will reduce the chances of shrinkage.

Blind baking

To blind bake your tart shell, line the base and side of the chilled tart shell with a large piece of foil, leaving the foil overhanging the side.

Fill to the top with uncooked rice *(3)*, dried beans or baking beads, then fold the foil over the top of the rice to leave the top edge of the tart shell exposed *(4)*. Filling with weights such as rice prevents the pastry from rising unevenly and blistering as it cooks. To a certain extent, it also reduces the possibility of the pastry sides shrinking, however, this will have more to do with how the pastry was made and rolled. You can buy baking beads from kitchenware shops, but I find rice works better as it gives a more consistent coverage (and it's considerably cheaper). You can reuse the rice or beans repeatedly.

Blind bake the tart shell at 180°C (350°F) for 20 minutes, or until the base is light golden. Remove the rice and foil and allow the tart shell to cool before filling.

cooking tip :

~ It is a good idea to reserve some of the pastry scraps in case your tart shell cracks a little during blind baking. If your filling is reasonably dry, a crack won't matter too much, but if it is runny, the liquid will seep through the crack, resulting in a soggy pastry base. Simply patch up any cracks on the hot tart shell with a small piece of reserved pastry and return to the oven for 5 minutes or so to allow it to dry out.

1

2

3

4

Rolling, lining and blind baking

This combination of ricotta, orange and chocolate is a classically Mediterranean one — you might have tried this filling in cannoli, a Sicilian dessert made of a fine, crunchy tube of pastry, filled with ricotta and various flavour combinations. In Provence, we typically add either orange blossom water or rosewater, anise or fennel flowers to the ricotta. This particular recipe uses pastis, an anise-based liqueur originating from Marseille, consumed profusely by the locals as a late-afternoon refreshment.

Tarte ricotta-orange au chocolat et au pastis

(Ricotta, orange, chocolate and pastis tart)

Serves 8–10

300 g (10^{1}/$_2$ oz) Pâte Sablée (pages 80–3)
600 g (1 lb 5 oz) fresh ricotta cheese, drained (see tip)
150 g (5^{1}/$_2$ oz) mascarpone
150 g (5^{1}/$_2$ oz) caster (superfine) sugar
75 g (2^{3}/$_4$ oz) honey
2 eggs

3 egg yolks
150 g (5^{1}/$_2$ oz) dark chocolate (65% cocoa solids)
finely grated zest of 2 oranges
30 ml (1 fl oz) pastis liqueur
pure icing (confectioners') sugar, for dusting
dried citrus zest (page 55), to serve (optional)

〜 You will need a 25 cm (10 in) tart ring or tart tin with a removable base. Roll out the pastry on a lightly floured work surface until 5 mm (^{1}/$_4$ in) thick, dusting with a little extra flour if necessary to stop the dough from sticking. Line the base and side of the tin with the pastry, then refrigerate for 30 minutes.

〜 Preheat the oven to 175°C (345°F). This tart can be cooked directly in the raw pastry shell but, just to be safe, you can begin the baking process by par-baking the crust. Line the pastry shell with foil, making sure the side of the shell is covered, then fill to the top with uncooked rice or baking beads. Bake for 15 minutes, or until the side of the pastry is golden. Unlike a full blind bake, which is usually reserved for very soft fillings, you want to stop baking as soon as the pastry around the side turns a light golden brown; the bottom should still be blonde. Remove the rice and foil and set aside to cool.

〜 Using an electric mixer fitted with a paddle attachment, beat the ricotta, mascarpone, sugar and honey until well combined. With the motor on low speed, add the eggs and egg yolks one at a time, then increase the speed to medium and beat for another 2–3 minutes, or until well combined.

〜 Using a large knife, finely chop the chocolate (don't use a food processor to do this or the chocolate will melt). Combine the chocolate with the orange zest and pastis, then add to the cheese mixture and beat for 30 seconds.

〜 Reduce the oven temperature to 130°C (265°F). Pour the filling into the tart shell, then bake on the bottom shelf of the oven for 35 minutes, or until the filling stops wobbling when the tart is gently shaken. Personally I find the brown skin usually found on cheesecakes and tarts a little unpalatable, so I always aim for a very blonde top. If you find that the top of the tart is browning too quickly, cover loosely with a piece of foil. This deflects the heat and slows down the colouration.

〜 Just before serving, dust with a little icing sugar and, if you like, sprinkle with dried citrus zest. This tart is delicious served either warm or cold with a peppermint tea or strong coffee in the morning. Personally, I prefer it warm, with a generous scoop of mascarpone and a drizzle of honey … but that's just me.

tip

When baking simple, wholesome food, always choose the best ingredients available. For this tart, I recommend using a soft Italian ricotta made of sheep's milk, preferably made fresh from a delicatessen, drained overnight in a cloth. Alternatively, use any fresh ricotta, but it needs to be drained in either a piece of muslin (cheesecloth) or on paper towel to remove the excess liquid.

For this very traditional cake, we are going to venture to the far south-west of France. This region is known as the Basque Country, and it sits deep in the Pyrenees mountains, right on the border of Spain. Food in this part of France uses many ingredients we think of as being typically Mediterranean, but because of the colder climate the cooking tends to be a lot richer and earthier.

This cake is a great example of those typical local characteristics, with a simple butter and almond custard sandwiched between a crumbly shortbread. It's perfect for those long winter evenings, eaten plain or with a few preserved cherries, with a bowl of hot chocolate, sitting in front of the fireplace (or, in my case, a small radiant heater).

Gâteau basque

(Almond custard Basque cake)

Serves 10

850 g (1 lb 14 oz) Pâte Sucrée (pages 86–7)
1 egg
1 egg yolk
pinch of fine salt

Almond custard

500 ml (17 fl oz) full-cream milk
2 tablespoons rum
50 g (1³⁄₄ oz) maize cornflour (cornstarch)
100 g (3¹⁄₂ oz) almond meal
120 g (4¹⁄₄ oz) caster (superfine) sugar
4 eggs
100 g (3¹⁄₂ oz) unsalted butter

~ To make the almond custard, bring the milk and rum to the boil in a saucepan over medium heat. Put the cornflour, almond meal and sugar in a heatproof bowl and combine well. Add the eggs and, using a hand-held whisk, beat until well combined and creamy. Whisking continuously, gradually add half of the boiling milk to the flour and egg mixture and combine well, then transfer the mixture to the pan with the remaining milk. Whisk continuously over medium heat until the custard comes to the boil, then continue whisking for another 2 minutes. Transfer the custard to the bowl of an electric mixer fitted with a paddle attachment. Add the butter and beat on low speed for 10 minutes, or until warm to the touch. Place the custard in a bowl, cover the surface with a piece of plastic wrap and set aside until cool to the touch.

~ Preheat the oven to 160°C (320°F). Lightly grease an 18 cm (7 in) round, 5 cm (2 in) deep tart tin with a removable base.

~ Divide the pastry in half. Roll out one portion on a lightly floured work surface until 3–4 mm (1/8 in) thick. Using the tart tin as a guide, cut out a circle of pastry about 5 cm (2 in) wider than the base of the tin. Line the base and side of the tin with the pastry. Pour the custard into the tart shell, filling it to the top. Make sure that the custard isn't too hot or the pastry will melt. Conversely, if it is too cold, it will set and become difficult to spread.

~ Roll out the second portion of pastry until 3–4 mm (1/8 in) thick, then cut out a circle of pastry about 1 cm (1/2 in) wider than the top of the tin. Roll the pastry around the rolling pin, then roll it over the top of the custard. Seal the lid to the base dough by running the rolling pin a few times over the top of the cake until the excess dough is cut off.

~ To make an egg wash, combine the egg, egg yolk and salt in a small bowl, then set aside for 5 minutes. Brush the egg wash over the top of the cake (see tip). Bake for 30 minutes, or until golden. It is crucial that this cake is baked at a low temperature to ensure that the pastry base is nicely cooked. If the cake becomes too brown before the recommended baking time, cover loosely with a piece of foil. Remove from the oven, set aside to cool, then refrigerate for at least 30 minutes before removing from the tin. Serve warm with a tablespoon of thick (double/heavy) cream or mascarpone, and with a small glass of Cognac in winter.

tip

In some versions of this traditional cake, the top is scored in a lattice pattern before baking. To do this, use the back of a paring knife to gently score the pattern over the top (after you have brushed the cake with egg wash), taking care that you don't cut right through the pastry.

Baked custards in one form or another have existed for hundreds of years, especially around the regions of Spain and Portugal, long before the first documented recipe for crème brûlée in the seventeenth century. A custard is made with a thickener, such as flour or cornflour, while a crème brûlée is more akin to a curd, where the thickness and texture is created by the coagulation of the eggs. This is why it requires a little more care during the baking process — you don't want your brûlée mix turning into an omelette! To do this tart justice, you really need a domestic blowtorch to achieve a crunchy and evenly caramelised top. A grill will tend to melt the sugar unevenly and burn the pastry.

Tartes crème brûlée à la lavande

(Lavender crème brûlée tarts)

Makes 12

8 egg yolks
200 g (7 oz) caster (superfine) sugar
250 ml (9 fl oz) full-cream milk
250 ml (9 fl oz) whipping cream (35% fat)
2 vanilla beans, halved lengthways, seeds scraped
900 g (2 lb) Pâte Sablée (pages 80–3)
lavender essence, to taste

〜 Put the egg yolks in a heatproof bowl, add half the sugar and whisk until well combined. Make sure you start whisking as soon as you pour the sugar into the egg yolks, to avoid 'burning' the eggs (see page 25).

〜 Put the milk, cream and vanilla beans and seeds in a saucepan and bring to the boil. Remove the pan from the heat and, whisking continuously, gradually pour the hot cream onto the egg mixture. Strain the custard mixture through a fine sieve into a jug. Set aside to cool, then return the vanilla beans to the mixture and refrigerate for 2 hours.

〜 You will need twelve 7.5 cm (3 in) diameter tartlet tins or a 25 cm (10 in) tart ring or tart tin with a removable base. Roll out the pastry on a lightly floured work surface until 4 mm (1/8 in) thick, dusting with a little extra flour if necessary to stop the dough from sticking. Using a 12 cm (4 1/2 in) round cutter, cut the pastry into twelve rounds. Line the base and side of the tins with the pastry, then refrigerate for 30 minutes.

〜 Preheat the oven to 180°C (350°F). Line each pastry shell with foil, making sure the side of the shell is covered, then fill to the top with uncooked rice or baking beads. Blind bake for 20 minutes, or until the base is golden (the cooking time is the same for both the small tarts and the single tart). Remove the rice and foil, then set the tart shells aside until cool. Reduce the oven temperature to 90°C (195°F).

〜 Remove the custard mixture from the fridge, remove and discard the vanilla beans, then add a few drops of lavender essence, to taste. Be careful not to overdo it; essences are very concentrated and can quickly overpower other flavours.

〜 To avoid spillage, place the tart shells on a baking tray and place in the preheated oven. Pour in the custard filling, being careful you don't overfill the shells or the filling will run over the side and the pastry will become soggy underneath. Bake for 30–40 minutes, or until the filling just wobbles when the tart is gently shaken. Set aside to cool to room temperature, then refrigerate for 3 hours. Remove from the fridge 15 minutes before serving and sprinkle the remaining sugar evenly over the tarts, including the pastry crust. Using a domestic blowtorch, brown the tops until caramelised.

The ingredients used in baking and cooking around the Mediterranean basin — from France to Greece, Spain and Sicily — have been greatly influenced by the invasion of the Moroccan Moors, around the eighth century. Common Middle Eastern spices, fruits and nuts, such as figs, saffron, almond and pistachio, have been used for centuries in Mediterranean cooking but have never really been associated with what is considered traditional French gastronomy. Despite its exotic oriental flavour profile, this tart has become a French classic, from Provence to Normandy.

Tarte à la pistache, aux figues et à l'eau de rose

(Fig and rose pistachio tart)

Serves 8–10

300 g (10¹/2 oz) Pâte Sablée (pages 80–3)
1 teaspoon rosewater, or to taste
350 g (12 oz) Pistachio Cream (page 260)
8 fresh figs

〜 Lightly grease a 25 cm (10 in) tart ring or tart tin with a removable base. The reason I recommend greasing the tart tin for this recipe (when I usually don't) is because the figs release a lot of sticky juices when cooking and they tend to caramelise around the base of the tin, making it impossible to remove the tart.

〜 Roll out the pastry on a lightly floured work surface until 4 mm (¹/8 in) thick, dusting with a little extra flour if necessary to stop the dough from sticking. Line the base and side of the tin with the pastry, then refrigerate for 30 minutes.

〜 Preheat the oven to 170°C (340°F). Stir the rosewater, to taste, into the pistachio cream. The amount you use will vary depending on the brand of rosewater and, of course, your personal taste. Remember that floral flavours such as rose, orange blossom, lavender, or any others, work best as an aroma; they are meant to add a subtle layer of complexity to your flavours, so don't be tempted to go overboard.

〜 Spoon the pistachio cream into the tart shell until two-thirds full. The volume of the pistachio cream will vary depending on how much it was beaten, so you might have some leftover. Cut the figs in half lengthways, then arrange them, cut side up, on top of the cream.

〜 Bake on the bottom shelf of the oven for 40 minutes, or until golden. You need to keep a close eye on the colour of this tart during cooking, as the fig juices released during cooking tend to caramelise before the tart is fully baked. If the top is browning too quickly, cover loosely with a piece of foil. This deflects the heat and slows down the colouration. Remove from the oven and set aside to cool a little. If you like, make a glaze (see tips, page 52) to brush over the tart. Serve warm with mascarpone or whipped cream, or cold with yoghurt.

This is such a simple, classic tart but it can be quite tricky to make. Not only do you have to deal with the uncertainty of whether the apple will stick to the mould, but you also have to think about offsetting the sweetness of the caramel and cooked apples. Let's assume that the first part is covered and the tart will come out in one piece — because it will — so then to address the sweetness issue, I have added some tart, slightly acidic rhubarb to balance the flavours. So, all hands on deck, we are doing it!

For this recipe you will need a 25 cm (10 in) ovenproof frying pan, as we are going to cook the apples directly over a high heat, then bake them in the same vessel. Alternatively, you can use a shallow, heavy-based sauté pan.

Tarte tatin à la rhubarbe

(Upside-down apple and rhubarb tart)

Serves 8

note : Start this recipe 3–4 hours in advance, to allow time for chilling.

100 g (3^{1}/$_{2}$ oz) unsalted butter
100 g (3^{1}/$_{2}$ oz) caster (superfine) sugar
3 stems rhubarb, chopped into small pieces
12 small granny smith apples (see tip)

1 tablespoon lemon juice
2 vanilla beans, halved lengthways, seeds scraped
500 g (1 lb 2 oz) Puff Pastry, 5 single turns (pages 145–9)

⌣ Melt 40 g (1^{1}/$_{2}$ oz) of the butter and 2 tablespoons of the sugar in a frying pan over high heat. Add the rhubarb, then cover and cook, stirring occasionally for 10 minutes, or until the rhubarb collapses into a thick purée. Remove from the heat and set aside until cool.

⌣ Preheat the oven to 180°C (350°F). Peel, halve and core the apples, then cut into 1 cm (^{1}/$_{2}$ in) thick slices. Sprinkle 2 tablespoons of sugar over the base of a 25 cm (10 in) heavy-based ovenproof frying pan or sauté pan. Arrange a layer of apple slices over the base of the pan, trimming the cut edges as needed so the slices fit snugly. Spread a thin layer of rhubarb purée over the apple, then repeat with the remaining apple and rhubarb. The apples will lose most of their water before they start to caramelise, so don't worry if the volume looks too big.

⌣ Melt the remaining butter in a saucepan, then add the remaining sugar, the lemon juice and vanilla bean seeds (discard the beans). Combine well, then pour over the top of the apples. Cover the pan with a lid and cook over high heat for about 10 minutes to 'sweat' the apples. When the apples have released their juices, reduce the heat to medium, then remove the lid and cook until the juices have evaporated and the apples begin to caramelise. Transfer the pan to the oven and bake for 10 minutes, or until the apples can be pierced easily with a small knife but are still firm. Remove from the oven, leave in the pan until cool, then refrigerate the apples in the pan for about 30 minutes, or until cold.

⌣ Roll out the puff pastry on a lightly floured surface into a circle about 3 mm (^{1}/$_{8}$ in) thick. Prick all over with a fork and then cut out a circle of pastry roughly 5 cm (2 in) wider than the diameter of the pan. Remove the pan with the cold apples from the fridge. Make sure the apples are cold, because any heat will melt the butter in the puff pastry. Cover the apples with the pastry, tucking the excess around the outside edges of the apples, like tucking in a blanket. Bake in a 180°C (350°F) oven for 20 minutes, or until the pastry is golden. Remove from the oven, set aside until cool, then refrigerate for 2–3 hours to allow the butter and sugar to crystallise — this will make it easier to turn out.

⌣ Before attempting the dreaded flip, heat the pan in a 200°C (400°F) oven for 5 minutes to soften the apples a little, then simply place a serving plate on top of the pan and invert the tart onto the plate. Serve warm with thick (double/heavy) cream or yoghurt or, even better, flambéed with Calvados (apple brandy) or rum.

tip

Use a firm-fleshed apple such as granny smith for this recipe, as they are more likely to retain their shape and texture during the baking process. Don't use overly ripe fruits; these will have lost some of their inherent tartness during the ripening process, giving you an overly sweet and unbalanced final product — the flesh will also be too soft when cooked.

For some unknown reason, liquorice is not as popular now as it was in the 1970s, when everything smelt of liquorice or was flavoured with it, from my toothpaste to the smell of pipe tobacco. Back then, one of the cheapest sweets available was a small piece of root from the liquorice tree. It looked like a thin, brown stick and it gave me a slight buzz when I chewed on it — I thought this made me look very rugged, just like Clint Eastwood did in the movie *A Fistful of Dollars*. Nowadays, however, I like liquorice for its versatility and complexity of flavour. It's slightly peppery yet sweet enough, and adds an amazing depth of flavour to both savoury and sweet dishes.

Tarte banane-réglisse
(Liquorice and banana tart)

Serves 8–10

300 g (10½ oz) Pâte Sablée (pages 80–3)
5 large bananas
juice of 1 lemon
100 g (3½ oz) unsalted butter
60 g (2¼ oz) caster (superfine) sugar

Liquorice custard

250 ml (9 fl oz) full-cream milk
250 ml (9 fl oz) whipping cream (35% fat)
80 g (2¾ oz) soft liquorice, thinly sliced
40 g (1½ oz) caster (superfine) sugar
25 g (1 oz) maize cornflour (cornstarch)
3 eggs

⁓ To make the liquorice custard, put the milk and cream in a saucepan over high heat and bring to the boil. Stir in the liquorice, then remove from the heat, cover and set aside until the liquorice is fully dissolved. Alternatively, you can speed up the process by using a stick blender. When cooled to room temperature, transfer to a medium bowl. Combine the sugar and cornflour in a small bowl, then add to the cooled cream mixture and whisk until smooth. Add the eggs and whisk until well combined, then strain the mixture through a fine sieve into a jug and refrigerate.

⁓ You will need a 25 cm (10 in) tart ring or tart tin with a removable base. Roll out the pastry on a lightly floured work surface until 4 mm (⅛ in) thick, dusting with a little extra flour if necessary to stop the dough from sticking. Line the base and side of the tin with the pastry, then refrigerate for 30 minutes.

⁓ Preheat the oven to 180°C (350°F). Line the pastry shell with foil, then fill to the top with uncooked rice or baking beads. Blind bake for 20 minutes, or until the base is golden. Remove the rice and foil, then set the tart shell aside until cool.

⁓ Cut the bananas into 5 mm (¼ in) slices and toss in a bowl with the lemon juice to stop them browning. Melt the butter and sugar in a frying pan over high heat. Shake the pan until the sugar caramelises to a light golden brown, then add the banana mixture and toss to combine. Do not stir the bananas; instead, hold the handle of the pan with both hands and toss the bananas occasionally until golden. Remove from the heat and allow to cool slightly.

⁓ Place the caramelised banana slices over the base of tart shell, arranging them in a circular pattern, starting on the outside edge of the shell and tightly overlapping each slice with another until you reach the starting point. Continue in this manner, working in circles until you reach the middle of the tart.

⁓ To avoid spillage, place the tart shell on a baking tray and place in the oven. Slowly pour the filling over the bananas, stopping just below the top. Don't overfill the tart shell, as the pastry may shrink a little during baking and the filling will run over the side of the shell, causing it to become soggy underneath. Bake for 30 minutes, or until the filling wobbles slightly when the tart is gently shaken. Cool to room temperature before serving.

Clafoutis originates from the Limousin region of France and is typically made with cherries, but there are numerous versions throughout many parts of France. In Provence, for example, it is known as a *flaugnarde*, and is usually filled with apples, apricots or fresh figs. When my sister and I visited my grandmother during the summer holidays, she used to bake this cherry clafoutis for us (as well as half the children in the village) for *le goûter*, a mid-afternoon pick-me-up snack.

Clafoutis aux cerises

(Cherry clafoutis)

Serves 8–10

290 ml (10 fl oz) full-cream milk

250 ml (9 fl oz) whipping cream (35% fat)

2 vanilla beans, halved lengthways

120 g (4$^1/_4$ oz) caster (superfine) sugar

60 g (2$^1/_4$ oz) plain (all-purpose) flour

4 eggs

300 g (10$^1/_2$ oz) Pâte Sablée (pages 80–3)

300 g (10$^1/_2$ oz) fresh black cherries, pitted

serving suggestion

To balance the tartness of the baked cherries, serve this clafoutis with a lightly sweetened whipped cream — add 1 tablespoon caster (superfine) sugar for every 100 ml (3$^1/_2$ fl oz) of whipping cream. The fat in the cream will also help to soften the taste and improve the overall flavour of the clafoutis.

~ Put the milk, cream and vanilla beans in a saucepan and bring to the boil over medium heat, then remove from the heat. Remove the vanilla beans and use the back of a small knife to scrape along the length of each cut side to remove the seeds. Add the seeds to the hot milk and discard the beans.

~ Put the sugar and flour in a bowl and stir until well combined (this will reduce the chance of the batter becoming lumpy). Add the eggs and, using a hand-held whisk, whisk until smooth. Whisking continuously, gradually add the hot milk mixture to the egg mixture until well combined. Cover with plastic wrap, set aside to cool, then refrigerate for at least 1 hour. Any batter made with flour needs to rest before baking to allow the gluten to relax. This will reduce the chewiness of the final product, and gives the starch time to absorb humidity and help it bloom (swell) properly during cooking.

~ Meanwhile, lightly grease a 25 cm (10 in) tart ring or tart tin with a removable base. I don't usually suggest that you need to grease the tin, but this is a very wet mixture and the custard may leak a little and stick to the tin. Roll out the pastry on a lightly floured work surface until 5 mm ($^1/_4$ in) thick, dusting with a little extra flour if necessary to stop the dough from sticking. Line the base and side of the tin with the pastry, then refrigerate for 30 minutes.

~ Preheat the oven to 175°C (345°F). Scatter the cherries over the pastry base. Don't be tempted to add more than this, as the cherries release their juices during baking and too many will make your pastry soggy. Pour the custard over the cherries, stopping about 2 mm ($^1/_{16}$ in) from the top. Bake on the bottom shelf of the oven for 30 minutes, or until golden brown. Place on a wire rack and leave to cool a little before removing from the tin. Clafoutis is best served at room temperature and tastes even better the day after.

Tarts filled with lemon have been around for centuries, but it wasn't until the nineteenth century that a Swiss baker had the idea of topping the pie with meringue. This very clever idea balances the tartness of the lemons with sweetness of the meringue, while the crunchy pastry base adds a textural layer. In this recipe I have added basil, bringing intonations of pepper, mint and anise, which softens the sweetness of the meringue and helps to refine the slightly harsh flavour of the lemon curd.

Tarte meringuée au citron et au basilic

(Lemon and basil meringue tart)

Serves 8-10

note : Start this recipe a day ahead.

300 g (10½ oz) Pâte Sablée (pages 80–3)
200 g (7 oz) egg whites (about 6–7)
300 g (10½ oz) pure icing (confectioners') sugar, sifted

Curd

100 g (3½ oz) basil leaves
ice cubes
140 ml (4¾ fl oz) lemon juice
1 vanilla bean, halved lengthways
190 g (6¾ oz) caster (superfine) sugar
1 tablespoon maize cornflour (cornstarch)
3 eggs
1 egg yolk
240 g (8½ oz) cold unsalted butter, chopped

To make the curd, bring a saucepan of water to the boil, add the basil and return to the boil. Remove the basil with a slotted spoon and quickly place on a bed of ice. When the leaves have cooled, place in a blender and blend into a fine purée. Transfer to a bowl, add the lemon juice and vanilla bean, then cover and refrigerate overnight, to allow the flavours to develop.

The following day, put the sugar and cornflour in a bowl and whisk until smooth. Add the eggs and egg yolk and combine well. Remove the vanilla bean from the lemon and basil mixture, then use the back of a knife to scrape along the length of each cut side to remove the seeds. Add the seeds to the egg mixture and combine well. Discard the vanilla beans. Add the lemon and basil mixture to the egg mixture, then, using a stick blender, process until smooth and well combined.

Strain the mixture through a fine sieve into a heatproof bowl and place over a bain-marie (see tips, page 37). Using a hand-held whisk, whisk the mixture until thick and opaque (about 70°C/160°F). At this temperature the egg yolk is cooked and the cornflour has fully gelatinised. Remove the bowl from the heat, add the butter, then use a stick blender to blend until smooth and creamy. Cover the surface with plastic wrap, leave to cool slightly, then refrigerate.

You will need a 25 cm (10 in) tart ring or tart tin with a removable base. Roll out the pastry on a lightly floured work surface until 5 mm (¼ in) thick. Line the base and side of the tin with the pastry, then refrigerate for 30 minutes.

Preheat the oven to 180°C (350°F). Line the pastry shell with foil, making sure the side of the shell is covered, then fill to the top with uncooked rice or baking beads. Blind bake for 20 minutes, or until the base is golden. Remove the rice and foil and set aside until cool.

Fill the tart shell with the cold curd and spread the top with a spatula until smooth. Make sure the curd is cold or your pastry will become soggy and lose its texture. Refrigerate while you make the meringue.

To make the meringue, use an electric mixer fitted with a whisk attachment to whisk the egg whites on high speed just until stiff peaks begin to form. Do not overwhip them or you will end up with a lumpy texture. Add half the icing sugar, reduce the speed to medium and whisk for 30 seconds, then add the remaining icing sugar and whisk for another 1 minute.

Using a spatula, spread the meringue generously over the tart. Don't make the meringue too flat; use the spatula to make small peaks in the meringue. Using a domestic blowtorch, lightly brown the meringue. Alternatively, place the tart under a preheated grill until the tips of the meringue have caramelised. The tart is best served on the day of making. If you like, serve with a coulis of lightly peppered raspberries.

tip

You can make the curd using other juices, but you need to maintain a good balance between the curd and the sweetness of the meringue, so stick to tart or acidic fruits such as pineapple, passionfruit or any other citrus fruit.

You just have to look at any cooking show, the display window of any pâtisserie or any cookbook on baking to realise how popular this tart is. It encompasses everything that a tart should be: rustic and appetising, very easy to make, and still delicious or even better the day after, for breakfast (as is the French way!), with a cup of coffee. The beautiful balance between the different textures of soft fruit, fluffy almond cream and crumbly shortcrust have ensured that this tart has remained unchanged for more than a 100 years and remains one of my favourite tarts to make when cooking at home.

Pear and almond tarts are commonly called *tarte Bourdaloue*, even though the original version was actually made with poached apricots. A French baker is credited with its creation at the end of the nineteenth century. His bakery was situated on a street called Rue Bourdaloue … and hence the name.

Tarte amandine aux poires et à la Williamine

(Pear and almond cream tart with pear liqueur)

Serves 8–10

300 g (10½ oz) Pâte Sablée (pages 80–3)
250 g (9 oz) Almond Cream (page 260)

Poached pears

240 g (8½ oz) caster (superfine) sugar
2 vanilla beans, halved lengthways
2–3 william (bartlett) pears (see tip)

Liqueur syrup

180 g (6¼ oz) caster (superfine) sugar
40 ml (1¼ fl oz) Williamine pear eau-de-vie, or any
  pear-based liqueur

⁓ To make the poached pears, put the sugar, vanilla beans and 500 ml (17 fl oz) water in a saucepan and bring to the boil. Peel the pears, then add to the syrup, cover the pan with a lid and simmer gently for 15 minutes, or until tender but still firm to the bite. Be careful not to overcook the pears; you need to feel a bit of resistance when piercing them with a knife. Drain and cool, then cut the pears in half lengthways and remove the cores but keep the stem of one of the pears attached.

⁓ You will need a 25 cm (10 in) tart ring or tart tin with a removable base. Roll out the pastry on a lightly floured work surface until 5 mm (¼ in) thick, dusting with a little extra flour if necessary to stop the dough from sticking. Line the base and side of the tin with the pastry, then refrigerate for 30 minutes.

⁓ Preheat the oven to 175°C (345°F). Tarts filled with almond cream don't need the pastry to be blind baked. Spoon the almond cream into the pastry shell until about three-quarters full. The volume of the almond cream will vary, depending on how much it was beaten, so you might have some leftover. Cut each pear half into four wedges and arrange on top of the almond cream. Place a wedge of pear with the stem attached in the centre of the tart. Bake for 40 minutes, or until golden.

⁓ Meanwhile, to make the liqueur syrup, put 250 ml (9 fl oz) water, the sugar and pear liqueur in a small saucepan and bring to the boil. As soon as the tart comes out of the oven, brush a small amount of syrup over the pears, but not too much or the tart will go soggy.

⁓ You have probably eaten this tart before, so you may have your preferred way to serve it. I am not a big fan of eating it warm, because the flavour of the pear tends to get overpowered by the sweetness of the almond cream, so I like to serve it cold, perhaps with a strong coffee or even a glass of crisp white wine.

tip

Williams (bartlett) pears are harvested in summer and are the most popular pear used in baking because of their sweet and dense, smooth flesh. If you are using buttery pears (such as beurre bosc) or watery pears (such as the popular nashi pear), bake them directly without poaching.

So, you've got guests arriving in a few hours and you need a stunning dessert. Don't look any further! While many people like raspberries and most people love chocolate, I can guarantee that everyone will love a chocolate and raspberry tart.

Although the recipe for this tart is quite simple, there is one important thing you need to know: tartness does not mitigate bitterness. By this I mean that the tartness of the raspberries will only exacerbate the bitterness of a chocolate that has a high percentage of cocoa (less sweet), so don't be tempted to fall into the trap of buying a bitter chocolate simply because it is often marketed as being a better chocolate. Each type and variety of chocolate has to be considered according to the taste and flavour requirements of the recipe. When using a tart or acidic ingredient, such as the raspberries used here, always increase the sugar content slightly by using a slightly sweeter chocolate (one with a lower percentage of cocoa), to balance out the flavours.

Tarte ganache aux framboises fraiches

(Chocolate ganache tart with fresh raspberries)

Serves 10

300 g (10¹/₂ oz) Chocolate Pâte Sablée (pages 80–3)
250 g (9 oz) fresh raspberries or strawberries
100 g (3¹/₂ oz) pistachios, slivered or coarsely chopped

Chocolate ganache

250 g (9 oz) dark chocolate (65% cocoa solids), chopped
90 g (3¹/₄ oz) honey
300 ml (10¹/₂ fl oz) whipping cream (35% fat)
30 g (1 oz) unsalted butter, at room temperature

tip

Do not use a whisk when making the ganache. Traditional ganache creams are emulsions of fat (cocoa butter and butter) and liquid (cream) and should not be aerated. Whipped ganaches are technically a very different type of cream; these are popular among professional pastry chefs as a filling for chocolate bonbons.

~ You will need a 25 cm (10 in) tart ring or tart tin with a removable base. Roll out the pastry on a lightly floured work surface until 4 mm (¹/₈ in) thick, dusting with a little extra flour if necessary to stop the dough from sticking. Line the base and side of the tin with the pastry, then refrigerate for 30 minutes.

~ Preheat the oven to 180°C (350°F). Line the pastry shell with foil, making sure the side of the shell is covered, then fill to the top with uncooked rice or baking beads. Blind bake for 10 minutes, then remove the rice and foil and bake for a further 10 minutes, or until the base is golden. Leave to cool, then refrigerate while you make the filling.

~ To make the ganache, put the chocolate and honey in a small heatproof bowl. Put the cream in a saucepan and bring to the boil over medium heat. Slowly pour the hot cream over the chocolate and honey and combine well with a flat spatula — do not use a whisk (see tip).

~ Stand the ganache at room temperature until cool to the touch. Add the butter, then use a stick blender to process until smooth and emulsified. Pour the ganache into the cold tart shell and leave at room temperature for 15 minutes, or until the ganache thickens. Decorate the top with berries, sprinkle with the pistachios, then refrigerate until ready to serve. Remove the tart from the fridge 15 minutes before serving and serve with mascarpone or thick (double/heavy) cream.

One of my first jobs as an apprentice chef was to make the *conversation*, not as a tart as it's typically seen, but as a slice. I remember being amazed at the mirror-like finish of the baked royal icing and the contrast between the light puff pastry, the fluffy almond cream and crumbly shell. The traditional recipe for *tarte conversation* is actually a little too heavy and sweet for my liking, so I have added spiced orange marmalade to offset some of the sweetness, and orange blossom water to add some floral notes. If you don't want to make the marmalade, use a good-quality ready-made marmalade or raspberry jam.

Conversation aux oranges épicées
(Almond and spiced orange tart)

Serves 8–10

500 g (1 lb 2 oz) Puff Pastry, 5 single turns (pages 145–9)
2–3 teaspoons orange blossom water, or to taste
250 g (9 oz) Almond Cream (page 260)

Marmalade

300 g (10^1/2 oz) caster (superfine) sugar
2 tablespoons Chinese five spice
3 teaspoons fine salt
2 oranges, washed

Royal icing

1 egg white
140 g (5 oz) pure icing (confectioners') sugar
few drops of lemon juice

To make the marmalade, put 1 litre (35 fl oz) water, 200 g (7 oz) of the sugar, five spice and salt in a heavy-based saucepan and bring to the boil. Add the whole oranges, then cover the pan and simmer over low heat for 35 minutes, or until the oranges crack open. Drain the oranges and discard the cooking syrup. When cool, cut open the oranges and remove the seeds. Place the unpeeled oranges in a food processor with the remaining sugar and process until a rough purée forms. Transfer to an airtight container and refrigerate until cold.

You will need a 25 cm (10 in) tart ring or tart tin with a removable base. Roll out the puff pastry on a lightly floured work surface until 3 mm (^{1}/8 in) thick. Line the base and side of the tin with the pastry. Reserve and refrigerate the offcuts to decorate the tart.

Stir the orange blossom water into the almond cream until well combined, then half-fill the tart shell with the almond cream. The volume of almond cream will vary depending on how much it was beaten, so you might have some leftover. Cover the almond cream with a layer of the cooled orange marmalade and refrigerate while you make the royal icing.

To make the royal icing, use an electric mixer fitted with a paddle attachment to beat the egg white on low speed for 30 seconds, then slowly add the icing sugar, waiting for it to dissolve fully before adding more. When the mixture firms up, add a few drops of lemon juice to soften it to a spreadable consistency.

Cover the marmalade with a thin layer of royal icing, about 2 mm (^{1}/16 in) thick. To decorate the tart with a lattice design, cut the reserved pastry offcuts into 1 cm (^{1}/2 in) wide strips. While you can get quite technical about the actual lattice work, you can simply lay parallel strips of pastry across the tart, spacing them about 3 cm (1^1/4 in) apart, then rotate the tart 45 degrees and repeat the process. Refrigerate the decorated tart for 30 minutes.

Meanwhile, preheat the oven to 190°C (375°F). Bake on the bottom shelf of the oven for 40 minutes, or until golden. If the top is browning too quickly, cover loosely with a piece of foil. Cool a little before removing from the tin. Serve at room temperature with crème fraîche.

tip

Serving a cake or tart either warm or hot will exacerbate the 'feeling' of sweetness. As a rule, when you bake a cake with a high sugar content, it is better to serve it cold, preferably with an unsweetened yoghurt, crème fraîche or sour cream. The fattiness and sourness of the yoghurt or sour cream will further reduce the perceived sweetness.

Silverbeet pies and tarts, either savoury or sweet, are specialties from Nice, a city located on the Côte d'Azur in the south of France. I was born there, as was my dad and his father, and was brought up on a steady diet of local specialties, such as Pissaladière (page 226), *socca niçoise* (chickpea crepe) and this silverbeet tart. I have chosen to feature the savoury version of this *torta de blea* (as it's called in the local dialect) because it has a broader appeal than its sweeter cousin, and because it is yet another example of how even the simplest and cheapest ingredients, when baked properly, can deliver amazing results.

Tarte aux blettes et aux raisins

(Silverbeet and raisin tart)

Serves 6–8

225 g (8 oz) Pâte Brisée (pages 84–5)

700 g (1 lb 9 oz) silverbeet (Swiss chard) leaves

2 teaspoons vegetable stock (bouillon) powder

1 teaspoon fine salt

60 g (2$^{1}/_{4}$ oz) white camargue rice or any round-grain rice, such as arborio

2 tablespoons virgin olive oil

1 onion, finely chopped

2 garlic cloves, finely chopped

120 g (4$^{1}/_{4}$ oz) speck or smoked bacon, diced

100 g (3$^{1}/_{2}$ oz) ham, diced

100 ml (3$^{1}/_{2}$ fl oz) whipping cream (35% fat)

100 ml (3$^{1}/_{2}$ fl oz) milk

3 eggs

$^{1}/_{2}$ teaspoon freshly grated nutmeg

40 g (1$^{1}/_{2}$ oz) gruyère cheese, grated

40 g (1$^{1}/_{2}$ oz) parmesan cheese, grated

85 g (3 oz) raisins or sultanas (golden raisins)

$^{1}/_{2}$ teaspoon ground black pepper

~ You will need a 25 cm (10 in) tart ring or tart tin with a removable base. Roll out the pastry on a lightly floured work surface until about 5 mm ($^{1}/_{4}$ in) thick, moving and fluffing up the dough with your hands so it doesn't stick. Line the tin with the pastry, leaving a little excess overhanging the side of the tin. Refrigerate for 30 minutes.

~ Preheat the oven to 180°C (350°F). Line the pastry shell with foil, making sure the side of the shell is covered, then fill to the top with uncooked rice or baking beads. Blind bake for 20 minutes, or until the base is golden. Remove the rice and foil and set aside until cool.

~ Meanwhile, cook the silverbeet leaves in a large saucepan of lightly salted boiling water for 3 minutes. Drain and refresh in a bowl of iced water to stop the cooking process. Place the leaves in a clean cloth and squeeze out as much water as possible. This process is called blanching and stops the leaves oxidising and turning brown.

~ Put the stock powder in a saucepan with 500 ml (17 fl oz) water and the salt and bring to the boil over high heat. Stir in the rice, then reduce the heat to medium and simmer for 10 minutes, or until the rice is *al dente*. Drain well and set aside.

~ Heat the olive oil in a saucepan over high heat. Add the onion and garlic and cook for 5 minutes, stirring continuously, until golden, then add the speck and ham and cook for another 5 minutes, or until golden brown. Remove from the heat and set aside.

tip.

As is the case for many tarts filled with a liquid, it is better to trim the excess pastry after the tart has cooked because the pastry tends to shrink a little during baking. Cutting the pastry afterwards does look a little less tidy than if you had cut it before cooking, but it ensures that none of the filling seeps over the side, which invariably leads to a soggy, raw pastry base.

~ Put the cream, milk, eggs and nutmeg in a bowl and beat together using a hand-held whisk. Strain the mixture through a fine sieve, then add the rice, silverbeet, cheeses, raisins and speck mixture. Add the pepper and season to taste with salt.

~ Pour the filling into the tart shell, smooth the top, then cook on the bottom shelf of the oven for 30 minutes, or until the filling is just set. Remove from the oven and immediately use a sharp knife to cut the excess pastry from around the top of the tin. Cool on a wire rack. This tart is usually served cold or at room temperature in summer. It is also delicious served the next day; simply reheat in a warm oven for a few minutes.

Boeuf bourguignon is another example of a traditional French peasant dish that has managed to find its way onto the menus of many Michelin-starred restaurants. Tenderising cheap cuts of meat by cooking them slowly is an age-old method that has been refined and polished over time, and opened the door to new trends. 'Nose to tail', 'paddock to plate' or 'slow cook' are popular terms in cooking circles nowadays, as meat cuts once considered of substandard quality, such as beef cheeks, oxtails or pork belly, are being served at premium prices across the tables of some of the best restaurants around the world.

Of all those stews, boeuf bourguignon reigns supreme in France and is one of the staples — along with crème brûlée and steak frites — you are likely to find in every café and bistro across the country. Serve the pie with a crisp leaf salad or use the filling as a topping for a bowl of pasta.

Tourte au boeuf bourguignon

(Beef burgundy pie)

Serves 6

2 eggs
1 egg yolk
pinch of fine salt
450 g (1 lb) Pâte Brisée (pages 84–5)

Filling

50 g (1¾ oz) maize cornflour (cornstarch)
300 ml (10½ fl oz) good quality red wine
2 tablespoons virgin olive oil
1 onion, finely chopped
100 g (3½ oz) smoked bacon, diced
2 garlic cloves, finely chopped
250 g (9 oz) button mushrooms, diced
2 small carrots, diced

1½ celery stalks, diced
1 tablespoon tomato paste (concentrated purée)
500 g (1 lb 2 oz) beef chuck steak, diced
125 ml (4 fl oz) beef stock, plus extra if needed
5 thyme sprigs
1 bay (laurel) leaf
1 teaspoon ground black pepper
2 teaspoons fine salt

∼ To make the filling, put the cornflour and 100 ml (3^{1}/2 fl oz) of the wine in a small bowl and stir until smooth, then set aside.

∼ Heat the olive oil in a heavy-based saucepan over high heat until the oil begins to smoke. Add the onion, bacon and garlic to the pan and stir until the mixture begins to brown. Add the mushrooms and carrots and stir until golden, then add all the remaining ingredients except the cornflour mixture. There should be enough liquid to just cover the beef; if not, simply add more stock. Stir to combine well, then reduce the heat to low, cover and simmer, stirring occasionally, for 1 hour. It is important to constantly check that the meat is submerged in the juices; if it appears too dry, add more stock and continue cooking. After 1 hour, check the beef by pressing one piece of meat between your fingers — if it doesn't break apart easily, cook for another 10 minutes and then check again, topping up with more stock if necessary.

∼ When the meat is tender, add the cornflour mixture and cook, stirring continuously until the sauce begins to boil and thicken. Remove from the heat, check the seasoning, then pour the beef filling over a flat tray with sides or into a large bowl. Cover the surface with a piece of plastic wrap and refrigerate for 2 hours, or until cool.

∼ Preheat the oven to 180°C (350°F). To make an egg wash, put the eggs, egg yolk and salt in a small bowl and whisk with a fork until well combined, then set aside.

∼ Divide the pastry in half, then cover the remaining half in plastic wrap and refrigerate. Roll out the pastry on a lightly floured work surface until about 4 mm (^{1}/8 in) thick, moving and fluffing up the dough with your hands so it doesn't stick. Line a 25 cm (10 in) pie or tart tin with the pastry, leaving a little excess overhanging the side of the tin. Pour the cooled filling into the pie shell.

∼ Remove the remaining portion of pastry from the fridge and roll out on a lightly floured work surface until about 4 mm (^{1}/8 in) thick. Brush a little egg wash around the rim of the pie shell. Roll the pastry up onto your rolling pin and place the pastry lid on top by resting one side of the pastry on the edge of the tin and then rolling it gently over the top of the filling, taking care that air doesn't get trapped underneath. Gently pinch the dough edges between your thumb and index fingers to make a good seal around the pie. Run a sharp knife around the outside edge of the tin to remove the excess pastry.

∼ Brush a generous amount of egg wash over the top of the pie and decorate it by gently scoring a geometric design into the top with the back of a knife (being careful not to cut all the way through the pastry). Use a skewer or small knife to make a hole in the centre to allow the steam to escape. Place the pie on a baking tray and bake on the bottom shelf of the oven for 30–40 minutes. To check if the pie is ready, lift it up slightly with a knife to check the base — the pastry should be golden brown. Serve hot.

Leeks, along with artichokes, are one of my favourite vegetables. They are subtle and sweet enough to be used as a discreet accompaniment to the most delicate ingredients, such as scallops or lobsters, but have enough earthiness and body to be used just as successfully in rustic pies and stews, or as a garnish for meats such as lamb and beef, as well as offal and game meat.

Chicken and leek pie flavoured with a few bay (laurel) leaves is one of the few traditional provincial recipes that you will routinely find in even the most up-market *traiteur* (delicatessen) in every city around France. It is the ideal meal to warm you up during the long winter nights.

Tourtes de poulet aux poireaux et au laurier

(Chicken, leek and laurel pies)

Serves 6

2 leeks, white part only, cut into 1 cm (¹/2 in) thick slices
200 ml (7 fl oz) whipping cream (35% fat)
2 tablespoons maize cornflour (cornstarch)
2 tablespoons olive oil
1 onion, finely chopped
2 garlic cloves, finely chopped
3 bay (laurel) leaves
¹/2 teaspoon ground black pepper

500 g (1 lb 2 oz) boneless, skinless chicken thigh fillets,
*   cut into 3 cm (1¹/4 in) pieces*
1 teaspoon fine salt
50 ml (1³/4 fl oz) white wine
450 g (1 lb) Pâte Brisée (pages 84–5)
2 eggs
1 egg yolk

～ Put the leek slices in a colander and rinse thoroughly under running water. Pat dry with a clean cloth or paper towel. Place the cream and cornflour in a small bowl and use a fork to whisk until smooth and well combined.

～ Heat 1 tablespoon of the olive oil in a large frying pan over high heat until the oil begins to smoke. Add the leek, onion, garlic, bay leaves and pepper, then reduce the heat to medium and stir continuously until the leek is light golden. Transfer to a bowl and set aside.

～ Heat the remaining tablespoon of oil in the pan over high heat until the oil begins to smoke. Add the chicken and salt and cook, stirring occasionally, until the chicken is golden all over. Add the wine and stir, scraping the base of the pan to remove any cooked pieces. Reduce the heat to medium, add the leek mixture and combine well. Stirring continuously, add the cream mixture, then reduce the heat to low and simmer for 10 minutes, or until reduced and thickened. Remove from the heat and set aside until cool, without covering.

～ You will need six 7.5 cm (3 in) diameter tartlet tins or a 25 cm (10 in) tart tin with a removable base. Divide the pastry in half, then cover one half in plastic wrap and refrigerate. Roll out the remaining pastry on a lightly floured work surface until about 4 mm (^{1}/8 in) thick, moving and fluffing up the dough with your hands so it doesn't stick. Using a 12 cm (4^1/2 in) round cutter, cut the pastry into six rounds. Line the base and side of the tins with the pastry, leaving a little excess overhanging the side of the tins. Refrigerate for 30 minutes.

～ Preheat the oven to 180°C (350°F). Line the pastry shells with foil, making sure the side of each shell is covered, then fill to the top with uncooked rice or baking beads. Blind bake for 20 minutes, or until the base is golden. Remove the rice and foil and set aside until cool. Pour the cooled filling into the pie shells.

～ To make an egg wash, put the eggs, egg yolk and a pinch of salt in a small bowl and whisk with a fork until well combined, then set aside. Remove the remaining portion of pastry from the fridge and roll it out on a lightly floured work surface until about 2 mm (^{1}/16 in) thick. Using a ruler and knife, cut the pastry into 1 cm (^{1}/2 in) wide strips, to use for the lattice top. Brush a little egg wash around the rim of the pie shell, then use the strips to make a lattice pattern over the top. Cut the strips to size by using your thumb to push them onto the edge of the tart to break off the excess.

～ Brush the egg wash generously over the top of the lattice. Place the pies on a large baking tray and bake on the bottom shelf of the oven for 30 minutes, or until the pastry is golden. Serve hot, with a green leaf salad and a glass of wine.

tip

When cooking pies and stews, always leave the herbs and leaves for the duration of the cooking process. It takes a long time for the aromatic oils to break down and dissipate through the sauce, especially if you are using dried herbs.

The problem of inviting friends over for dinner when you are a pastry chef or baker is that your guests tend to have the preconceived idea they are going to be taken on a magical gastronomical *journée*, when the fact is (and I can only talk for myself here) their expectations are bound to exceed my skills when it comes to cooking anything savoury.

My solution is simply to stick to the basics, use the best and freshest ingredients, and try to identify two flavours that work perfectly together, such as blue cheese and meat, as used here. The following recipe is a homage to this perfect combination of salty and sharp flavours, with the cheese providing subtle hints of pepper and hazelnuts. This is my idea of a perfect entrée.

Tarte au jambon cru et au roquefort
(Blue cheese and prosciutto tart)

Serves 6–8

225 g (8 oz) Pâte Brisée (pages 84–5)
200 ml (7 fl oz) whipping cream (35% fat)
200 ml (7 fl oz) full-cream milk
4 eggs
1/2 teaspoon freshly grated nutmeg
1 teaspoon ground black pepper
fine salt, to taste
100 g (3 1/2 oz) gruyère cheese, grated
150 g (5 1/2 oz) roquefort cheese, finely chopped
250 g (9 oz) prosciutto, finely chopped

~ You will need a 25 cm (10 in) tart ring or tart tin with a removable base. Roll out the pastry on a lightly floured work surface until about 5 mm (1/4 in) thick, moving and fluffing up the dough with your hands so it doesn't stick. Line the tin with the pastry, leaving a little excess overhanging the side of the tin. As is the case for many tarts filled with a liquid, it is better to trim the excess pastry after the tart has cooked because the pastry tends to shrink a little during baking. Refrigerate for 30 minutes.

~ Preheat the oven to 180°C (350°F). Line the pastry shell with foil, making sure the side of the shell is covered, then fill to the top with uncooked rice or baking beads. Blind bake for 20 minutes, or until the base is golden. Remove the rice and foil and set aside until cool.

~ Put the cream, milk, eggs and nutmeg in a bowl and beat together using a hand-held whisk. Strain the mixture through a fine sieve into a jug, then add the pepper and season to taste with salt. When seasoning the filling for any savoury tart, consider the salt content of your ingredients and adjust the amount of salt accordingly.

tip

You can replace the roquefort with any other blue cheese made of sheep's milk, such as gorgonzola or stilton. As a general rule, subtle meats such as veal or rabbit will work better with younger, sweeter blue cheese such as gorgonzola dolce, while game meat or dried meats will work better with darker, older and more pronounced cheeses such as roquefort or gorgonzola picante.

~ Scatter the gruyère, roquefort and prosciutto evenly over the base of the tart shell. Place on a baking tray on the bottom shelf of the oven, then carefully fill the shell to the top with the egg mixture.

~ Bake the tart for 40 minutes, or until the filling is just set. Remove from the oven and immediately use a sharp knife to cut the excess pastry from around the top of the tin. Cutting the pastry after cooking it does look a bit less tidy than if you had cut it beforehand, but it ensures that none of the filling seeps over the side, which invariably leads to a soggy, raw pastry base. Serve warm, perhaps with a glass of chilled rosé and a crisp green salad.

It would be difficult to overlook this classic tart in the long list of so-called 'French specialties' and while its name suggests it originated from Lorraine, a French region in the far north of France, the first version of a quiche was called *kuchen* and was German in origin. The method of adding vegetables, meats and condiments to a curd made of eggs and cream cooked in pastry dates back over 500 years and was a very popular technique used throughout Anglo-Saxon gastronomy.

This versatile and delicious dish can be eaten for breakfast, lunch or dinner, or even served as canapés at a cocktail party.

Quiche lorraine

Serves 6–8

225 g (8 oz) Pâte Brisée (pages 84–5)
200 ml (7 fl oz) whipping cream (35% fat)
200 ml (7 fl oz) full-cream milk
4 eggs
1 teaspoon ground black pepper
fine salt, to taste
250 g (9 oz) speck or smoked bacon, cut into 1 cm (^{1}/2 in) pieces
100 g (3^1/2 oz) gruyère cheese, grated

~ You will need a 25 cm (10 in) tart ring or tart tin with a removable base. Roll out the pastry on a lightly floured work surface until about 5 mm (^{1}/4 in) thick, moving and fluffing up the dough with your hands so it doesn't stick. Line the tin with the pastry, leaving a little excess overhanging the side of the tin. Unlike fillings for sweet tarts, which are often firmer, fillings for savoury tarts are often runny and more likely to spill over the rim and down the side, especially as the pastry tends to shrink a little during baking, so it is better to trim the excess pastry after the tart has cooked. Refrigerate for 30 minutes.

~ Preheat the oven to 180°C (350°F). Line the pastry shell with foil, making sure the side of the shell is covered, then fill to the top with uncooked rice or baking beads. Blind bake for 20 minutes, or until the base is golden. Remove the rice and foil and set aside until cool.

~ Put the cream, milk and eggs in a bowl and beat together using a hand-held whisk. Strain the mixture through a fine sieve into a jug, then add the pepper and season to taste with salt. When seasoning the filling for any quiche, consider the salt content of your ingredients and adjust the amount of salt accordingly.

~ Heat a small frying pan over high heat and add the speck, without adding any extra fat. Stir continuously until golden, then remove with a slotted spoon and drain on paper towel. Spread the speck evenly over the tart shell, then scatter with the gruyère. Place on a baking tray on the bottom shelf of the oven, then carefully fill the shell to the top with the egg mixture. Filling tarts already sitting inside the oven means you won't need to precariously walk around the kitchen balancing a quiche full of liquid cream.

~ Bake the quiche for 40 minutes, or until the filling is just set. Remove from the oven and immediately use a sharp knife to cut the excess pastry from around the top of the tin. Serve cold or warm. The quiche can be stored, covered in plastic wrap, in the fridge for 3–4 days.

tip
Here's an easy formula for making a quiche when you can't find the recipe: 1+1+1. The basic recipe consists of 1 part milk, 1 part cream and 1 part egg. Whatever else you add is up to you.

Pâte à choux

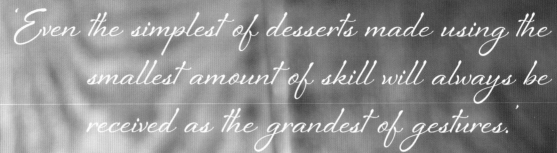

'Even the simplest of desserts made using the smallest amount of skill will always be received as the grandest of gestures.'

Pâte à choux

(Choux pastry)

I remember the first time I ever made choux pastry. I was only a few weeks into my apprenticeship when I was given the task of making *pâte à choux* — I will never forget that moment of sheer panic. Not only did I have to make this puzzling pastry, but I also had to face the challenging task of piping it into an array of different shapes and sizes. Ever since I was a child, I had always wondered how anyone made those delicate little puffs, so thin and light, pumped full of air. To me they were more about engineering than cooking and while this isn't quite the case, choux pastry is a good illustration of how the chemistry of each ingredient works together in baking, reinforcing the point that a good baker is first and foremost a technician.

The invention of an early form of choux pastry is credited to the very creative pastry chefs at the French court of Catherine de Medici in the sixteenth century, who were also responsible for the amaretti, the ancestor of the famous macaron. Over time, the recipe for choux was improved upon, and finally cemented its place in French gastronomy in the early nineteenth century when the famous pastry chef Marie-Antoine Carême created the *croque-en-bouche* ('crunch in the mouth'), or croquembouche as it's also known.

Unbeknown to most amateur bakers, choux pastry is actually an amazingly simple concoction to make at home. It is also very versatile and can be turned into a wide range of pastries — from éclairs to croquembouche (baked), churros to doughnuts (fried), and even savoury dishes, such as the famous Parisian gnocchi (poached).

Pets de nonne citronnés à l'anis (Anise and lemon nun's puffs) ~ page 135

Pâte à choux

(Choux pastry)

There are just three easy steps when making choux pastry: boil the liquids with the butter, dry it up with the flour, then incorporate the eggs. It is almost failproof, providing you follow the recipe precisely — the real challenge lies in the baking. Choux pastry rises due to the evaporation of the liquids when exposed to the high temperature in the oven. The steam is subsequently trapped within the puff due to the coagulation of the eggs early in the baking process, and the flour, once cooked, will provide the thin supporting structure of the skin. This batter is used for both sweet pastries and savoury dishes.

Makes 750 g (1 lb 10 oz)

125 ml (4 fl oz) water
125 ml (4 fl oz) full-cream milk
100 g (3^1/2 oz) unsalted butter
2.5 g (^{1}/16 oz) fine salt
150 g (5^1/2 oz) plain (all-purpose) flour
3 eggs, plus 1 extra (lightly beaten), if needed

Making the choux paste

Put the water, milk, butter and salt in a saucepan (*photo 1*) and stir over medium heat until the butter has melted. Increase the heat to high, then add the flour all at once and begin stirring with a wooden spoon until the mixture comes together into a thick buttery paste. Continue mixing for 2–3 minutes, or until the mixture comes away from the side of the pan (*2*). Remove from the heat.

Transfer the mixture to the bowl of an electric mixer fitted with a paddle attachment (*3*) and beat on medium speed until cool to the touch. Reduce the speed to low and add the 3 eggs, one at a time (*4*), scraping the side of the bowl from time to time and allowing each egg to be fully incorporated before adding the next.

To check if the choux paste has the right consistency, lift the paddle attachment; if the dough stretches about 5 cm (2 in) before it breaks, it is ready (*5*). Alternatively, take a small teaspoon of the dough; if it stays upright but collapses at the tip, it is ready. If the dough tip breaks off or stays in a stiff peak, you will need to add ^{1}/2 of the extra egg.

Piping choux

Once made, the choux paste needs to be piped straight away. Lightly grease a baking tray, then line with baking paper. The paper will stick to the oil on the tray, making it easier to pipe the sticky choux.

To make éclairs, fill a piping bag fitted with a 1 cm (^{1}/2 in) plain nozzle (*6*) and pipe 10 cm (4 in) lengths of choux onto a lined baking tray. To pipe puffs or *gougères* (cheese puffs), pipe small mounds of the mixture onto the tray (*7*). For savoury *gougères*, brush over the tops with an egg wash (*8*), then use a fork to make a crosshatched pattern on the top (*9*). These raised ridges will brown quickly, allowing the puff to crack evenly during baking.

Cooking choux

In order for the choux to develop properly and get the maximum lift, it needs to be baked in a hot oven at 180°C (350°F) early in the process. Never open the door during the initial stages of baking. After the first 15 minutes of baking, reduce the heat to 170°C (340°F) and cook for at least 30 minutes to allow the choux pastry to dry out. The oven door should be left slightly ajar after the first 25 minutes of baking, to rid the oven of the large amount of steam created while cooking. If the steam is unable to escape, this will lengthen the drying process.

Choux pastry can be tricky to cook perfectly, so I always recommend cooking a few samples before cooking the whole mixture.

1

2

3

4

Pâte à choux

5

6

7

8

9

Chouquettes really are an exercise in restraint for any budding baker, just as they are for the professional pastry chef. Their look can only be described as rustic, and they are filled with … well, air, and rely on nothing more than their sweet and crunchy pearl sugar for taste and texture. If you can't trust me as to how wonderful they are, then at least know that Parisians would not wait in long queues outside their local bakery every weekend for their bags of freshly baked *chouquettes* if they were anything else but deliciously addictive.

Chouquettes

(Pearl sugar puffs)

Makes 50

2 eggs
pinch of fine salt
750 g (1 lb 10 oz) Choux Pastry (pages 122–5)
200 g (7 oz) pearl sugar (see tip)

tip

Pearl sugar is made from highly refined caster (superfine) sugar that has been compacted during the manufacturing process, then crushed and sifted into large (2 mm/^{1}/$_{16}$ in) crystals. The advantage of this sugar is that it is highly resistant to heat and water and therefore does not melt during the baking process — perfect for when you want to add a crunchy element to your biscuits or pastries. Pearl sugar is available from specialist food stores. Alternatively, you can crush and sieve sugar cubes to an almost identical result.

⌣ Preheat the oven to 180°C (350°F). Lightly grease two large baking trays, then line with baking paper. The paper will stick to the oil on the trays, making it much easier for you to pipe the sticky choux paste.

⌣ To make an egg wash, put the eggs and salt in a small bowl and lightly beat with a fork until well combined, then set aside.

⌣ Spoon the choux pastry into a piping bag fitted with a 1 cm (^{1}/$_2$ in) plain nozzle. Pipe balls of about 3 cm (1^1/$_4$ in) in diameter on the trays, spacing them about 5 cm (2 in) apart. Don't be tempted to make them any bigger — the best part of eating a *chouquette* is fitting a whole one, or even two, into your mouth! If you don't have a piping bag, use a tablespoon and simply push them off the spoon onto the tray with your fingers or another spoon.

⌣ Brush a thin layer of egg wash over the puffs, then sprinkle a generous amount of pearl sugar over the top. Try to cover the whole puff with as much sugar as you can, because the choux will double in size during baking. Remove the excess sugar by gently tipping each tray on its side while holding onto the sheet of paper.

⌣ Bake for 15 minutes, then reduce the oven temperature to 170°C (340°F) and bake for another 20 minutes, or until golden brown. Remember not to open the oven door during the initial stages of cooking, as the puffs need the steam in the oven to build up in order to rise properly. Remove from the oven and place on a wire rack to cool. Repeat with the remaining pastry.

For many decades, éclairs were simply one of many classic cakes that you would expect to find in your local bakery, usually filled with either coffee or chocolate custard, or maybe fresh cream. Nowadays, however, thanks largely to the very talented pastry chef Christophe Adam, éclairs have enjoyed a resurgence, even dethroning the famed macaron for the title of 'most popular new (old) must-have pâtisserie'.

The reason behind their massive success is their wonderful versatility (as was the case for the macaron). They can be filled with all manner of creams, curds and ganache, of an almost infinite combination of flavours and textures, and can be coated with every colour under the sun. Feel free to use this recipe as inspiration for your own ideas or flavours.

Éclairs à la fraise et à la mandarine

(Strawberry and mandarin éclairs)

Makes about 35

750 g (1 lb 10 oz) Choux Pastry (pages 122–5)

Custard

40 g (1^1/$_2$ oz) maize cornflour (cornstarch)

100 g (3^1/$_2$ oz) caster (superfine) sugar

1 egg

2 egg yolks

500 ml (17 fl oz) strawberry purée (frozen or blended from fresh)

finely grated zest of 2 mandarins

1 vanilla bean, halved lengthways, seeds scraped

100 g (3^1/$_2$ oz) cold unsalted butter, chopped

50 ml (1^3/$_4$ fl oz) whipping cream (35% fat)

Crumble

120 g (4^1/$_4$ oz) plain (all-purpose) flour

30 g (1 oz) almond meal

150 g (5^1/$_2$ oz) raw (demerara) sugar

150 g (5^1/$_2$ oz) unsalted butter, at room temperature

red food colouring (see tip)

To decorate (optional)

strawberries, quartered

mandarin segments

pistachio nuts, very finely chopped

small mint leaves

small edible flowers, such as violas

To make the custard, put the cornflour and sugar in a heatproof bowl and stir until smooth, then add the egg and egg yolks and whisk until smooth. Put the strawberry purée, mandarin zest and the vanilla bean and seeds into a saucepan over medium heat and stir continuously until the mixture comes to the boil. Remove from the heat and immediately add to the egg mixture in the bowl, whisking vigorously until combined well. Return the custard to the pan and whisk over low–medium heat until the custard thickens and returns to the boil. Remove from the heat, then remove and discard the vanilla bean.

Transfer the custard to the bowl of an electric mixture fitted with a whisk attachment. Add the butter and beat on low speed for 20 minutes, or until the custard is cool to touch (about 40°C/105°F). Add the cream and beat until well combined. Transfer the custard to a bowl and cover the surface with plastic wrap. When refrigerating a warm mixture such as this custard, make sure the plastic wrap sits directly on the surface to avoid the formation of a skin. Set aside for 1 hour, then refrigerate until needed.

Meanwhile, to make the crumble, put the flour, almond meal, sugar and butter in a food processor and process for 2–3 minutes, then add a few drops of food colouring and process just until the dough comes together. Shape into a disc, cover in plastic wrap and refrigerate for 30 minutes.

Roll out the coloured pastry between two sheets of baking paper until 2–3 mm ($^1/_{16}$–$^1/_8$ in) thick. Remove the top sheet of paper. Then, using a sharp paring knife, cut the dough into 4 x 11 cm ($1^1/_2$ x $4^1/_4$ in) rectangles. Press all the scraps together, re-roll and repeat the process until you have 35 rectangles. Store the pastry flat in the refrigerator for at least 10 minutes, or until needed, before trying to lift it off the baking paper.

Preheat the oven to 180°C (350°F). Lightly grease two baking trays, then line with baking paper. The paper will stick to the oil on the trays, making it much easier for you to pipe the sticky choux paste.

Spoon the choux pastry into a piping bag fitted with a 1 cm ($^1/_2$ in) plain nozzle. Pipe éclairs about 10 cm (4 in) long and 2.5 cm (1 in) wide, spacing them about 5 cm (2 in) apart. Carefully place one chilled pastry rectangle on each éclair, then bake for 15 minutes. Reduce the oven temperature to 170°C (340°F) and bake for another 20 minutes. Remove from the oven, leave to cool a little on the tray, then transfer to a wire rack to cool completely.

Using the tip of a paring knife or a skewer, make two holes (one in each end) in the base of each éclair. Remove the custard from the fridge and whisk vigorously until smooth. Spoon the custard into a piping bag fitted with a 4 mm ($^1/_8$ in) plain nozzle and pipe the custard into the éclairs. Make sure that the custard (or any filling for choux puffs) is cold or your éclairs will become soggy almost immediately.

You can serve the éclairs as they are, but I like to decorate them with fruit, nuts and small mint leaves and edible flowers — all held on with a small dollop of left-over custard. Feel free to experiment with whatever you have on hand. The éclairs must be kept refrigerated until serving and are best eaten the day they are baked.

tip.

All food colourings are not the same. Some are much more concentrated than others, some are sold as liquids or gels, paste or even dry pigments. In order to control the amount of colour you add to your cakes, always bind all your ingredients together first, then add the smallest amount of colouring. You can then add more at any time during the mixing process. As a rule, strong colours tend to give a modern look, while lighter colours tend to be associated with a more sophisticated look.

Éclairs à la fraise et à la mandarine
(Strawberry and mandarin éclairs)

Choux beurre de cacahouète-chocolat au lait
(Peanut butter and milk chocolate puffs)

This mixture of peanut butter and chocolate is a twist on the Italian *gianduja*, a confectionery made of milk chocolate and hazelnut, which is also very popular in France.

I always thought of peanut butter as a little sickening and the poor cousin of praline paste, so it took months of negotiations from my team to convince me to make a peanut ganache macaron. As it turned out, and it pains me to admit it, this has become one of my favourite flavour combinations, so much so that I thought I would use it for these choux puffs as well. This recipe calls for a peanut and chocolate custard rather than a straight ganache, which would be too rich for the serving portion and too hard once refrigerated.

Choux beurre de cacahouète-chocolat au lait

(Peanut butter and milk chocolate puffs)

Makes about 40

2 eggs
pinch of fine salt
750 g (1 lb 10 oz) Choux Pastry (pages 122–5)
200 g (7 oz) salted peanuts, finely ground
700 g (1 lb 9 oz) Custard (page 261), at room temperature

Peanut ganache

200 g (7 oz) milk chocolate (40% cocoa solids), finely chopped
85 g (3 oz) smooth peanut butter
220 ml (7¾ fl oz) whipping cream (35%)
50 g (1¾ oz) cold unsalted butter, cut into small cubes

To decorate (optional)

caramel coating (page 72)
toasted or caramelised peanuts
shards of dried meringue
chocolate biscuit crumbs

〜 To make the peanut ganache, put the chocolate and peanut butter in a heatproof bowl. Put the cream in a small saucepan and bring to the boil over high heat. This is a small amount of liquid and it will boil over very quickly, so pay close attention. As soon as the cream comes to the boil, pour half the cream over the peanut butter mixture and whisk until it begins to come together. At this stage, your ganache should look like a thick paste. Add the remaining cream and gently whisk until well combined. Be careful not to whisk the ganache too much, as this pushes air into the mixture and makes it hard and grainy. Set aside until just warm to the touch (about 30°C/85°F).

〜 Add the butter and use a stick blender to blend until smooth and well combined. Cover the surface with plastic wrap, then set aside in a cool place, but not in the fridge.

〜 Preheat the oven to 180°C (350°F). Lightly grease two large baking trays, then line with baking paper. The paper will stick to the oil on the trays, making it much easier for you to pipe the sticky choux paste.

〜 To make an egg wash, lightly beat the eggs and salt together in a small bowl, then set aside. Spoon the choux pastry into a piping bag fitted with a 1 cm (^{1}/2 in) plain nozzle. Pipe 4 cm (1^1/2 in) rounds onto the lined trays, spacing them about 5 cm (2 in) apart. Brush the egg wash all over the puffs, then sprinkle generously with the ground peanuts. Remove the excess nuts by gently tipping each tray on its side while holding onto the sheet of paper.

〜 Bake for 15 minutes, then reduce the oven temperature to 170°C (340°F) and cook for another 20 minutes, or until golden. Remove from the oven, leave to cool a little on the trays, then transfer to a wire rack to cool for at least 20 minutes.

〜 Meanwhile, place the custard and the cooled peanut ganache together in a small bowl. Using a stick blender, process until smooth and well combined. Using a small bowl for this helps the peanut custard to stay glossy and smooth by reducing the risk of any air bubbles getting into the mixture.

〜 Using a serrated knife, cut the choux puffs in half and keep the top of each puff close to its base so they don't get mixed up. Spoon the filling into a piping bag fitted with a 1 cm (^{1}/2 in) plain nozzle and pipe a generous dollop of peanut custard into the bottom half of the puff. As you do this, try to pull the bag in an upward direction as you press the mixture out, to give a bit of height to the custard. Put the other half of the puff on top.

〜 If you like, you can coat the top of each puff with a blonde (pale) caramel, then decorate with some crushed toasted or caramelised peanuts, some small shards of dried meringue and a pinch of chocolate biscuit crumbs. Alternatively, you could simply coat the puffs with melted chocolate, sprinkle with some crushed peanuts and decorate with a small edible flower.

tips

When cooking a large quantity of choux puffs, I recommend that you cook a few samples before cooking the whole mixture, so you can be confident about the cooking times. Each oven will cook a little differently.

While you are advised to closely follow the recipes when baking, I recommend that you also add your personal touch, especially when it comes to decorating.

These delicious bite-sized fritters are one of the rare French specialties that failed to gain widespread popularity overseas, probably due in part to their slightly irreverent name (which literally translates as 'nun's fart'). *Pets de nonne* first appeared in gastronomic literature around the sixteenth century and while the origin of its name is steeped in folklore, it at least gives us an insight into the dubious sense of humour at the time. Serve these little morsels as a delicious mid-afternoon snack or for breakfast, dunked into a large bowl of *café au lait*.

Pets de nonne citronnés à l'anis

(Anise and lemon nun's puffs)

Makes 100

300 g (10½ oz) caster (superfine) sugar
1 teaspoon ground star anise
375 g (13 oz) Choux Pastry (pages 122–5), rested at room
   temperature for 1 hour
finely grated zest of 2 lemons
2 vanilla beans, halved lengthways, seeds scraped
½ teaspoon baking powder
vegetable oil, for deep-frying

tip

Caster (superfine) sugar flavoured with various spices, teas and fragrant flowers (lavender, jasmine tea, vanilla bean seeds, citrus zests) can be sprinkled on many desserts and sweet breads, including these puffs. Pour caster sugar and the flavouring of choice into an airtight container, then cover with the lid and shake well. Keep the sugar in your pantry, shaking it from time to time. If you are using fragrant flowers or leaves, always use dried, edible flowers, remembering that a lot of beautifully fragrant flowers can be poisonous, such as frangipanis or azaleas.

～ Put the sugar and star anise in a large bowl, combine well and set aside. Put the choux pastry in another bowl, then add the lemon zest, vanilla bean seeds (discard the beans) and baking powder and beat with a wooden spoon until well combined.

～ Heat the oil in a deep-fryer or a deep saucepan until 180°C (350°F). Spoon the choux pastry into a piping bag fitted with a 1 cm (½ in) plain nozzle. Hold the filled piping bag in one hand and a small paring knife in the other hand and, working in batches of 10 to 15 at a time, pipe the mixture into the hot oil, cutting close to the nozzle every 2 cm (¾ in) to make small balls. During cooking, make sure that the temperature of the oil stays at 180°C (350°F) — if it cools too much, the puffs may become greasy. Be aware that the further you are from the oil, the more likely you are to get scalded when the choux is dropped into the hot oil.

～ Using a flat spatula, gently move the puffs around in the oil, constantly pushing them down into the oil so they cook evenly. It is important to fry the puffs reasonably slowly so that they cook all the way through.

～ When they are golden, remove with a slotted spoon, drain on paper towel, then immediately toss the puffs in the bowl with the sugar and star anise mixture until well coated. Serve warm or cool on wire racks until at room temperature.

Pets de nonne citronnés à l'anis (Anise and lemon nun's puffs) ～ photo page 120

This is the most popular recipe for these savoury choux, often served as an *apéritif* with drinks. The fact that they can be served plain, very much like you would a *chouquette*, or filled with any manner of creams and sauces, makes them an incredibly versatile *amuse-bouche*, perfect for any occasion, from the most formal wedding function to a casual family picnic.

These béchamel-filled *gougères* are the most popular and classically French version but, of course, feel free to add your own personal touches by swapping nutmeg for cardamom or dried herbs, or adding mushrooms cooked with garlic and parsley to the béchamel.

Gougères fourrées à la béchamel au gruyère
(Gruyère béchamel-filled puffs)

Makes about 40

2 eggs
pinch of salt
750 g (1 lb 10 oz) Choux Pastry (pages 122–5)
200 g (7 oz) gruyère cheese, finely grated

Gruyère béchamel

1 litre (35 fl oz) full-cream milk
120 g (4¼ oz) unsalted butter
80 g (2¾ oz) plain (all-purpose) flour
100 g (3½ oz) gruyère cheese, grated
½ teaspoon ground nutmeg
½ teaspoon ground black pepper
fine salt, to taste

∽ To make the gruyère béchamel, put the milk in a saucepan over high heat and bring to a simmer. Remove from the heat and set aside. Put the butter in a medium heavy-based saucepan and cook over low heat until melted. Add the flour and begin stirring with a wooden spoon until the mixture begins to thicken. This butter and flour paste is called a roux and is used to thicken sauces, stocks or soups. Cook the roux for 2 minutes, stirring continuously and never allowing it to brown. Swap the spoon for a whisk, then, whisking continuously, add half the hot milk, a little at a time and waiting for each addition to be fully incorporated before adding the next. Increase the heat to medium and continue adding the remaining milk, a little at a time.

∽ Bring to the boil, then remove from the heat and continue whisking for another minute. Add the 100 g (3½ oz) gruyère, the nutmeg, pepper, and salt to taste, and combine well. Pour the béchamel sauce into a shallow container, cover the surface with a piece of plastic wrap to prevent a skin forming and refrigerate for 1 hour.

∽ Preheat the oven to 180°C (350°F). Lightly grease two large baking trays, then line with baking paper. The paper will stick to the oil on the trays, making it much easier for you to pipe the sticky choux paste. To make an egg wash, put the eggs and a pinch of salt in a small bowl and lightly beat with a fork until well combined, then set aside.

∽ Spoon the choux pastry into a piping bag fitted with a 1 cm (½ in) plain nozzle. Pipe 4 cm (1½ in) rounds onto the lined trays, spacing them about 5 cm (2 in) apart. Brush the egg wash over the top of each round, then use a fork to make a crosshatched pattern on the top of each one (see photo, page 125). Sprinkle the finely grated gruyère over the top. Bake for 15 minutes, then reduce the oven temperature to 170°C (340°F) and bake for another 25 minutes. Remove from the oven and allow to cool for at least 20 minutes. Using the tip of a paring knife or a skewer, make a small hole in the bottom of each puff.

∽ When you are ready to serve, use an electric mixer fitted with a whisk attachment to whisk the cold béchamel on low speed until smooth. Spoon the béchamel into a piping bag fitted with a 4 mm (⅛ in) plain nozzle and fill each puff with the béchamel. *Gougères* are best eaten the day they are made, although unfilled puffs can be stored in an airtight container for a few hours until you are ready to fill them.

Béchamel is usually referred to as 'white sauce' in English. The inherent characteristics of this sauce, with its beautiful creamy texture and relatively neutral flavour, have made it a popular ingredient in many dishes, including Greek moussaka and Italian cannelloni and lasagne.

Parisian gnocchi, which are made from choux pastry, are quite different from the more popular Mediterranean potato gnocchi, but they're just as versatile and even easier to make.

When I was an apprentice, Parisian gnocchi was my boss's idea of an up-market staff meal. Simply boil the left-over choux pastry, soften cold béchamel leftovers with milk, then add a few mushrooms and everybody wins. By 'everybody' I mean mostly my boss, because that version was as light and refined as a 1970s mayonnaise-laden prawn cocktail! For this recipe, I am suggesting a lighter, healthier Provençal alternative by swapping the heavy béchamel for a zingy clam and basil sauce. This is delicious served as a hot dish for winter or as a summery cold entrée for a relaxed lunch in the sun.

Gnocchi au pistou et aux palourdes
(Clam and pesto gnocchi)

Serves 6

750 g (1 lb 10 oz) Choux Pastry (pages 122–5), rested for
    at least 1 hour in the fridge
2 tablespoons extra virgin olive oil, plus extra, for drizzling
1 onion, finely chopped
1 garlic clove, finely chopped
80 g (2³⁄₄ oz) thyme (about ¹⁄₂ bunch), leaves picked
200 ml (7 fl oz) whipping cream (35% fat)
400 ml (14 fl oz) dry white wine
1.25 kg (2 lb 12 oz) clams (vongole), soaked in cold water
    for 1 hour to disgorge any sand
40 g (1¹⁄₂ oz) unsalted butter
juice of 1 lemon

Pesto

120 g (4¹⁄₄ oz) basil (1 large bunch), leaves picked
4 garlic cloves, peeled
50 g (1³⁄₄ oz) parmesan cheese, finely grated
30 g (1 oz) pine nuts, toasted
200 ml (7 fl oz) extra virgin olive oil, refrigerated until cold
salt and ground black pepper, to taste

tips

When making pesto in a food processor, be careful not to overprocess it. The machine can heat up the mixture and causes rapid oxidation of the chlorophyll in the basil leaves, turning their vibrant colour into a dark olive green mess. If the pesto starts to feel tepid to the touch, stop blending and refrigerate for about 10 minutes before resuming.

You can flavour your gnocchi by adding finely chopped basil leaves, thyme or pepper during the final stage of mixing the choux dough. This will give not only an additional touch of flavour but also a tinge of colour to the dish.

⌒ To make the pesto, put the basil, garlic, parmesan, pine nuts and half of the olive oil in a food processor and process for 30 seconds, before drizzling in the remaining oil. Process just until smooth, then season to taste with salt and pepper (see tips). Transfer the pesto to a small bowl, cover the surface with a piece of plastic wrap and refrigerate.

⌒ Fill a medium saucepan two-thirds full of water and bring to the boil over high heat, then reduce the temperature to low–medium to maintain a gentle simmer. Spoon the choux pastry into a piping bag fitted with a 1 cm (¹⁄₂ in) plain nozzle. Place the filled piping bag in one hand and a small paring knife in the other and, working in batches, pipe the mixture into the simmering water, cutting close to the nozzle every 3 cm (1¹⁄₄ in) to make small gnocchi. As soon as the gnocchi rise to the top, remove with a slotted spoon, drain well and place in a bowl. Drizzle the gnocchi with a little olive oil. Repeat with the remaining mixture.

⌒ Heat 1 tablespoon of the olive oil in a large frying pan over medium heat. Add the onion, garlic and thyme and cook, stirring, for 5 minutes, or until the onions are dark golden. Add the cream and wine and simmer for 5 minutes, then add the clams, cover and cook for another 5 minutes, or until all the shells have opened. Turn off the heat and cover the pan.

⌒ Heat the remaining tablespoon of olive oil and the butter in another large frying pan over high heat. When it begins smoking, add the cold gnocchi and cook, tossing the pan continuously, until the gnocchi are golden. Add the clams and cream sauce, reduce the heat to medium, then add the lemon juice and season to taste. Shake the pan with both hands until everything is well combined. Remove from the heat and set aside for 2 minutes with the lid on. Divide the gnocchi and clams among serving plates and add a few tablespoons of pesto randomly over the top. Serve hot with a green salad and a glass of rosé.

Pâte feuilletée

'The fine arts are five in number, namely: painting,
sculpture, poetry, music and architecture,
the principal branch of the latter being pâtisserie.'
MARIE-ANTOINE CARÊME

Pâte feuilletée

(Puff pastry)

The puff pastry we are familiar with today

is thought to be an adaptation of filo pastry, where layers of thin, unleavened buttered dough were stacked to make desserts such as baklava and strudel. The actual process of folding a dough around a block of butter to achieve those impossibly thin and flaky layers is credited to a seventeenth-century painter and pastry chef named Claude Gellée. Since then, puff pastry has infused every corner of French gastronomy, and in myriad forms: sweet, savoury, coated, filled, twisted — it's the most versatile dough of all. As an added bonus, *pâte feuilletée* freezes very well raw, a privilege not afforded by any yeasted doughs.

Along with the dough for croissant, puff pastry is often considered one of the trickiest doughs to master, but I have actually always found it the least technically challenging of all bakers' doughs. It consists of wrapping a base mixture of plain flour, salt and water (sometimes with the addition of melted butter) around a block of butter. What it does require, however, is time and a lot of elbow grease to achieve those amazingly thin and buttery layers so typical of puff pastry. The dough needs to be folded and laminated several times (turned), just as you would a croissant dough, except you have to do this for almost double the number of times. Unlike the dough for a croissant or Danish, which has a propensity to begin proving at room temperature (due to its yeast content) and is usually a softer, more fragile dough, puff pastry is made of a dry and stiff batter that does not stick or break easily during the laminating process. This is providing, of course, that you work patiently, allowing time between each 'turn' for the gluten to relax.

Palmiers aux noisettes (Hazelnut palmiers) ~ page 151

Pâte feuilletée

(Puff pastry)

There are three different methods of making puff pastry:

Traditional puff :

This is the method I use in this book. The pastry is made from a stiff water-and-flour dough (called *détrempe*) wrapped over a layer of butter. It requires five or six single turns (a series of rolling, folding and turning the dough) and a bit of patience, but it will take just as long to finish as the other two methods. This method will give you beautifully thin and regular layers throughout your pastry that will rise evenly during the baking process.

Flaky puff (rough puff) :

This is a supposedly quicker version of the traditional puff pastry, although you still have to turn the dough as you would when making a traditional puff. This type of puff is used to make pie and quiche bases where the consistency of the layers is not really critical to the look of the finished product. To speed the process up a little, the pastry can be made with three turns instead of five. For this method, you actually mix the butter with the dough right at the end of the process, before laminating.

Inverted puff :

This method is called inverted because it requires the butter to be wrapped around the dough, the exact opposite to the traditional method. Once turned, this will give you more (but thinner) layers of butter and a more refined texture. In my opinion, the added difficulties of rolling the butter directly (which can be difficult when the butter starts to melt and stick to the work surface) instead of rolling the dough are far outweighed by the perceived benefits, especially for an amateur baker.

Pâte feuilletée

(Traditional puff pastry)

The following method is for a puff pastry made using the traditional method, with five single turns (note that a few of the recipes in this chapter require six turns). Before starting, it's important to read through the instructions several times to familiarise yourself with the process.

Makes about 1 kg (2 lb 4 oz)

500 g (1 lb 2 oz) plain (all-purpose) flour
10 g (¼ oz) fine salt
50 g (1¾ oz) unsalted butter, melted and cooled
250 ml (9 fl oz) cold water
250 g (9 oz) block cold unsalted butter

How to mix the dough and prepare the butter

Using an electric mixer fitted with a dough hook attachment, mix the flour and salt on low speed until well combined. Add the melted butter and cold water and knead for 2–3 minutes, or until smooth. The time it takes for the dough to (détrempe) become smooth will vary depending on the size of your bowl and the speed of the mixer, however you should never overmix a puff pastry dough because this will develop the gluten, making the dough elastic and very hard to roll. Shape the dough into a ball (photo 1), cover with plastic wrap and refrigerate for at least 2 hours.

When the dough is cold, you will need to prepare the butter for the laminating process. Place the block of cold butter on a piece of baking paper. Cover with another piece of baking paper and use a rolling pin to pound the butter, turning it regularly by 90 degrees, into a rectangle that measures about 18 x 20 cm (7 x 8 in). Cover the butter with plastic wrap and set aside.

The laminating process

Place the dough on a lightly floured work surface and dust the top with flour. Using the rolling pin, roll the dough starting from the middle and working out towards the edges (2), to form a 16 x 30 cm (6¼ x 12 in) rectangle. Keep moving the dough and dusting with a little extra flour to stop it sticking — but be frugal with the flour. If you can't roll out your dough to the exact dimensions, use your hands to stretch it into shape (3, 4). Unwrap the butter and place it in the centre of the dough rectangle (5). Fold both ends of the dough over the top so they meet in the middle of the butter and pinch the ends together (6). You should end up with a 16 x 15 cm (6¼ x 6 in) rectangle, with the butter exposed at two ends and a tightly sealed seam over the top.

With one short end facing you, begin rolling the dough from the middle to the top (7, 8), flouring as needed. Rotate the block 180 degrees and repeat the process until you have a rectangle that measures about 20 x 65 cm (8 x 25½ in). Fold one-third of the rectangle over into the middle of the block (9), then fold the other end over the top (10). This will give you a single turn.

Repeat this process once more to get the first two single turns. During the process of 'turning', make sure that you maintain your original rectangular shape either by rolling the dough (11) or stretching it into shape, as this ensures an even distribution of butter throughout the dough.

Cover the pastry block (pàton) in plastic wrap and refrigerate for at least 3 hours. When the pastry is cold and rested, repeat the process by giving the dough another two single turns, then refrigerate for another 2 hours. Finally, turn it once more — this is the last of five single turns (note that some recipes require six single turns, so add the extra turn at this point, if required). You've done it! Refrigerate overnight.

1

2

3

4

5

Pâte feuilletée

6

7

8

9

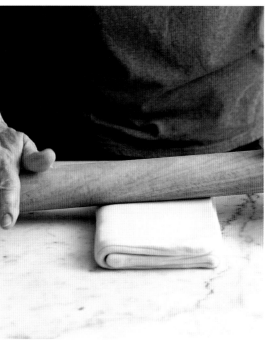

10

11

freezing puff pastry :

~ By now you probably better understand what I meant about needing patience and elbow grease to make this dough, but there is good news! Puff pastry dough freezes very well, so I suggest you make the whole batch even if the recipe requires only half, and freeze the leftover for later (it will freeze for 1–2 months). However, you will need to make some minor adjustments.

As I have mentioned before, wheat flour contains a protein called gluten (responsible for the dough's elasticity), which, along with the coagulation of the starches, traps the steam created during the baking process, underpinning its ability to develop while baking. Unfortunately flour also contains an antioxidant called glutathione, which weakens the gluten over time (denaturation process), reducing the dough's ability to retain its elasticity.

To slow down the denaturation process and extend the life span of any dough (if you are going to freeze it or use it a few days later), add a small amount of vitamin C (ascorbic acid) — the same vitamin C sold in health food stores. Simply dissolve a 500 mg tablet in the water for your dough and prepare the dough in the usual way. The addition of vitamin C will also stop the flour from oxidising and developing brown spots.

Ascorbic acid is one of the main ingredients in many powdered 'bread improvers' used by professional bakers, and while other antioxidants such as vinegar (acetic acid) or citric acid (found in lemon juice) do slow down the oxidation process, they do not slow the denaturation process of the gluten.

In summary: If you are going to freeze your dough or keep it refrigerated to use at a later stage, dissolve one 500 mg vitamin C tablet into the water for your dough (0.1 per cent of the weight of flour). Remember to allow time for the frozen pastry to defrost before baking.

Pâte feuilletée

Make a batch of these elegant bite-sized treats for afternoon tea or your next cocktail party. Use some left-over puff pastry from the freezer, roll it out, then spread some *glace royale* over the top of them and what you will end up with is a simple but stunning, light and airy pastry, delicious with a cup of tea or a glass of wine or Champagne. More importantly, with their smooth, shiny finish and long delicate shape, they will make an otherwise routine gathering with friends seem like quite a sophisticated affair (not guaranteed by this author).

Allumettes glacées
(Iced puff pastry fingers)

Makes 40

500 g (1 lb 2 oz) cold Puff Pastry, 5 single turns (pages 145–9)

Royal icing
1 egg white
250 g (9 oz) pure icing (confectioners') sugar, sifted
squeeze of lemon juice

tip.

Royal icing is traditionally used to pipe intricate decorations on wedding or Christmas cakes and gingerbread houses. To get the best results always follow these rules:
～ Never whisk the mixture. Any air pushed into the mix will make it very brittle and difficult to pipe, so always use a flat spatula and a bit of elbow grease.
～ The lemon juice helps to bind the albumen cells (egg protein) together. This improves the elasticity of the icing, but also enables you to work with a softer mixture that will set quickly and neatly. Alternatively, you can replace the lemon juice with cream of tartar or vinegar (acetic acid).

～ Roll out the puff pastry on a lightly floured work surface into a 2.5 mm (^{1}/8 in) thick rectangle measuring about 18 x 40 cm (7 x 16 in). Remember to keep moving the dough and dust with extra flour when necessary so that it doesn't stick to your work surface. If you haven't achieved a perfectly shaped rectangle with your rolling pin towards the end of the rolling process, simply stretch and pull the dough into shape using your hands. Place the rolled-out dough (*abaisse*) on a tray lined with baking paper and refrigerate for 30 minutes.

～ Meanwhile, to make the royal icing, put the egg white and a little icing sugar in a small bowl and mix with a spatula until the sugar has dissolved (see tip). Gradually stir in the rest of the icing sugar until a firm paste forms. Add ^{1}/2 teaspoon lemon juice and stir vigorously for about 3 minutes, or until smooth and glossy. To check the consistency of your icing, lift the spatula from the mixture and look for a soft peak. If the icing is too firm, add a few more drops of lemon juice (conversely, if it's too soft, add more icing sugar). Cover the bowl with a damp cloth and set aside at room temperature.

～ Remove the pastry on the tray from the fridge. Using a flat spatula, spread a 1 mm (^{1}/32 in) thin layer of royal icing over the top, taking care that the icing is spread evenly all over the surface. You may not need the whole amount of icing. Place the pastry in the freezer for 30 minutes.

～ Preheat the oven to 180°C (350°F). Line two large baking trays with baking paper. Transfer the frozen pastry to a cutting board. Using a large knife, cut the pastry into 2 x 9 cm (^{3}/4 x 3^1/2 in) rectangles. To ensure neat edges, dip the knife in hot water before cutting the pastry so the icing doesn't stick to the knife, wipe the knife clean, then repeat the process.

～ Place on the lined trays and bake for 20 minutes, or until the bases of the pastries are golden. If you notice that the top is browning too quickly, cover loosely with a piece of foil and continue baking. Leave to cool a little on the trays before transferring to a wire rack to cool for 30 minutes before serving.

It wasn't until I began working in a bakery that I actually tried one of these simple, heart-shaped pastries. Compared to all the other brightly coloured, decadent-looking alternatives that lined the shelves of pâtisseries, I thought they looked a little sad and boring. I finally relented and tried one and was so surprised to find how clever they actually were — light and subtly flavoured and filled with layers of crystallised sugar. Nowadays, palmiers come in all manner of sizes and flavours, from the traditional sugared ones to those filled with jam, and even some savoury versions.

For this recipe I've used a filling of soft chocolate and hazelnut spread, sprinkled with roasted hazelnuts, which not only brings an additional layer of texture but also gives the pastries a slightly more rustic edge. If you don't want to make your own hazelnut spread, then buy a good-quality praline or hazelnut paste and not the more readily available versions that are high in sugar and fat, as these don't hold up as well during baking.

Palmiers aux noisettes

(Hazelnut palmiers)

Makes about 25

note : You will need to give an additional single turn to the puff pastry, to refine the layers of pastry and to stop the palmier from expanding excessively during the baking process.

150 g (5¹/2 oz) raw hazelnuts, roasted and skinned (see tip)
1 kg (2 lb 4 oz) cold Puff Pastry, 6 single turns (pages 145–9)
300 g (10¹/2 oz) Hazelnut and Chocolate Spread (page 257)

roasting and skinning hazelnuts

Preheat the oven to 200°C (400°F). Put the hazelnuts on a baking tray and roast for 10–15 minutes, or until they begin to turn dark brown. Use a spatula to move the nuts around every 5 minutes or so. Every oven cooks differently, so keep an eye on them, especially towards the end of cooking. Remove from the oven and when cool enough to handle, roll the hazelnuts around in your hands to rub off the skins.

～ Preheat the oven to 180°C (350°F). Wrap the skinned hazelnuts in a clean cloth, then smash the nuts in the cloth with the base of a heavy-based saucepan until coarsely crushed. Set the nuts aside.

～ Roll out the puff pastry on a lightly floured work surface into a 4 mm (¹/8 in) thick rectangle measuring 40 x 50 cm (16 x 20 in). Remember to keep moving the dough and dust with extra flour when necessary so that it doesn't stick to your work surface. If you haven't achieved a perfectly shaped rectangle with your rolling pin towards the end of the rolling process, simply stretch and pull the dough into shape using your hands.

～ Using a flat spatula, spread the hazelnut and chocolate paste evenly over the pastry, right to the edges, then sprinkle with the crushed hazelnuts. Don't be tempted to apply a thicker layer; the palmier is made of four layers of pastry, so if the hazelnut spread is too thick the dough won't cook properly, and there's nothing worse than undercooked puff pastry! With one long side of the rolled-out dough (*abaisse*) facing you, use your hands to roll the two long sides of the pastry towards each other to meet in the middle. Fold the bottom half over the top to form a log. If the pastry is too soft to handle, refrigerate it for 30 minutes, or until firm.

～ Line two baking trays with baking paper. Using a large knife, cut the roll into 2 cm (³/4 in) thick slices and place on the lined trays, leaving a 10 cm (4 in) gap between each as they are going to double in size during cooking. As you will need to cook the palmiers in batches, it is a good idea to refrigerate the remaining pastries while the first batch is cooking.

～ Bake for 10 minutes, then reduce the oven temperature to 160°C (320°F) and bake for another 30 minutes, or until the bottom of the pastries are golden brown. Puff pastry needs an initial burst of heat to develop, but the majority of the cooking time is designed to dry it up as much as possible. If the tops darken too fast, cover loosely with a piece of foil. Repeat with the remaining pastries. Transfer to a wire rack to cool for 1 hour before serving.

Feuilleté is a general term used to describe sweet or savoury pastries made from puff pastry. It usually refers to a simple square of pastry topped with a fruit, cream or whatever else tickles your fancy and is a great way to use up your offcuts — simply roll out the dough, cut it to shape and freeze for later use. This is a great example of the fact that, more often than not, the best pastries are often the result of restraint and simplicity.

Feuilletés ricotta-figue
(Ricotta and fig pastries)

Makes 18

400 g (14 oz) fresh ricotta cheese, drained well
200 g (7 oz) Greek-style yoghurt
finely grated zest of 1 lemon
100 g (3^{1}/$_{2}$ oz) caster (superfine) sugar, plus extra, for sprinkling
3 vanilla beans, halved lengthways, seeds scraped
200 g (7 oz) honey, preferably lavender
9 ripe figs, halved lengthways
2 eggs
1 egg yolk
pinch of fine salt
500 g (1 lb 2 oz) cold Puff Pastry, 5 single turns (pages 145–9)

〜 Put the ricotta, yoghurt, lemon zest, sugar, vanilla bean seeds and 2 tablespoons of the honey in a food processor and process for 1 minute, or until smooth. Transfer to a bowl, cover and refrigerate. Sprinkle the figs generously with the extra sugar and set aside.

〜 Preheat the oven to 180°C (350°F). Line two baking trays with baking paper. To make an egg wash, lightly beat the eggs, egg yolk and salt together in a small bowl, then set aside.

〜 Roll out the puff pastry on a lightly floured work surface into a 3 mm (^{1}/$_{8}$ in) thick rectangle measuring about 25 x 35 cm (10 x 14 in). Remember to keep moving the dough and dust with extra flour when necessary so that it doesn't stick to your work surface. If you haven't achieved a perfectly shaped rectangle with your rolling pin towards the end of the rolling process, simply stretch and pull the dough into shape using your hands.

〜 Using a large knife, cut the pastry into eighteen 6 x 8 cm (2^{1}/$_{2}$ x 3^{1}/$_{4}$ in) rectangles. Try not to run the knife through the dough when you cut the shapes, as this damages the fragile layers of pastry. Instead, push the tip of the knife through the dough first, then let the knife roll down, following the curvature of the blade. Using a flat spatula, carefully place the pastries on the lined trays, spacing them about 4 cm (1^{1}/$_{2}$ in) apart.

〜 Put 1 tablespoon of the ricotta mixture in the centre of each rectangle, leaving as much exposed pastry as possible around the sides. Gently push a fig half into the ricotta mixture, placing them cut side up. Carefully brush the exposed puff pastry with the egg wash. When brushing egg wash over puff pastry, try not to drip any of the egg mixture over the sides, because this will make it harder for the pastry to rise evenly. Drizzle 1 teaspoon honey over the figs on each pastry.

〜 Bake for 20 minutes, or until the pastry has risen and is golden. The cooking times will vary a little depending on your oven, so always check that the bottom of the pastries are golden before removing them from the oven. Serve at room temperature with a cup of coffee, or warm with thick (double/heavy) cream or yoghurt.

I was eight years old when my family moved from Nice to Petit-Couronne, a small town in the Normandy region. Normandy is a mostly agricultural area, dotted with apple orchards and lush green dairy and cattle pastures, so much of the produce is very rich and earthy, with lots of creams, butters and hearty stews. Although I had already travelled with my family around most of Eastern and Central Europe, sampling exotic foods and specialties far removed from what I was accustomed to, it was not until we moved to Normandy that I began to realise how diverse the food was within my own country, and just how much our food and recipes are shaped by and intimately connected to so many things — our local landscape, the weather, our history and traditions.

It was in Normandy that I tried my first *douillon de pommes*, a beautifully sweet and flaky apple pie, packed full of caramel and butter. It was also the first time I drank raw milk straight from the farm, ate a tarte tatin — and the cheeses ... ! These dishes were all made from local and seasonal ingredients, perfectly designed to keep you warm during those long winter nights, the likes of which I'd never experienced before.

Douillons de pommes au Calvados et gousse de vanille

(Baked apples in pastry with Calvados and vanilla bean)

Serves 6

1 kg (2 lb 4 oz) cold Puff Pastry, 5 single turns (pages 145–9)
finely grated zest and juice of 2 oranges
100 ml (3$^{1}/_{2}$ fl oz) Calvados
6 small apples (reinette or red delicious)
100 g (3$^{1}/_{2}$ oz) soft unsalted butter
100 g (3$^{1}/_{2}$ oz) caster (superfine) sugar
2 eggs
1 egg yolk
pinch of fine salt
3 vanilla beans

⌒ Roll out the puff pastry on a lightly floured work surface into a 2.5 mm (¹/₈ in) thick rectangle measuring about 40 x 70 cm (16 x 27¹/₂ in). Remember to keep moving the dough and dust with extra flour when necessary so that it doesn't stick to your work surface. Using a 9 cm (3¹/₂ in) round cutter, stamp out six rounds for the bases, then use a 20 cm (8 in) round cutter to stamp out six rounds for the tops. Don't be tempted to divide the pastry in half before you do this, because you will need more pastry for the tops than the bases. Dust each round with a little flour, then place on a tray lined with baking paper. Cover with plastic wrap and refrigerate for 1 hour.

⌒ Meanwhile, put the orange zest, orange juice and 50 ml (1³/₄ fl oz) of Calvados in a large bowl and set aside. Peel the apples and core them with an apple corer or a sharp paring knife, then place in the bowl with the orange juice mixture. Turn the apples in the mixture to make sure they are coated in the liquid, to stop them oxidising. Set aside, turning the apples around in the bowl occasionally.

⌒ Using an electric mixer fitted with a paddle attachment, beat the butter and the remaining Calvados until combined. If the mixture looks split, heat the bowl a little over a hot flame or run the outside of the bowl under very hot water, then beat again until well combined.

⌒ Preheat the oven to 200°C (400°F). Line a large baking tray with baking paper. Place one of the pastry bases (the smaller rounds) on the lined tray, leaving the rest in the fridge. Drain one apple and pat dry, then fill the hollowed-out core with a generous amount of Calvados butter. Place a teaspoon of the butter on top and sprinkle generously with sugar. Remove one of the pastry tops (the larger rounds) from the fridge and use a 1 cm (¹/₂ in) round pastry cutter or a paring knife to cut out a small hole in the middle. Place the pastry over the apple and fold the pastry around it, trying not to create too many overlaps of pastry towards the bottom. Using a sharp knife or a pair of scissors, cut off the excess pastry around the bottom.

⌒ To make an egg wash, lightly beat the eggs, egg yolk and salt in a small bowl. Brush a little egg wash over the pastry base, then sit the apple in the middle of the base. Press down firmly to join the top and base together, then brush all over with egg wash. Using the back of a paring knife, score a geometric design over the pastry, being careful not to cut all the way through. To finish, cut the vanilla beans in half and push a half through the hole in the top, to resemble an apple stem. Repeat the process with the remaining apples and pastry rounds.

⌒ Place the *douillons* in the oven and bake for 20 minutes, then reduce the oven temperature to 190°C (375°F) and bake for another 45 minutes, or until golden. If you find your pastry is browning too quickly, cover loosely with a piece of foil. Remove from the oven and serve hot with mascarpone or thick (double/heavy) cream.

For this pie, we will travel north to the municipality of Pithiviers in the Loire Valley region. This very traditional pie, baked for the Epiphany on the sixth of January, is also called 'kings' cake' or *galette des rois*, referring to *les rois mages*, or the three wise men (kings). The galette is made of puff pastry and frangipane, a moist almond cream, and always contains a small ceramic figure called a *fève* (meaning broad bean, as this is what was originally used). The idea is that the person who finds the *fève* is then crowned king or queen for the day. I have never forgotten that wonderful sense of anticipation I felt as a child, just before we cut the cake, hoping it would be me who found the *fève*.

A word of warning: if you are baking this pie for a French person, never forget the *fève* and a paper crown, or the small child inside your guest will be shattered!

Pithiviers

(Frangipane pie)

Serves 8

1 kg (2 lb 4 oz) cold Puff Pastry, 5 single turns (pages 145–9)
1 egg
pinch of fine salt

Frangipane

200 g (7 oz) Almond Cream (page 260)
100 g (3^1/2 oz) Custard (page 261)
few drops of almond essence, to taste

~ Roll out the puff pastry on a lightly floured work surface until 5 mm (^{1}/4 in) thick. Remember to keep moving the dough and dust with extra flour when necessary so that it doesn't stick to your work surface. Using a cake tin or dinner plate as a guide, cut out a 25 cm (10 in) circle for the base and a slightly larger 26 cm (10^1/2 in) circle for the top. Place the pastry rounds on two baking trays lined with baking paper and freeze for 15 minutes.

~ Meanwhile, to make the frangipane, use a hand-held whisk to beat the almond cream and custard together until smooth, then add the almond essence and combine well. Be frugal with your almond essence, as it can overpower the main flavour of your dish.

~ Preheat the oven to 185°C (365°F). To make an egg wash, lightly beat the egg and salt together in a small bowl and set aside. Remove the pastry from the freezer and spread the frangipane mixture onto the smaller circle, leaving a 3 cm (1^1/4 in) border around the edge. Gently push the *fève* into the frangipane. Lightly brush around the edge with egg wash, then place the larger pastry circle over the top and gently press around the edge to seal. Brush the top with egg wash, taking care not to drip any of the egg mixture over the side, because this will make it harder for the pastry to rise evenly. Using the back of a paring knife, score curved lines on the top, radiating from the centre to the outside edge.

~ Bake on the bottom shelf of the oven for 40 minutes, or until the base of the pie is golden. Puff pastry needs to be cooked at a relatively high temperature for a long time to get the best height and flakiness. If you find the top is browning too quickly, cover loosely with a piece of foil and continue baking. Transfer to a wire rack to cool and serve at room temperature, with a crown for the lucky finder of the *fève*.

Frangipane or almond cream?
These creams are often confused or, at least, almond cream is often erroneously called frangipane. While they both use similar ingredients, their texture and taste are very different. Almond cream is made of almonds, butter, sugar and eggs, sometimes with flour or custard added to it. It contains a proportionally large amount of dry ingredients and is used as a base cream for all kinds of fruit tarts. Frangipane, on the other hand, uses less dry ingredients and always includes bitter almonds or almond essence for flavour and fragrance. Frangipane is used as a filling and resembles a dense custard.

A typical French breakfast usually consists of a croissant or a toasted baguette *tartine* with jam, or some other sweet pastry — I, for one, would never think to eat anything savoury such as these cheese sticks, instead reserving them for an *apéritif* or afternoon snack, maybe with a few green olives and a glass of red wine. In Australia, however, they have become very popular as a quick snack for breakfast. I remember how I used to shake my head in bewilderment as I watched customers walking out of the shop early in the morning with a few cheese sticks in one hand and a coffee in the other. It didn't take me long to change my mind. Now, I am often caught early in the morning, scavenging all the broken cheese sticks and nibbling on the burnt gruyère left over on the baking trays.

Batons gruyère-parmesan
(Cheese sticks)

Makes 15

300 g (10¹/2 oz) gruyère cheese, grated
80 g (2³/4 oz) parmesan cheese, grated
3 eggs
pinch of fine salt
1 kg (2 lb 4 oz) cold Puff Pastry, 5 single turns (pages 145–9)
2 teaspoons finely ground black pepper

⌣ Combine the gruyère and parmesan in a small bowl and put in the freezer for 1 hour. When the cheese has frozen, place on a chopping board and chop into the smallest pieces possible, then return to the freezer.

⌣ Meanwhile, to make an egg wash, lightly beat the eggs and salt in a small bowl and set aside. Preheat the oven to 180°C (350°F). Line two baking trays with baking paper.

⌣ Roll out the puff pastry on a lightly floured work surface into a 3 mm (¹/8 in) thick rectangle measuring about 20 x 60 cm (8 x 24 in). Remember to keep moving the dough and dust with extra flour when necessary so that it doesn't stick to your work surface. Towards the end of rolling, feel free to use your hands to stretch the pastry into shape.

⌣ Brush a small amount of egg wash over the top of the pastry, then sprinkle a generous amount of the chopped cheese evenly over the top, going all the way to the edges. Using a rolling pin, gently roll over the top of the cheese to make sure it sticks to the dough during the twisting process. Sprinkle the pepper evenly over the top of the cheese.

⌣ With one long side of the pastry facing you, and using a large knife, cut the pastry into fifteen 4 cm (1¹/2 in) wide strips. Take one strip and place it on the work surface, cheese side down and with the long side facing you. Using your palms, gently roll one end of the strip in a downwards direction while rolling the other end in an upwards direction. Lengthen the twist to about 20 cm (8 in) by rolling it with both your hands, working from the middle out. Place on the lined trays, spacing them about 4 cm (1¹/2 in) apart.

tip

Gruyère is the perfect cheese to use in cheese sticks because it has a mild flavour with just the right amount of salt, it adds a hint of sweetness and, more importantly, it stays relatively dry during baking. The only other cheese suitable for cheese sticks is cheddar. Never use a soft pizza cheese, such as provolone or mozzarella, because they are too soft when melted and will stop the puff pastry from drying out properly.

⌣ Bake on the bottom shelf of the oven for 20 minutes, then reduce the oven temperature to 160°C (320°F) and cook for another 15 minutes, or until dry. It is essential that the cheese sticks are crisp and flaky so make sure they are cooked through. If you find they are browning too quickly, place a piece of foil loosely over the top and continue baking until crisp. Remove from the oven and cool on a wire rack for at least 30 minutes before serving. These cheese sticks, as well as most pastries made from puff, freeze very well prior to being baked, so make more than you need and freeze the rest to use another time.

Olive tapenade has been used in Provençal cooking for over 2000 years, probably because the olive tree was one of the few trees resilient enough to survive the harsh climatic conditions of the area. Olives have been cultivated for millennia and used in all manner of products, from olive oils and pickles, to hair conditioners and herbal medicines. I have loved eating olives since I was a child, but it wasn't until I started working in a Michelin-starred restaurant in Marseille (which featured olives and tapenades in many of its fine dishes) that I realised how versatile they truly were and how, with a little bit of imagination, they could be used in almost any capacity, from condiments for meats and fish, to spreads for breads and crackers, and even desserts.

These roulades are made with a green olive tapenade — a name derived from the Provençal word for capers, *tapenas* — which is made by crushing olives, capers and anchovies with olive oil. This miraculous concoction can be stored almost indefinitely in your fridge, and used on toast, spread over a grilled steak, used as you would pesto on pasta, or as a condiment to flavour sauces and creams.

Roulades à la tapenade et au haloumi

(Olive tapenade and haloumi swirls)

Makes about 80

note : You will need to give an additional single turn to the puff pastry, to refine the layers of pastry and to stop the roulade from expanding excessively during the baking process.

500 g (1 lb 2 oz) cold Puff Pastry, 6 single turns (pages 145–9)
olive oil, for pan-frying
300 g (10½ oz) haloumi cheese, roughly chopped

Olive tapenade

300 g (10½ oz) green olives, pitted
50 g (1¾ oz) small capers in brine, drained
50 g (1¾ oz) anchovy fillets
juice of 1 lemon
½ teaspoon ground black pepper
80 ml (2¾ fl oz) virgin olive oil, plus extra, if needed

~ To make the tapenade, put the olives, capers, anchovies, lemon juice and pepper in a food processor. With the motor running, gradually add the olive oil and process until a thick, spreadable paste forms. You may need to add a little extra oil to achieve the right consistency. Transfer to a small bowl, cover with plastic wrap and refrigerate until needed.

~ Roll out the puff pastry on a lightly floured work surface into a 2 mm ($1/16$ in) thick rectangle measuring about 35 x 40 cm (14 x 16 in). Remember to keep moving the dough and dust with extra flour when necessary so that it doesn't stick to your work surface. Towards the end of rolling, feel free to use your hands to stretch the pastry into shape. For these small roulades, it is important that the pastry is rolled no thicker than 2 mm ($1/16$ in) or the spiral will come undone during baking. Cut the rectangle in half lengthways so you end up with two 40 cm (16 in) long strips, then dust a little flour over the top. Place on a lined tray and refrigerate for 30 minutes.

~ Heat a drizzle of olive oil in a frying pan over high heat. As soon as the oil begins to smoke, add the haloumi and cook for 1 minute, stirring continuously until light golden all over. Remove and drain on paper towel and set aside until cooled to room temperature.

~ Lightly dust the work surface with flour. Take one half of the pastry out of the fridge and place it on the work surface, with one long side facing you. Using a spatula, spread half of the tapenade evenly over the top of the pastry, then scatter with half of the haloumi. Use the palm of your hand to gently push down on the haloumi. Roll the pastry up into a tight roulade, starting from the top left-hand corner and working your way across to the right. Put the roulade in the freezer for 30 minutes to firm up. Repeat the process with the remaining pastry, tapenade and haloumi.

~ Preheat the oven to 180°C (350°F). Line two large baking trays with baking paper. Remove one roulade from the freezer and place it, seam side down, on a cutting board. Using a large knife, cut the roulade into 1 cm ($1/2$ in) thick slices, holding it in shape while cutting. Pick up one piece at a time, then place on the lined baking trays, spacing them about 3 cm ($1 1/4$ in) apart. Place a piece of baking paper on top of the pastries and cover with another baking tray. Bake for 15 minutes, then reduce the oven temperature to 170°C (340°F), remove the top tray and paper and bake for another 15 minutes, or until golden. Remove and cool on wire racks. Repeat with the remaining roulade.

~ Serve warm or at room temperature. The subtle saltiness of the tapenade and delicate flakiness of the puff pastry make these roulades an ideal canapé. Serve them with some cheese and a glass of wine, or with pâté or pork rillettes.

tips

If you want to freeze the roulades, do so before cooking them: wrap the sliced roulade pieces in plastic wrap. To cook, place the frozen roulade slices in the fridge to thaw, then bake as per the recipe instructions.

To achieve a perfectly circular shape, use a round cutter that best fits the size of your roulades and use that to cut the excess pastry off as soon as they come out of the oven.

Roulades à la tapenade et au haloumi
(Olive tapenade and haloumi swirls)

Tarte au potiron et aux lardons
(Speck and pumpkin tart)

This speck and pumpkin savoury tart is very common in the south of France, mainly due to the fact that pumpkin favours a more temperate climate. Pumpkin tart is largely a provincial specialty, found mostly in small village bakeries or on the shelves of fresh food markets rather than in the more cosmopolitan bakeries of large towns and cities.

If you overlook its understated and decidedly rustic look, you will be rewarded with a perfectly balanced and moist tart, with undertones of hazelnuts and honey that can be enjoyed as a mid-afternoon treat, or served as our family likes to do, as an accompaniment for a Sunday roast.

Tarte au potiron et aux lardons

(Speck and pumpkin tart)

Serves 6–8

500 g (1 lb 2 oz) cold Puff Pastry, 5 single turns (pages 145–9)
1 egg
1 egg yolk
pinch of fine salt

Filling

600 g (1 lb 5 oz) butternut (squash), jap or kent pumpkin
50 g (1³/4 oz) unsalted butter
150 ml (5 fl oz) whipping cream (35% fat)
2 eggs, lightly beaten
¹/4 teaspoon freshly grated nutmeg
¹/4 teaspoon ground black pepper
fine salt, to taste
200 g (7 oz) piece speck, bacon or prosciutto, cut into
   1 cm (¹/2 in) cubes

~ You will need a 25 cm (10 in) tart ring or tart tin with a removable base. Roll out the puff pastry on a lightly floured work surface until 5 mm (¼ in) thick. Remember to keep moving the dough and dusting with extra flour when necessary so that it doesn't stick to your work surface. Line the base and side of the tin with the pastry, reserving the pastry scraps. Refrigerate both the tart shell and scraps for 30 minutes.

~ Meanwhile, to make the filling, peel the pumpkin, remove the seeds and cut it into 4 cm (1½ in) cubes. Bring a large saucepan of lightly salted water to the boil over high heat. Add the pumpkin, then reduce the heat to medium, cover and cook for 15 minutes, or until tender. Remove from the heat and drain. Put the hot pumpkin into a food processor with the butter, cream, eggs, nutmeg and pepper and process until smooth and creamy. Season to taste with salt, then set aside to cool.

~ Preheat the oven to 190°C (375°F). Remove the tin from the fridge and line the tart shell with foil, making sure the side of the shell is covered, then fill to the top with uncooked rice or baking beads. Blind bake for 20 minutes, or until the bottom of the tart shell is golden. Remove the rice and foil and set aside until cool. Reduce the oven temperature to 180°C (350°F).

~ Meanwhile, place a frying pan over high heat for 2 minutes or until hot, then add the speck and cook, stirring continuously, for 8–10 minutes, or until the speck is golden and the fat has melted. Remove with a slotted spoon and drain on paper towel. This process is called rendering and it is designed to melt the fat in your meat, remove impurities and improve the overall flavour and texture. Stir the speck into the cooled pumpkin purée, then pour the pumpkin filling into the tart shell.

~ To make an egg wash, lightly beat the egg, egg yolk and salt together in a small bowl and set aside. Roll out the reserved puff pastry scraps on a lightly floured work surface into a 2 mm (¹/₁₆ in) thick rectangle that measures at least 25 cm (10 in) wide. Cut the pastry into thin 5 mm (¼ in) strips. Lay the strips over the filling, arranging them parallel to each other and spacing them about 2 cm (¾ in) apart. Rotate the tart 45 degrees and repeat the process. This simplified lattice design is a lot faster and easier to execute than a weaved lattice on a large tart and still looks rustic and elegant after baking. If you prefer the traditional lattice design, refer to the photograph on page 114 as a guide. Brush the egg wash neatly over the lattice top and around the edge of the pie, then bake for 30 minutes, or until the pastry is golden. Serve warm with a tablespoon of thick (double/heavy) cream, and a green salad.

salt to taste

I rarely recommend a dosage for salt in savoury recipes, because the amount of salt you need can vary dramatically, depending on how long you reduced a sauce to the type of ingredients you chose (even if they are the same as those I have recommended, different products can vary in saltiness) and, of course, your personal taste. Most foods need a little salt to enhance the flavour, but as with most other spices and condiments, the right amount is mostly based on your own preferences. For this reason, I usually suggest 'salt, to taste' or, when making anything where the volume of sauce will reduce as it cooks, it is best to season at the end of cooking.

This tart is based on the recipe for *gratin dauphinois*, which was developed over 300 years ago by Auguste Escoffier, one of the pioneers of French gastronomy. This recipe for *tarte gratinée* differs somewhat from the original as it contains a small amount of cheese and eggs. The idea behind using this version over the traditional one is because the cheese and eggs will help bind the tart together, making it a lot easier to serve, transforming this delicious, if somewhat messy, gratin into an easy-to-handle picnic treat.

Tarte gratinée

(Potato and cream tart)

Serves 6–8

500 g (1 lb 2 oz) cold Puff Pastry, 5 single turns (pages 145–9)
500 g (1 lb 2 oz) potatoes, such as russet (idaho), desiree or pontiac
700 ml (24 fl oz) whipping cream (35% fat)
$1/2$ teaspoon freshly grated nutmeg
3 teaspoons fine salt, or to taste
$1/2$ teaspoon ground black pepper
3 eggs
150 g ($5^1/2$ oz) gruyère cheese, grated

technical tip

There are two types of non-enzymatic browning and the terms for each are often erroneously used. You might have noticed that throughout this book I tend to use the word 'golden' and not 'caramelised' to describe the browning of cheese (as for this tart), meats or fish. This is because 'caramelising' describes the browning that occurs when sucrose (not protein) is heated. This is different from the Maillard reaction, a term used to describe a series of chemical reactions that occur between amino acids and reducing sugars when proteins (meat, fish, dairy products) are heated. Sweet vegetables such as carrots, beetroot (beets) or sweet potatoes will be subjected to both caramelisation and the Maillard reaction during the browning process, because they contain both sucrose and protein.

You will need a 25 cm (10 in) tart ring or tart tin with a removable base. Roll out the puff pastry on a lightly floured work surface until 5 mm ($1/4$ in) thick. Remember to keep moving the dough and dusting with extra flour when necessary so that it doesn't stick to your work surface. Line the base and side of the tin with the pastry. Refrigerate for 30 minutes.

Preheat the oven to 190°C (375°F). Remove the tin from the fridge and line the tart shell with foil, making sure the side of the shell is covered, then fill to the top with uncooked rice or baking beads. Blind bake for 20 minutes, or until the base of the tart shell is golden. Remove the rice and foil and set aside until cool. Reduce the oven temperature to 160°C (320°F).

Meanwhile, peel, wash and dry the potatoes. Using a mandolin or the slicing attachment on a food processor, cut the potatoes into 2 mm ($1/16$ in) thin slices. You can use a large knife to slice the potatoes, but you need to make sure they are all the same thickness, to ensure the potato cooks evenly.

Put the cream, nutmeg, salt and pepper in a large saucepan and bring to the boil over high heat. As soon as the cream comes to the boil, remove from the heat and add the sliced potatoes. Cover with a lid and set aside for 15 minutes, or until cool to the touch, then pour the potatoes into a sieve placed over a bowl. Whisk the eggs into the cream mixture, then stir in half the gruyère.

Starting from the outside edge, arrange the potato slices, slightly overlapping, around the circumference of the tin. Repeat with the remaining potatoes, working all the way to the middle of the tart. Place the tart on the oven shelf, then pour in the cream mixture, leaving the top edges of the potato slices exposed. Sprinkle the remaining gruyère over the top.

Bake for 45 minutes, then increase the oven temperature to 190°C (375°F) and bake for another 10–15 minutes, or until the potatoes are cooked through and the cheese is golden. To check if the potatoes are cooked, insert the tip of a paring knife into the tart — if you feel any resistance, cook for another 5 minutes, then check again. Remove from the oven and cool for at least 15 minutes before removing from the tin. This is delicious served hot or cold, with a green salad tossed with a sharp vinegar dressing.

When my sister and I were young, we spent our summer holidays at my grandparents' house in Ongles, a tiny Provençal village surrounded by fields of lavender, wild thyme and sunflowers. Every weekend they took us to Banon, a small township famous worldwide for its traditional specialties, including a donkey sausage and the very well renowned Banon goat's cheese, a small circular cheese made of raw goat's milk, wrapped in chestnut leaves. This tart reminds me of those happy summer weekends, when we would huddle under the yellow awning of the local café to escape the scorching heat, sipping on a refreshing orgeat syrup, hungrily scoffing down a cold *tartelette de Banon*. I love this tart for the fact that it is so representative of Provençal cooking: simple, almost rustic and made with locally sourced ingredients.

Tarte au fromage de Banon
(Goat's cheese, tomato and basil tart)

Serves 6–8

500 g (1 lb 2 oz) cold Puff Pastry, 5 single turns (pages 145–9)
2 roma (plum) tomatoes, very thinly sliced
10 black olives
180 g (6¼ oz) Banon goat's cheese, or other fresh goat's cheese, crumbled
2 tablespoons extra virgin olive oil

Sauce

1 tablespoon extra virgin olive oil
1 onion, finely chopped
400 g (14 oz) cherry tomatoes, quartered
2 garlic cloves, thinly sliced
3 thyme sprigs, leaves picked
1 teaspoon ground black pepper
10 large basil leaves, plus extra, to serve
fine salt, to taste

〜 You will need a 25 cm (10 in) ring tin or tart tin with a removable base. Roll out the puff pastry on a lightly floured work surface until 5 mm (¼ in) thick. Remember to keep moving the dough and dusting with extra flour when necessary so that it doesn't stick to your work surface. Line the base and side of the tin with the pastry. Refrigerate for 30 minutes.

〜 Meanwhile, to make the sauce, heat the olive oil in a saucepan over medium–high heat. As soon as the oil begins to smoke, add the onion, then reduce the heat to medium and cook for 10 minutes, stirring regularly until the onion is golden. Add the tomatoes, garlic, thyme and pepper, then cover and simmer, stirring occasionally, for 15 minutes, or until thickened and reduced. Towards the end of cooking, tear the basil leaves into the sauce and season to taste with salt. Remove from the heat, cover with a cloth and set aside until cooled to room temperature.

〜 Preheat the oven to 190°C (375°F). Remove the tin from the fridge and line the tart shell with foil, making sure the side of the shell is covered, then fill to the top with uncooked rice or baking beads. Blind bake for 20 minutes, or until the base is golden. Remove the rice and foil and set aside until cool. Reduce the oven temperature to 180°C (350°F).

〜 Spread the cooled sauce over the base of the tart shell. Make sure your sauce is cool, as a warm sauce will soften the thin layers of puff pastry, resulting in a soggy base. Place the sliced tomatoes over the top, arranging them in slightly overlapping concentric circles, then scatter over the olives and goat's cheese. Bake on the bottom shelf of the oven for 25 minutes, or until the pastry is golden. Drizzle the olive oil over the tomatoes, then scatter with the extra basil leaves and serve warm. If you prefer to serve it cold (my personal favourite) as a mid-afternoon treat or for dinner, refrigerate until needed and only garnish with the basil when you are ready to serve.

tip

The thyme and basil will take a while to infuse the sauce properly, so this tart will taste even better after a few days. Simply reheat it in a 180°C (350°F) oven for 5 minutes.

Croissants

'Nothing is created, nothing is lost,
all is transformed.'

ANTOINE LAVOISIER

Croissants

From a freshly baked baguette to a bowl of *café au lait,* the croissant is so much a part of the fabric of daily French life that it's hard to believe it isn't really French. There are countless stories about how and where this pastry originated, with most theories suggesting that it was Marie Antoinette, originally from Vienna, who introduced the Austrian *kipferl* (a rolled-up plain brioche) to the French Royal Court. It wasn't until later that a French baker invented the method of layering butter in a sweet bread dough, which, in turn, led to the creation of puff pastry, Danish pastry and, of course, the famed butter croissant we know and love today. It is not entirely clear why the croissant has become so closely associated with French culture; however, what is clear is that there really is no such thing as a true 'local' creation. As much as we might think otherwise, all our favourite specialties are in fact just the last step in a long line of small improvements that have been made over many years, all subjective and bearing witness to the various influences of a long line of bakers.

As a small boy, I remember looking longingly at the baskets filled with golden brown pastries that adorned the window of my local pâtisserie, and even now I can still remember the warm, buttery smell that wafted out the door. I loved trying to catch a glimpse of the pale and dishevelled baker inside, rolling those small triangles of dough into croissants at warp speed, the trays of perfectly shaped crescents of dough glistening under the fluorescent lights. Now, every time I see a small child looking up at me when I am in the kitchen rolling croissants, the same way it's been done for a hundred years, I wonder if he sees the magic of the moment as I did all those years ago, or if all he sees is a pale and dishevelled middle-aged man playing with flour.

Croissant ～ pages 174–81

Pâte à croissant

(Croissant dough)

This *viennoiserie* is notoriously tricky to make because it encompasses not only the art of mixing a yeasted dough, but also the fiddly process of laminating, or 'turning', the dough with butter. Unlike puff pastry, the croissant dough contains yeast and has a propensity to start proving during the laminating process if your working environment is too warm. Added to that are the problems you will face if your butter begins to soften too much. So be patient and familiarise yourself with your ingredients by reading the chapter on Essential Ingredients (pages 10–19) and the entire process described in this step-by-step section before you begin. Trust me, the rewards of looking at your croissants slowly developing in the oven and the pride you will feel when you serve these beautifully flaky pastries to your friends and family will far exceed the effort spent in making them.

Makes about 1 kg (2 lb 4 oz)

500 g (1 lb 2 oz) plain (all-purpose) flour ('0'/T55)
60 g (2¼ oz) caster (superfine) sugar
2 teaspoons fine salt
10 g (¼ oz) dried yeast
300 ml (10½ fl oz) full-cream milk
270 g (9½ oz) block cold unsalted butter

How to mix the dough and prepare the butter

Using an electric mixer fitted with a dough hook attachment, mix the flour, sugar, salt and yeast (*photo 1*) on low speed until well combined. Gradually add the milk (*2*) and mix for 5 minutes. At this stage the dough should be firm but not dry. If the mixture looks too hard or if your mixer finds it hard to mix properly, add 1–2 tablespoons of extra milk to soften it up. Some types of flour or flours made from different types of wheat have different rates of absorption and may require more liquid than others.

After 5 minutes, increase the speed slightly and mix for another 10 minutes, or until the dough is smooth and comes away from the side of the bowl (*3*). Be careful when increasing the speed of your mixer; this dough can be hard on small mixers, so if you feel like your mixer is struggling, reduce the speed and mix for a few minutes longer.

Stop the mixer, remove the dough and place in a bowl. Lightly dust with flour (*4*) and cover with a clean cloth. Set aside in a warm place for the first prove (*pointage*) for 1 hour, or until increased in size by half. Always check on how fast your dough is proving. The first prove is meant to stimulate the yeast only, so as soon as the dough increases by roughly half of its original size, transfer to a tray lined with baking paper. Flatten the dough over the tray as much as you can to remove as many gas bubbles as possible. Cover the tray with plastic wrap and refrigerate on the top shelf for at least 1 hour.

When the dough (*détrempe*) is cold, you will need to prepare the butter for the laminating process. This involves pounding the cold butter into a rectangle roughly half the size of your dough. To do this, place the block of cold butter on a piece of baking paper, cover with another piece of baking paper and use a rolling pin to pound the butter, turning it regularly by 90 degrees, into a rectangle about 18 x 20 cm (7 x 8 in). Cover the butter in plastic wrap and set aside.

cooking tip :

~ Ideally, the proving process should be done in a humidity-controlled environment because the dough has a tendency to dry out when exposed to dry air so, if you can, prove your croissants in an enclosed space such as a cupboard or your oven (turned off) to stop them drying out.

1

2

3

4

Pâte à croissant

The laminating process

Place the dough on a lightly floured work surface and dust the top with flour *(5)*. Roll the dough from the middle all the way to the edges into a 20 x 35 cm (8 x 14 in) rectangle. Keep moving the dough and dusting with a little extra flour to stop it sticking (be frugal with the flour you use during this process). If you can't roll your dough out to the exact dimensions, use your hands to stretch it into shape. Rotate the dough 90 degrees.

Unwrap the butter and place it in the centre of the dough rectangle. Fold both ends of the dough over the top so they meet in the middle of the butter and pinch the ends together *(6, 7)*. You should end up with a 20 x 18 cm (8 x 7 in) rectangle, with the butter exposed at two ends, and a tightly sealed seam over the top.

With one short end facing you, begin rolling the dough from the middle to the top *(8)*, flouring as needed. Rotate the block 180 degrees and repeat the process until you have a rectangle that measures about 20 x 65 cm (8 x $25^{1}/_{2}$ in). Fold one-third of the rectangle over the middle of the block *(9)*, then fold the other end over the top *(10)*. This will give you a single turn. During the process of 'turning', make sure that you maintain your original rectangular shape either by gently rolling or stretching the dough into shape, as this will ensure an even distribution of butter throughout the croissant.

Use your finger to mark one dot in the dough *(11)*, as a reminder that this is the first turn. (Increase the number of dots for subsequent turns.) Cover the dough in plastic wrap and refrigerate for 1 hour, or until the butter is firm.

The next and final turn is a double turn, or book turn, and for this the dough will need to be rolled out thinner to accommodate the additional fold *(12)*. Repeat the process as for the first turn but continue rolling until you get a larger rectangle measuring 20 x 90 cm (8 x $35^{1}/_{2}$ in). Once you have rolled and stretched the dough into the correct dimension *(13)*, fold both ends up to meet in the middle of the rectangle *(14, 15)*, then fold it in half again to end up with a block roughly the original size of the butter *(16)*.

Wrap the croissant dough (*pâton*) in plastic wrap and refrigerate for 2 hours. Resting the dough in the fridge enables the gluten (protein in the flour) to relax and also helps the butter harden. This not only makes it a lot easier to work with the dough but also ensures that the butter isn't absorbed into the thin layers of dough, which would effectively negate most of the work you have just done.

cooking tip :

～ Croissant dough does not freeze very well due to its live culture content (yeast), and domestic freezers are not designed to maintain the cold temperatures required to stabilise the yeast properly. My advice is to bake all the croissants on the day and keep any leftover to make Almond Croissants (page 184) or Bread and Butter Pudding (page 63).

Ever wondered how many layers of butter there are in a croissant?

～ Croissants are made using two different types of turns, or folds: a single turn and a double turn, or book turn. Even though a book turn is generally referred to as a double turn, it is not entirely mathematically correct. To save you the trouble of having to count each and every layer of your croissant or puff pastry at breakfast, here is a simple equation that illustrates the mechanics of laminating:

Single turns:
First turn: 3 layers of butter
Second turn: 3 x 3 = 9 layers
Third turn: 9 x 3 = 27 layers
Fourth turn: 27 x 3 = 81 layers
Fifth turn: 81 x 3 = 243 layers
Sixth turn: 243 x 3 = 729 layers

Double (book) turns:
First turn: 4 layers of butter
Second turn: 4 x 4 = 16 layers
Third turn: 16 x 4 = 64 layers
Fourth turn: 64 x 4 = 256 layers

So if you've ever wondered how many layers of butter are in your croissant, the answer is 12: three layers for a single turn x four layers for a double turn.

5

6

7

8

Pâte à croissant

9

10

11

12

13

14

15

16

Pâte à croissant

Making the croissants

Croissants are a homage to the wonderment of geometry and how a simple triangle can be shaped into a multi-layered, perfectly shaped croissant with a single roll of the hand. Remember that every baker and pastry chef in the world has their own personal style when it comes to the shape of their croissant, a style honed over many years of practice, so don't be too daunted if yours end up a little fat, or a little short. Regardless of their shape, they are yours and that, in itself, is a beautiful thing.

Makes 10–12

1 kg (2 lb 4 oz) cold Croissant Dough, 1 single and 1 double turn (pages 174–9)
3 eggs
pinch of fine salt

Cutting the croissants

Line two baking trays with baking paper. Remove the croissant dough from the fridge and place on a lightly floured work surface with one short, open side facing you. Dust the top with a little extra flour and begin rolling lengthwise, regularly moving the dough and dusting with flour to ensure it doesn't stick to the work surface. This final process is the most demanding one. If you're getting tired or if the dough softens up too much, simply sprinkle the top of the dough with flour, fold it gently over itself and refrigerate until it sets again. Continue the rolling process until you get a long rectangle *(photo 1)* that measures about 20 x 60 cm (8 x 24 in) and is about 5 mm ($^{1}/_{4}$ in) thick.

Before you begin cutting your rolled-out dough (*abaisse*), fluff it up by running your hand underneath it and lifting it up gently on all sides. This allows the gluten time to relax and stops your cut pieces from shrinking and losing their shape during the cutting process.

Use a large knife to cut the dough into alternating triangles with a 10 cm (4 in) base *(2)*. Gently lift each triangle and stretch it with your hands until they are lengthened by about 10 per cent, to roughly 22 cm (8$^{1}/_{2}$ in) long *(3)*. Remove any excess flour from the work surface, as the dough needs to adhere to the surface for the croissants to be rolled properly. Place one triangle on the work surface with the pointed end facing you. Using both palms, roll the wide end (the base) of the croissant towards you, all the way to the tip of the triangle *(4)*. When the croissant is rolled, simply bend it in the shape of a crescent and place it on a lined baking tray, leaving a 5 cm (2 in) gap between each.

Cover the croissants with a damp cloth and place in a warm place to prove for 2 hours, or until doubled in size. To check if your pastries are ready to bake, poke them with your index finger; they should feel soft but still elastic. If the pastry doesn't bounce back after being poked, they are probably slightly overproved, so occasionally check on their progress towards the end of the recommended proving time.

Baking the croissants

To make an egg wash, lightly beat the eggs and salt together in a small bowl, then set aside for 5 minutes.

Preheat the oven to 185°C (365°F). When the croissants have proved, brush them generously with the egg wash and bake for 25 minutes, or until golden brown. Unlike puff pastry, croissant dough has a leavening agent (yeast), so does not rely solely on the steam created by water evaporation during the baking process to develop. Croissants should have a flaky skin and a soft, fleshy centre, so they need to be cooked at a much lower temperature for a shorter period — don't be tempted to leave them for too long in the oven. Generally speaking, if you respect the cooking temperature, the colour will be a great indicator of whether the croissants are ready or not.

1

2

3

4

Making the croissants

Pains au chocolat, or *chocolatines* as they are called in some areas, are one of many pastries made with croissant dough. They seem to have made their way onto the shelves of French bakeries, probably as an improvement of the much-loved, and 'imaginatively' named, *baguette beurre et chocolat* — a crunchy stick of — as per the literal translation — chocolate sandwiched in a buttered bread stick.

For this recipe I recommend you use a good-quality, low-sugar chocolate with a 70 per cent cocoa content and some chopped hazelnuts to add a bit of texture. However, as always, feel free to use any type of chocolate to suit your personal taste, or remove the nuts altogether to make a traditional *chocolatine*.

Pains au chocolat et aux noisettes

(Chocolate and hazelnut croissants)

Makes 10–12

1 kg (2 lb 4 oz) cold Croissant Dough, 1 single and 1 double turn (pages 174–9)
300 g (10½ oz) dark chocolate (70% cocoa solids), coarsely chopped
200 g (7 oz) hazelnuts, roasted and skinned, coarsely chopped (see tip, page 151)
3 eggs
pinch of fine salt

⌒ Following the method on page 180, roll out the croissant dough on a lightly floured work surface, dusting with extra flour when needed to ensure the dough doesn't stick to the surface. The sticking creates resistance, which means you will need to apply more pressure, thus damaging the delicate layers of butter. You need to make the rectangle slightly wider — about 30 cm (12 in) wide and 5 mm (¼ in) thick.

⌒ Line two baking trays with baking paper and set aside. Before you begin cutting your rolled-out dough (*abaisse*), fluff it up by running your hands underneath it and lifting it up gently on all sides. This allows the gluten time to relax and stops your cut pieces from shrinking and losing their shape during the cutting process. Cut the rectangle in half lengthways to form two long, 15 cm (6 in) wide, rectangles. Place one piece on a lined tray and refrigerate while you cut and roll the other half.

⌒ Using a large knife, cut the dough into 10 x 15 cm (4 x 6 in) rectangles. In order to preserve the integrity of the fine layers of butter, try to cut the pastry using one single motion of the knife, and avoid dragging the knife through the dough. Place 1 tablespoon chopped chocolate on each rectangle, along the top of one short side, then sprinkle some hazelnuts over the whole rectangle. Feel free to increase or decrease the amount of chocolate, nuts or whatever else you decide to use. Starting from the end with the chocolate, tightly roll up each rectangle of dough to enclose the filling. Place on the lined trays, leaving a 7 cm (2¾ in) gap between each. Cover with a damp cloth and place in a warm place to prove for 2 hours, or until doubled in size.

⌒ Preheat the oven to 185°C (365°F). To make an egg wash, lightly beat the eggs and salt together in a small bowl, then set aside for 5 minutes.

⌒ To check if your pastries are ready to bake, poke them with your index finger; they should feel soft but still elastic. If the pastry doesn't bounce back after being poked, they are probably slightly overproved, so it's a good idea to occasionally check on their progress towards the end of the recommended proving time. Brush the egg wash generously over the top of each pastry, then bake for 25 minutes, or until golden. Serve warm or at room temperature.

tip

Pastries will increase in size after they have been baked, sometimes as much as twice their original size, so be very thorough when brushing the egg wash over your pastries before cooking them. Start from the top and brush the egg wash all the way to the very bottom of each piece, to ensure maximum coverage and the best finish possible.

Considering how much work goes into making a simple croissant, and keeping in mind that each of the millions of croissants baked every day across the world need to be sold within hours of being baked, it was inevitable that bakers were going to come up with a clever way of recycling them. As far as I know, there is no documented way of making a 'typical' French almond croissant; some are made by lining the croissant dough with almond cream prior to baking, some are soaked in syrup and some aren't. Once again, it is a matter of personal preference.

This recipe follows the exact process that I have stuck to since my apprenticeship. As a wise man eloquently told me when I first moved to Australia, 'If it ain't broke, don't fix it'. The recipe requires only a few ingredients: some left-over croissants (or use *pain au chocolat* if you like), some almond cream and a syrup, and what you'll end up with is an incredibly moist and tasty pastry, with a delicately crunchy layer of almonds. This is recycling at its best!

Croissants aux amandes
(Almond croissants)

Makes 10

200 g (7 oz) caster (superfine) sugar
50 ml (1³/4 fl oz) rum (optional)
10 day-old croissants
500 g (1 lb 2 oz) Almond Cream (page 260)
200 g (7 oz) flaked almonds
pure icing (confectioners') sugar, to dust

~ Put 1 litre (35 fl oz) water, the sugar and rum, if using, in a saucepan and bring to the boil over high heat. Remove from the heat and set aside to cool for at least 15 minutes, or until about 60°C (140°F).

~ Preheat the oven to 180°C (350°F). Line a large baking tray with baking paper. Cut the croissants three-quarters of the way through, from the back to the front. Not cutting them in half completely will stop the tops from falling off during soaking. Working with one at a time and using your hands (see tip), submerge the croissants into the warm syrup, opening them up slightly to allow the liquid to soak all the way to the middle of the pastry. Gently squeeze to remove the excess syrup and place on the lined tray.

~ Spoon the almond cream into a piping bag fitted with a 1 cm (¹/2 in) plain nozzle. Lift up the top of each croissant and pipe a thick line of almond cream inside the croissant, from one end to the other. When all the croissants are filled, pipe another layer of almond cream along the top of each one. Sprinkle with a generous amount of almonds, then use your palm to press the almonds onto the cream and flatten the cream on the top of the croissants.

~ Bake for 25 minutes, or until the almond cream filling begins to set. To check, use a pair of kitchen tongs to carefully lift open a croissant; if the cream is still runny, cook for another 5 minutes. Remove from the oven, allow to cool a little, then dust generously with icing sugar. Serve warm or at room temperature.

~ Like most pastries, almond croissants are best when they are freshly cooked, however, in the unlikely event that they won't all be eaten on the day, they can be kept for up to 1 week if they are wrapped individually and stored on the bottom shelf of the fridge. Simply reheat them in a 180°C (350°F) oven for 10 minutes.

tip

Always check the temperature of your syrup before putting your hands into the pan! If you don't have a thermometer, allow the syrup to cool for 15 minutes, then dip one finger in the syrup to assess the temperature. You will get the best result if your syrup is hot, because a cold syrup won't soak into the pastry as well as it should. If the syrup is getting too cold, reheat it for 1–2 minutes on high heat.

Nothing says summer more than the arrival of the first stone fruits in the baskets of your local fruit and vegetable shop. Let's be honest, if you are talking about temptation, the humble apple pales in comparison to a beautiful velvety peach with its sweet and moist pulp and tangy skin, or a perfectly ripe plum with its shiny, translucent-burgundy colour and juicy flesh. In this recipe I have used well-ripened peaches (or you could try apricots or plums) and have added a small amount of lemon zest to balance out the sweetness of the fruit.

Fourrés aux pêches et au citron
(Peach and lemon pastries)

Makes 18

350 g (12 oz) cold Custard (page 261)
finely grated zest of 2 lemons
2 tablespoons whipping cream (35% fat)
1 kg (2 lb 4 oz) cold Croissant Dough, 1 single and 1 double turn (pages 174–9)
2 eggs
pinch of fine salt
9 ripe peaches, halved, stones removed and cut into 4 mm (¹/8 in) thick slices

∼ Using an electric mixer fitted with a whisk attachment, whisk the custard on low speed until smooth. Add the lemon zest and cream and whisk for another 3–5 minutes, or until smooth and shiny. Transfer to a small bowl, cover and refrigerate until needed.

∼ Following the method on page 180, roll out the croissant dough on a lightly floured work surface into a 30 x 60 cm (12 x 24 in) rectangle, dusting with extra flour when needed to ensure the dough doesn't stick to the surface. If you haven't achieved a perfectly shaped rectangle with your rolling pin towards the end of the rolling process, simply stretch and pull the dough into shape using your hands.

∼ Before you begin cutting your rolled-out dough (*abaisse*), fluff it up by running your hand underneath it and lifting it up gently on all sides. Using a large knife, cut the dough into eighteen 10 cm (4 in) squares. Try to cut the pastry using one single motion of the knife, and avoid dragging the knife through the dough. Place the squares on a baking tray lined with baking paper and refrigerate for 20 minutes, or until cold and firm.

∼ Working with one pastry square at a time, and keeping the others refrigerated, place it on the work surface. Fold in each corner so they meet in the centre, then use your thumb to press the ends together to seal. Place on a lined baking tray and repeat with the remaining squares, leaving a 10 cm (4 in) gap between each. Cover with a damp cloth and place in a warm place to prove for 2 hours, or until doubled in size.

∼ Preheat the oven to 180°C (350°F). To make an egg wash, lightly beat the eggs and salt together in a small bowl and set aside.

∼ To check if your pastries are ready to bake, poke them with your index finger; they should feel soft but still elastic. If the pastry doesn't bounce back after being poked, they are probably slightly overproved, so it's a good idea to occasionally check on their progress towards the end of the recommended proving time. Using your fingertip, make a small indent in the centre of each pastry square. This will stop the folded pastry corners from opening up during the baking process and will force the dough to rise around the peaches rather than pushing the filling out from underneath. Spoon 1 tablespoon custard into each indent, then arrange the peach slices in a circular pattern on the custard. Brush the egg wash over the exposed pastry (see tips). Bake on the bottom shelf of the oven for 20–25 minutes, or until golden brown. Transfer to a wire rack to cool slightly. Serve warm or at room temperature.

tips

While it might be a little fiddly, always fill your pastries before you apply the egg wash so that the custard sticks to the dough; otherwise, the custard (and the peaches) might slide off during the baking process.

Citrus rinds always need to be cooked to make them more palatable and, more importantly, so that they release their oils; however, they will burn very quickly when exposed to direct heat, so always mix them in a cream, or place them under any fruit, prior to baking.

The word *roulade* literally means 'rolled up' and, as such, refers to a method rather than a specific dough or flavour combination. This *viennoiserie* can be tweaked to suit the season, a specific celebration or just personal preference — if ever there was a blank canvas for you to experiment with your flavour combinations, this is it.

This roulade with pistachio and raspberry is one of my favourites, with its beautifully flaky pastry, sweet pistachio cream and tart berry infusion, it is perfect for dunking in your cup of coffee in the morning, and it is also the simplest way to use croissant dough.

Roulades pistache-framboise
(Pistachio and raspberry swirls)

Makes about 15

1 kg (2 lb 4 oz) cold Croissant Dough, 1 single and 1 double turn
 (pages 174–9)
300 g (10¹/2 oz) Pistachio Cream (page 260)
300 g (10¹/2 oz) frozen raspberries
2 eggs
pinch of fine salt
finely chopped pistachios, to decorate (optional)
finely chopped freeze-dried or fresh raspberries,
 to decorate (optional)

⌣ Following the method on page 180, roll out the croissant dough on a lightly floured work surface into a 25 x 50 cm (10 x 20 in) rectangle, dusting with extra flour when needed to ensure the dough doesn't stick to the surface. The sticking creates resistance, which means you will need to apply more pressure, thus damaging the delicate layers of butter in the dough. If you haven't achieved a perfectly shaped rectangle with your rolling pin towards the end of the rolling process, simply stretch and pull the dough into shape using your hands.

⌣ Line two baking trays with baking paper and set aside. Before you begin cutting your rolled-out dough *(abaisse)*, fluff it up by running your hands underneath it and lifting it up gently on all sides. This allows the gluten time to relax and stops your cut pieces from shrinking and losing their shape during the cutting process.

⌣ With one long side nearest to you, spread the pistachio cream all over the dough, right up to the edges, then sprinkle the frozen raspberries evenly over the cream. Starting from the top left-hand corner of the dough and working your way across to the top right-hand corner, roll the dough into a tight log. Using a large knife, cut the log into 3–4 cm (1¹/4–1¹/2 in) thick rolls and place on the lined trays, leaving a 10 cm (4 in) gap between each. Cover with a damp cloth and place in a warm place to prove for 2 hours, or until doubled in size.

⌣ Preheat the oven to 175°C (345°F). Lightly beat the eggs and salt together in a small bowl and set aside for 5 minutes.

⌣ To check if your pastries are ready to bake, poke them with your index finger; they should feel soft but still elastic. If the pastry doesn't bounce back after being poked, they are probably slightly overproved, so it's a good idea to occasionally check on their progress towards the end of the recommended proving time. Brush the egg wash generously over the top of each roulade and bake on the bottom shelf of the oven for 25 minutes, or until the bases are golden. If the tops are browning too quickly, cover loosely with a piece of foil and continue baking until ready. Remove from the oven and transfer to a wire rack to cool for 20 minutes. If you like, sprinkle with finely chopped pistachios and raspberries before serving.

tip

Any dough that is layered with butter, such as doughs used for croissants or Danish pastries, tends to taste a lot richer and more buttery than a brioche dough (even though they usually contain a lot less fat), because the butter is used raw, sandwiched inside the dough. This rich, fatty taste is exacerbated when the butter is hot and melted. I therefore always recommend eating any layered pastry at room temperature, never warmed up.

Brioches

If they don't have bread, let them eat brioche!

Brioches

Since its first written reference in the Middle Ages, this *viennoiserie* was always going to be special, with its soft and fluffy texture, its buttery undertones and beautifully coloured crust. It was, and still is, considered the most decadent of all *viennoiseries*.

In order for this dough to be called a brioche, it has to be made of the whitest flour, preferably with a high-protein wheat, butter, eggs and sugar. While these ingredients are now readily available from any supermarket, it is not until we think of them in their historical context — when the cost of a kilogram of flour was around 40 per cent of a peasant's daily salary, sugar had to be imported from various exotic places from around the world, and butter was the preserve of the rich upper class — that we can begin to understand how brioche rapidly cemented itself as an epicurean product.

The fact that the infamous quote (top left), often erroneously translated as 'let them eat cake', was wrongly attributed to Marie Antoinette, the last queen of France at the time of the French Revolution, actually had more to do with propaganda, to reinforce the glaring disparities between the ruling elite and its subjects than regards for historical accuracy. It nonetheless helped propagate and cement the image of the humble brioche as a luxurious and decadent product.

Brioche au sucre et aux écorces d'oranges
(Candied orange peel and pearl sugar brioche) ~ page 198

Pâte à brioche

(Brioche dough)

Generally speaking, in a traditional bakery you will find two brioche recipes: butter brioche, which contains a very high percentage of butter and a relatively small amount of sugar, and sugar brioche, which contains less fat but is slightly sweeter. The recipe I have chosen to include here is the butter brioche. The advantage of this recipe over the sugar version lies not so much in the fact that it contains more butter (although that alone should be enough!) but rather that it contains very little sugar, making it a versatile brioche that can be used for both savoury or sweet *viennoiserie*.

Makes 1 kg (2 lb 4 oz)

note : The dough for this brioche has to be prepared a day ahead and can only be used when cold.

500 g (1 lb 2 oz) plain (all-purpose) flour ('00'/T45)
150 g (5$^{1}/_{2}$ oz) caster (superfine) sugar
3 teaspoons fine table salt
15 g ($^{1}/_{2}$ oz) dried yeast
5 cold eggs
150 ml (5 fl oz) water chilled with 5 ice cubes, refrigerated
230 g (8 oz) unsalted butter, at room temperature, cubed

Making the dough

Using an electric mixer fitted with a dough hook attachment, combine the flour, sugar, salt and yeast on low speed until well combined.

Break the eggs into a bowl and add them to the flour mixture *(photo 1)*, along with 100 ml (3$^{1}/_{2}$ fl oz) of cold water strained from the ice cube bath. Mix on low speed for 5 minutes, or until a soft, sticky dough forms.

Increase the speed to medium and mix for 15 minutes, scraping the dough hook from time to time, until the mixture comes away from the side of the bowl and begins to 'slap' around the bowl *(2)*. Always check the temperature of the brioche dough during the mixing process. The friction created during kneading will generate heat, which can damage the yeast and potentially break the strands of gluten (which give the dough its elasticity), leaving you with a soft, unworkable paste. If the dough starts to feel warm, reduce the speed of the mixer to low.

If you are still on medium speed, reduce the speed to low, then add the butter a little at a time, allowing each addition to be incorporated before adding the next *(3)*. When all the butter has been added, increase the speed to medium and mix for 10 minutes, or until the dough is glossy and smooth.

Windowpane test

To check whether the dough is kneaded properly, use the 'windowpane' test. Hold a small piece of dough in your hands and stretch the dough until it is almost thin enough to see through *(4)*. If you can't see through it, continue kneading for another 2 minutes.

cooking tip :

Any dough enriched with butter will require the fat to be added last. Gluten (the protein in the flour) needs water to develop its elasticity, a crucial requirement in yeasted dough, and the fat reduces the ability for the gluten to absorb water (which is why we put the butter in first for doughs such as shortbread where elasticity is undesirable). So, for brioche dough, it is essential to first add the water, which allows the gluten strands to develop before introducing the butter.

1

2

3

4

Pâte à brioche

First prove

Remove the dough hook from the mixer, then sprinkle a little flour over the dough in the bowl. Cover with plastic wrap and set aside in a warm place to prove for 2 hours, or until the dough has doubled in size *(1)*.

When the dough has risen, knock it down with your fist, then remove as much gas as you can by folding the dough over a few times. Place the dough in another bowl, sprinkle with a little flour, then cover with plastic wrap and refrigerate overnight.

Dividing and balling the dough

All breads (ameliorated or not) need to be divided into the appropriate size and 'balled', a process aimed at tightening the dough prior to the final shaping of each individual product. This is especially important when working with soft, buttery doughs, as it helps to lengthen the strands of gluten (the protein in flour) weakened by the inherent fat content in the brioche and increases the dough's elasticity, helping it to retain its shape during the proving process.

Remove the proved dough from the fridge. Place the dough on a lightly floured work surface, then shape it into an even log — it doesn't matter what size, this is just to help you cut even portions of dough. Use a plastic scraper or small knife to cut the dough into the size needed *(2)*. If you are making one single loaf, skip this cutting step.

Remove any excess flour from the work surface. Take a portion of dough in the cupped palm of your hand and flatten slightly, then bring the outside edges into the middle and pinch the centre to seal *(3)*. Turn the ball over and drag the base over the work surface several times *(4)* — this will ensure any air bubbles trapped in the middle are released and you don't end up with a big hole in the middle of the bread.

If you are making a full loaf, apply the same balling technique as above, but use the whole amount of dough. Use both your hands to run the dough ball over the work surface, to stretch the dough and tighten up your loaf.

Place the balls, seam-side down, on a lightly floured tray, cover with a cloth and set aside to rest for 15 minutes.

more on proving :

~ Most yeasted doughs requires two proving stages. The first prove is designed to kick start the effect of the yeast. It should only be a very moderate prove, because overdoing your *pointage*, or first prove, weakens the protein in the flour and adds an undesirable taste (ethanol). After knocking the dough down following the first prove and refrigerating it overnight, the dough is then proved again, to give it time to develop a more refined texture and small, even air pockets. If you skip the second proving stage, you'll end up with a substandard product, filled with large air bubbles.

1

2

3

4

Dividing and balling the dough

When it comes to any food prepared with only a few ingredients, the rule is this: use good-quality ingredients and let them shine. If ever there was a product that illustrates this concept, then it is the brioche. Floral aromas such as orange blossom, rosewater or lavender add a subtle but very effective layer of dimension to your dough, and I think these are perfect for accentuating the underlying flavours of the brioche without overdoing it. Orange blossom water is widely used in southern France and this brioche invariably reminds me of Christmas, when I was a fifteen-year-old apprentice going to work in the middle of those bitterly cold winter's nights, then walking into the kitchen and being enveloped in a wave of hot orange-blossom steam emanating from the hundreds of freshly baked, golden *brioches des rois*. All the chefs were there, sitting silently and blank-faced in front of the ovens to warm up, sipping on cups of strong coffee as they contemplated yet another long, hard day ahead.

Brioche au sucre et aux écorces d'oranges

(Candied orange peel and pearl sugar brioche)

Makes 12–13

note : The method for making the dough for this brioche is the same as the basic recipe, but you need to reduce the amount of water by 20 ml ($^1/_2$ fl oz) and substitute it with the orange blossom water. Add the candied orange peel at the end of the mixing process.

1 kg (2 lb 4 oz) Brioche Dough (page 194)
1 tablespoon orange blossom water
200 g (7 oz) good-quality candied orange peel,
   very finely chopped
2 eggs
pinch of fine salt
200 g (7 oz) pearl sugar (see tip, page 126)

~ Prepare the brioche dough following the method on pages 194–6, to the end of the first prove. Cover with plastic wrap and refrigerate overnight.

~ Following the dividing and balling steps on pages 196–7, divide the dough into small 80 g ($2^3/_4$ oz) pieces, then roll the pieces into tight balls. Place the brioche balls on two baking trays lined with baking paper, spacing them about 10 cm (4 in) apart. Cover with a dry cloth and set aside in a warm place to prove for 2 hours, or until doubled in size.

~ Preheat the oven to 190°C (375°F). To make an egg wash, lightly beat the eggs and salt together in a small bowl, then set aside for 5 minutes. Brush the egg wash liberally over the top of the brioche balls then, using a pair of scissors dipped in the egg wash, make a small cross in the top of each brioche. Sprinkle liberally with pearl sugar. Bake for 15–20 minutes, or until golden. Transfer to a wire rack to cool a little, then serve warm or at room temperature. Brioche are best eaten within 1–2 days.

The literal translation of *pain perdu* is 'lost bread', and describes a method of recycling day-old bread into a palatable, sweet dish. Today we tend to take our daily loaf of bread for granted, but many years ago when wheat was scarce and bread production required an incredible amount of work, it was unthinkable that a loaf of bread could ever be wasted, so it was put to good use in dishes such as this. Nowadays, French toast is made out of almost any dough, from bread to croissants, and it is still the best way to use up your old pastries. I have decided to use brioche here because, unlike bread, brioche has a high fat and egg content, so it is less likely to break apart and remains soft and silky when soaked in milk.

Pain perdu

(French toast)

Serves 6

500 g (1 lb 2 oz) Brioche Dough (page 194)
1 litre (35 fl oz) full-cream milk
150 g (5½ oz) caster (superfine) sugar
2 vanilla beans, halved lengthways, seeds scraped

5 eggs
pinch of fine salt
unsalted butter, for pan-frying
pure icing (confectioners') sugar, for dusting

~ Prepare the brioche dough following the method on pages 194–6, to the end of the first prove. Cover with plastic wrap and refrigerate overnight.

~ Lightly grease and flour a 15 x 25 cm (6 x 10 in) loaf (bar) tin. Place the cold dough on a lightly floured work surface and use your hands to shape it into a 25 cm (10 in) long roll. Don't spend too much time trying to make the roll smooth and regular — overworking your dough will make it very soft and sticky and, more importantly, we are only using this brioche as slices, so its initial shape is not a great concern. Place the roll in the prepared tin, cover with a damp cloth and set aside in a warm place to prove for 2 hours, or until doubled in size.

~ Preheat the oven to 180°C (350°F). When the brioche has proved, remove the cloth and cover with a heavy baking tray. This forces the brioche to rise evenly into a neat rectangle. Bake for 40 minutes, then remove the brioche from the oven, remove the tray from the top, then turn the tin upside down and remove it. Return the brioche loaf to the oven (directly on the oven rack) and bake for another 15 minutes, or until the brioche is golden and springs back to the touch. Remove from the oven and cool to room temperature, then refrigerate for at least 2 hours. Cooling it in the fridge will harden the fat in the brioche, which makes it easier to cut into neat and regular slices.

~ Put the milk, sugar and vanilla beans and seeds in a saucepan and stir continuously over medium heat until the milk begins to simmer. Remove and discard the vanilla beans, then pour the milk into a flat-bottomed bowl. Cool slightly, then refrigerate until cold. I like to use cold milk when making French toast with fresh brioche; however, if you are using day-old brioche or other bread, there's no need to refrigerate the milk, just leave it to cool a little in the bowl and use warm.

~ Lightly beat the eggs and salt together in a separate flat-bottomed bowl, then set aside for 5 minutes. Using a serrated knife, cut the chilled brioche into 4 cm (1½ in) thick slices. Soak two slices of bread in the sweetened milk for a few seconds, turning the bread over to soak on the other side as well (don't soak the slices for too long or they will fall apart during cooking). Transfer the soaked bread to the egg mixture and soak for a few seconds on both sides.

~ Heat a large heavy-based frying pan over high heat. Add a small knob of butter and, when the butter starts to foam, add the soaked brioche and cook for 4 minutes on each side, or until golden brown and caramelised. Transfer to a wire rack. Repeat with the remaining brioche, milk and egg. Just before serving, dust the French toast with icing sugar. Serve with fresh, tangy fruits such as berries or a dollop of Greek-style yoghurt, to balance the sweetness of the toast.

tip

You will need to vary the amount of sugar in the recipe according to the type of bread you are using. If using ready-made brioche, which is already quite sweet, follow the recommended amount given in the recipe; however, if using croissants or an unsweetened bread, increase the sugar content of your milk recipe by about 50 g (1¾ oz) to 150 g (5½ oz).

The word *beignet* can be roughly translated as 'fritter', a generic term referring to a deep-fried dough, and while it is traditionally made from fried choux pastry, they can be made from almost any dough, from sweet bread made with olive oil (*chichi au pommes*) to brioche made with butter (*beignet italien*), or even from croissant dough.

Although I have included a few different variations of fritters in this book, brioche doughnuts are by far the best, especially when it comes to plain sugar doughnuts. If you have ever been to the beaches in the south of France during summer, you would have invariably been approached by overtanned vendors carrying large cane baskets, spruiking their apple doughnuts and caramelised peanuts. There really is nothing quite like sitting in the sand in a pair of glorified underpants, munching into a soft, buttery doughnut, with the smell of iodine and coconut oil in the air!

Beignets à la cannelle
(Cinnamon doughnuts)

Makes 10–12

300 g (10½ oz) caster (superfine) sugar
2 teaspoons ground cinnamon
1 vanilla bean, halved lengthways, seeds scraped
1 litre (35 fl oz) canola oil, for deep-frying

Brioche dough

500 g (1 lb 2 oz) plain (all-purpose) flour ('0'/T55)
100 g (3½ oz) caster (superfine) sugar
2 teaspoons fine salt
2 eggs
15 g (½ oz) dried yeast
175 ml (5½ fl oz) cold full-cream milk
2 teaspoons natural vanilla extract
finely grated zest of 2 lemons
75 g (2¾ oz) unsalted butter, at room temperature

~ To make the brioche dough, put the flour, sugar, salt, eggs and yeast into the bowl of an electric mixer fitted with a dough hook attachment and mix on low speed until well combined. Add the milk, vanilla and lemon zest and combine, then add the butter, following the method on pages 194–6 to make the dough (to the end of the first prove). The amount of butter used for this recipe has been drastically reduced from the basic recipe, so it will cook through more quickly, and to offset some of the additional fat that is absorbed during the frying process. Cover with plastic wrap and refrigerate overnight.

~ Following the dividing and balling steps on pages 196–7, divide the cold dough into small 70 g (2½ oz) pieces, then roll them into tight balls. Place the brioche balls on two baking trays lined with baking paper, spacing them about 10 cm (4 in) apart. Cover with a dry cloth and set aside in a warm place to prove for 2 hours, or until doubled in size.

~ Put the sugar, cinnamon and vanilla bean seeds in a bowl and mix thoroughly by rubbing the mixture between the palms of your hands. This ensures the vanilla seeds infuse properly into the sugar and cinnamon. Set aside.

~ Heat the oil in a deep-fryer or heavy-based saucepan to 170°C (340°F). Working in batches, use the palm of your hand to gently flatten each dough ball before gently sliding it into the hot oil. Be extremely careful not to drop the dough balls from a height or you will splash yourself with hot oil. Don't fry too many balls at once or the oil temperature will drop and the doughnuts will absorb too much oil. Fry one side for about 30 seconds, then flip them over and cook for another 1 minute, or until golden. Flip them back again to finish cooking the first side. Remove with a slotted spoon and drain on paper towel. Toss the hot doughnuts in the cinnamon sugar and serve.

serving tip

These cinnamon doughnuts can be served as they are, or filled with a custard such as crème pâtissière, strawberry jam or hazelnut and chocolate spread (page 257), as pictured here. Spoon the filling into a piping bag fitted with a 4 mm (⅛ in) plain nozzle. Use the tip of the nozzle to poke a small hole in the side of the doughnut, then pipe the filling into the centre.

Not to be confused with the much maligned, but nonetheless delicious, garlic snail, these snails (the literal translation is raisin bread) are a delicious *viennoiserie* made from a buttered pastry dough, custard and sultanas, rolled together into a tightly spiralled bun. Every region of France has its preference as to what type of dough they use, from the rich and flaky croissant dough used in the south, to the fluffy brioche in the north. Although a *pain aux raisins* always relates to a custard and raisin filling, you will find a similar-looking product called a roulade, which comes with an almost infinite combination of fillings, from pistachio and chocolate to praline and chocolate.

In keeping with the underlying philosophy of this book, this classic snail recipe is simply a blueprint for you to experiment with different types of fillings and textural combinations, from almond creams or crushed nuts, to fresh fruits and exotic spices. Whatever filling you choose, you will (hopefully) always end up with a fantastically moist and delicious pastry.

Pains aux raisins

(Snails)

Makes 10

500 g (1 lb 2 oz) Brioche Dough (page 194)
250 g (9 oz) sultanas (golden raisins) or raisins
2 vanilla beans, halved lengthways
50 ml (1¾ fl oz) rum
350 g (12 oz) cold Custard (page 261)
80 ml (2¾ fl oz) cold whipping cream (35% fat)
2 eggs
pinch of fine salt

~ Prepare the brioche dough following the method on pages 194–6, to the end of the first prove. Cover with plastic wrap and refrigerate overnight.

~ You will also need to rehydrate your sultanas or raisins the day before. Put the sultanas in a heatproof bowl. Put the vanilla beans, rum and 500 ml (17 fl oz) water in a small saucepan and bring to the boil over high heat. Pour over the sultanas, then immediately cover with plastic wrap. Set aside until cool, then refrigerate overnight.

~ Using an electric mixer fitted with a paddle attachment, beat the custard on medium speed for 1 minute, then add the cream and beat until smooth and shiny. Mixing in the cold cream helps prevent the mixture from setting again.

~ Line two baking trays with baking paper and set aside. If you are not very experienced with rolling dough, you can divide the brioche dough in half to make life a little easier. Brioche is softer and stickier than most other bread doughs, including croissant dough, so you will need to use a bit more flour and try to be quick! Roll out the cold brioche dough on a lightly floured work surface into a rectangle about 3 mm (¹/8 in) thick. If necessary, stretch the dough using your hands to achieve a rectangular shape. As a guide, the shape should be twice as long as it is wide — about 15 x 30 cm (6 x 12 in).

~ Using a spatula, spread the custard over the dough, right to the edges. Don't spend too much time trying to achieve a perfectly smooth, even layer of custard, as your priority is to work fast while the brioche is still cold and firm. Drain the sultanas well, then sprinkle them evenly over the custard. Starting from one long side, roll the dough into a tight, long roll. The roll should be 6–7 cm (2^1/$_2$–2^3/$_4$ in) in diameter; if it is any bigger, use your hands to gently stretch it out until you reach the right thickness. Using a large knife, cut the roll into 3 cm (1^1/$_4$ in) thick slices and place on the lined trays, spacing the slices about 10 cm (4 in) apart. Cover with a dry cloth and set aside in a warm place to prove for 1 hour, or until risen by half.

~ Preheat the oven to 180°C (350°F). To make an egg wash, lightly beat the eggs and salt in a small bowl, then set aside for 5 minutes. When the rolls have proved, brush them liberally with the egg wash. Bake for 15–20 minutes, or until golden. Remove from the oven and transfer to wire racks to cool. Depending on the size of your oven and how many trays you can bake at one time, keep your unbaked snails in the fridge, to stop them overproving while they are waiting to go into the oven.

Bakers and pastry chefs routinely add a small amount of alcohol to their creams and pastries, to help reduce the perceived sweetness (such as the sultanas used here) or fattiness of an ingredient or cream. Don't be concerned about the alcohol content, because most of the alcohol will evaporate during the baking process once the temperature reaches 78°C (172°F). When making ganaches and creams, always make sure you add any liquors to boiling liquids.

I know what you're thinking … this sounds more like the latest gimmick from a large fast-food pizza conglomerate than a typical provincial French recipe. It may sound unusual, but I have actually seen a chocolate pizza listed on the menu of a large pizza chain restaurant, as well as macarons, *crème brûlée*, flans and many other French specialties that you wouldn't expect to find. In fact, making a pizza out of brioche dough leftovers has been a common practice for centuries. Today, these sweet pizzas are typically sold from small vendor stalls at local markets or fairs, adorned with fresh seasonal fruits or chocolate-hazelnut paste.

Pizzas banane-chocolat

(Chocolate and banana pizzas)

Makes 2

250 g (9 oz) Brioche Dough (page 194)
2 large ripe bananas
50 g (1³/4 oz) caster (superfine) sugar
100 g (3¹/2 oz) unsalted butter
100 g (3¹/2 oz) dark chocolate (70% cocoa solids), finely chopped
80 ml (2³/4 oz) whipping cream (35% fat)

> Prepare the brioche dough following the method on pages 194–6, to the end of the first prove. Cover with plastic wrap and refrigerate overnight.

> Divide the brioche dough in half, then roll each portion out on a lightly floured work surface into a 15 cm (6 in) round. Place on a large baking tray lined with baking paper, then cover with a dry cloth and set aside in a warm place to prove for 1 hour, or until the dough has doubled in size.

> Meanwhile, cut the bananas into 1 cm (¹/2 in) thick slices. Put the sugar and half of the butter in a large frying pan and cook over medium heat until the butter has melted. Add the sliced bananas in a single layer and cook for 3–5 minutes, or until golden brown. Turn the bananas over and cook until golden on the other side, then remove from the pan and place in a single layer on a plate to cool.

> Put the chocolate and the remaining butter in a small saucepan and stir over very low heat until melted and smooth. Remove from the heat and set aside.

> Preheat the oven to 180°C (350°F). When the dough has proved, use your fingertips to make small craters all over the pizza bases; this prevents the cream from running off the pizza during baking. Arrange the caramelised bananas evenly over the top of the pizzas.

> Bake for 10 minutes, then open the oven, slide out the pizzas on the tray and drizzle the cream over the top. Bake for another 10 minutes, or until golden and bubbling. If the pizza tops caramelise before the bases are cooked, cover loosely with a piece of foil; this will deflect the heat from the top and stop the caramelisation. Remove from the oven, drizzle with the melted chocolate mixture and serve immediately.

tip

As an alternative, you can replace the bananas with pears, and the chocolate with a hazelnut spread. Other flavour combinations you might like are apple, rhubarb and almond cream; or honey, ricotta cheese and orange zest.

Not to be confused with the alcoholic beverage from Provence of the same name, the *pastis* referred to in this brioche means 'cake,' a translation of the local dialect of Landes de Gascogne, a region in the south-west of France. Unlike the other brioches in this chapter, *pastis landais* is made using a poolish starter (see page 212), a method traditionally used in the manufacture of semi-sour breads, some of which are included in the bread chapter. While a little more complicated to make, *brioche sur poolish* are well worth the additional effort. With their dense, creamy texture and slight touch of sourness, they have the added advantage of staying soft for far longer than their traditional yeast-proved cousins. This recipe is actually almost identical to the famed Italian Christmas brioche, panettone, but doesn't contain any of the candied fruits and raisins typically used — just lots of butter and eggs, a generous dash of orange blossom water, and some rum for good measure.

Pastis landais

(French panettone)

Makes 1 large or 18 small

2 eggs
pinch of fine salt
200 g (7 oz) pearl sugar (see tip, page 126)

Poolish

100 g (3½ oz) plain (all-purpose) flour ('0'/T55)
10 g (¼ oz) dried yeast
100 ml (3½ fl oz) tepid water

Brioche

125 ml (4 fl oz) full-cream milk
2 vanilla beans, halved lengthways
40 ml (1¼ fl oz) rum
250 g (9 oz) caster (superfine) sugar
40 ml (1¼ fl oz) orange blossom water
5 eggs
750 g (1 lb 10 oz) plain (all-purpose) flour ('0'/T55)
3 teaspoons fine salt
130 g (4½ oz) unsalted butter, melted and cooled

～ To make the poolish, put the flour, yeast and tepid water in a bowl and stir until a soft, sticky paste forms. Cover with a cloth and set aside in a warm place to prove for 1 hour, or until doubled in size.

～ To make the brioche dough, put the milk, vanilla beans, rum and sugar in a saucepan and stir over medium heat for 2–3 minutes, or until warm, then remove from the heat. This process is only meant to dissolve the sugar and soften the vanilla beans, so don't be tempted to bring it to the boil. Remove the vanilla beans and use the back of a small knife to scrape the seeds out. Add the seeds to the milk and discard the beans, then stir in the orange blossom water and set aside.

～ Using an electric mixer fitted with a whisk attachment, whisk the eggs on medium speed for 2 minutes, or until the mixture begins to foam. Reduce the speed to low and gradually add the tepid milk. Be careful; if the milk is hotter than 65°C (150°F) the eggs will cook, so to ensure it is at the right temperature, dip your finger into the milk for 30 seconds — if it is too hot for you, it is too hot for the eggs!

～ Still on low speed, add the proved poolish and mix until well combined. Swap the whisk for the dough hook attachment, then add the flour and salt and mix for another 2–3 minutes, or until the dough comes together. Increase the speed to medium and knead, scraping the side of the bowl occasionally, for 10–12 minutes, or until smooth and glossy. Add the melted butter and continue mixing on low speed, scraping the side of the bowl, until fully combined. Cover the bowl with a cloth and set aside in a warm place to prove for 2–3 hours, or until doubled in size.

～ Scrape the dough out of the bowl onto a generously floured work surface. Knock out as much gas as you can by punching down the dough, then fold the sides over to the middle, dusting with extra flour when necessary.

～ Preheat the oven to 180°C (350°F). Grease a deep 12 x 26 cm (4^{1}/2 x 10^{1}/2 in) cake tin or use 18 individual panettone or muffin paper cups (these are sturdy and don't need to sit in a tin). Unlike traditional brioche, this dough is a lot softer and cannot be balled into shape. To divide, simply soak your hands in cold water and shake off the excess water, then take a small handful of dough and drop it in the prepared tin or muffin cases until two-thirds full. You can use any mould, tin or paper cup, but never fill them higher than two-thirds or the brioche will overflow during baking. Cover with a cloth and set aside in a warm place to prove for 2–3 hours, or until the dough has reached the top of the tin or paper cups.

～ To make an egg wash, lightly beat the eggs and salt together in a small bowl, then set aside for 5 minutes. Brush the egg wash over the top of the brioche, then, using a pair of scissors dipped in egg wash, cut a cross shape about 2 cm (^{3}/4 in) deep on the top. Sprinkle with pearl sugar and bake for 45 minutes for a large brioche, or 20–25 minutes for individual brioches. Remove from the oven and place on a wire rack to cool. If you have baked the brioche in a tin, remove it from the tin as early as possible, but don't burn yourself in the process.

Pains

'With bread, all sorrows are less.'

DON QUIXOTE, MIGUEL DE CERVANTES

Pains

(Breads)

While not all of the local specialties included in this book have enjoyed the same level of global recognition as the croissant or lemon tart, they are nonetheless based on age-old recipes that have, over the years, cemented themselves deeply in the local gastronomic psyche. None of them, however, will ever achieve the notoriety that bread has enjoyed. Bread is so much a part of the French gastronomic and cultural landscape that it's easy to forget that, for thousands of years, people from every civilisation around the world have included bread, in one form or another, as an integral part of their daily diet. It is truly remarkable that such a seemingly simple concoction has not only withstood the test of time, but also managed to play such a crucial role in the development of so many civilisations.

It is easy to overlook the fact that the humble loaf of bread we just bought from an artisan baker is the result of years of practice with countless trials and errors. More importantly, the recipes used to make these breads have often been perfected, sometimes over generations, based on the bakery's own climatic environment, local ingredients and equipment. That being said, making bread is an incredibly rewarding exercise that can be enjoyed by the whole family, and providing that you start at the beginning and take the time to familiarise yourself with the subtleties of your ingredients and equipment, your bread-making journey will reward you with some of the same simple pleasures that people have enjoyed for so many years.

Pain de campagne (Country bread) ~ page 223

Nowadays, there are countless types of bread, each with their own flavour and texture profiles, varying degrees of difficulty and timeline constraints. To simplify things, I have divided breads into three basic categories.

Pain méthode directe (Bread, direct method):

This is by far the simplest and most popular method of making bread. It relies entirely on the addition of yeast for the fermentation process (proving). This is an ideal method for amateur bakers to use, because it is very predictable, fast and almost failproof. Breads made with this method, such as the baguette, are usually very light and airy, with a thin, crispy crust, but they have a short shelf life and don't have the same depth of flavour as breads made using the other methods.

The taste and texture of breads made using the direct proving method can be further improved by reducing the amount of yeast, but this process will dramatically lengthen the proving process and the breads will be much more vulnerable to environmental factors such as variations in temperature or humidity (for more information on yeast, see page 218).

Pain sur poolish (Semi-sourdough bread):

This is my favourite method. This bread relies on the addition of a poolish, a very lightly yeasted levain (starter) for its fermentation process. It is still very quick to prove, but it produces a bread that is more 'creamier' and full-bodied, with a light sour tang and crunchy crust. This method is usually called *à l'ancienne*, probably due to its more rustic appearance and gives you the best of both worlds — a quick and predictable fermenting process and a beautifully crispy and tasty loaf.

The poolish is a pre-ferment method routinely used in France for the manufacture of anything yeasted, from brioche to croissants, breads to fougasse. Personally, I think the slightly heavier crumb and sour taste that you get when using this method is better suited to rustic bread loaves more so than subtle *viennoiseries* such as croissants or brioche, where the added sourness, however small, detracts from their wonderfully buttery undertones and fluffiness. Once again, it's a personal preference and first and foremost, the poolish method is a great way to gently transition into the complex world of bacterial fermentation and its wonderful flavours and textures.

Pain au levain (*Full sourdough bread*):

Making bread with a full levain (starter) was the only method available until the invention of commercial yeast early in the twentieth century. The fermentation process relies on a *levain chef*, a pre-ferment made of flour and water without addition of yeast, which has been left to age over four or five days. Making full sourdough bread requires time, patience (five days for the pre-ferment and up to 20 hours proving), dedication and, most important of all, a heavy firebrick oven. Breads made with a full starter will tend to have a denser and much sourer crumb and a chewier crust.

~

I have been fortunate enough to have worked with some amazing bakers, both in France and Australia, over the course of my career and I am yet to taste an 'OK' loaf of full sourdough bread. Loaves that rely entirely on a *levain chef* for their fermentations are either amazing or just plain bad, and when considering the fact that most home bakers won't have access to the equipment required to make a successful loaf, the inevitable conclusion is that you will most likely be disappointed with the result. I am aware that this is probably going to get me in trouble, but I truly believe that cookbooks should be motivational tools, aimed at gradually building the skills and confidence of their readers by providing achievable goals, taking into account the level of skill required and the type of equipment required.

Consequently, I have chosen to include only the quick and almost failproof bread recipes that are based on the direct and semi-sourdough methods. I feel these recipes are easily achievable for the home cook and will hopefully provide you with the skills and confidence to experiment with more technically challenging sourdoughs in the future.

All ferments are not created equal

Not to put too fine a point on my reluctance to include full sourdoughs in this book … but, remember that yeasts and bacteria are all around us — in the water and air — and in all the ingredients used in the manufacture of the bread. As such, each levain will ferment based on its own indigenous yeast and bacterial content, so therefore a recipe designed in France will not taste or prove with the same characteristics as one made anywhere else.

Pain méthode directe

(Bread, direct method)

Practical, fast and almost failproof, the direct method is the best way to start your bread-baking journey. These breads, with their thin crispy crust, white crumb and relatively mild flavour, have a much broader appeal in France than the more pungent sour breads, which tend to overpower the subtleties of the food they are supposed to complement. The following steps will clarify how to knead your dough and, just as importantly, how to shape it.

Makes 800 g (1 lb 12 oz)

500 g (1 lb 2 oz) plain (all-purpose) flour ('0'/T55 or '1'/T65)
350 ml (12 fl oz) cold water (20°C/70°F)
8 g (¹/4 oz) dried yeast
10 g (¹/4 oz) fine salt

Making the dough

By mixer Using an electric mixer fitted with a dough hook, mix the flour and 300 ml (10¹/2 fl oz) of the cold water on low speed for 2–3 minutes, or until a rough dough forms. Cover the bowl with a clean damp cloth and set aside to rest for 15 minutes (see tip below).

Put the yeast and the remaining water in a small bowl and whisk until fully dissolved. Add to the hydrated dough, then add the salt and knead on low speed for 10 minutes. Increase the speed to medium and knead for another 2 minutes, or until the dough is smooth and elastic and comes away from the side of the bowl. Be careful not to overheat the dough; regularly check for any sign of heat by testing it with the back of your index finger. Stop kneading if the dough feels like it is warming up. Shape the dough into a ball.

By hand Put the flour on the work surface and make a well in the middle. Slowly add 300 ml (10¹/2 fl oz) of the water *(photo 1)*. Using your fingertips, start to incorporate the flour into the water *(2)*. At this stage, don't worry if some of the water escapes from the well; simply scrape it back inside your flour well and continue incorporating and binding the dough together. Using the heel of your hand, press the dough roughly together *(3)*,

then cover with a damp cloth and rest for 35–40 minutes (see tip below).

Shape the dough into a disc with slightly elevated sides. Put the yeast and remaining water into a small bowl and whisk until fully dissolved *(4)*. Pour the dissolved yeast onto the dough *(5)*, then add the salt and gently pull the sides of the dough towards the middle *(6)* to incorporate the liquid into the dough. At this stage the dough will be soft and tacky, so begin the kneading process by gently pushing the dough across the work surface with the palm of your hand, folding the dough over itself *(7)* until it becomes more elastic. Then, push the dough away from you with the heel of your hand and bring the outside edges of the dough towards the middle *(8)*, until the dough is smooth and stops sticking. This process should take 15–20 minutes. Shape the dough into a ball *(9)*.

Windowpane test

To check whether the dough is kneaded properly, use the 'windowpane' test. Hold a small piece of dough in your hands and stretch the dough until it is almost thin enough to see through (see page 195, photo 4). If not, continue kneading for another 2 minutes.

cooking tip :

~ After the flour and water have been kneaded, the dough must be left to rest. This crucial step is 'autolyse' and is designed to hydrate the flour and improve gluten development. Dough kneaded without this step will need a longer mixing time, which often leads to a weakening of the yeast.

1

Pain méthode directe

2

3

4

5

6

7

8

9

Pain méthode directe

First prove

Place the dough in a lightly floured bowl and cover with a cloth. Set aside in a warm place to prove for 1 hour, or until risen by half. The time this takes will depend on the temperature of the dough and your kitchen.

When the dough has risen, knock it down with your fist, then remove as much gas as you can by folding the dough over a few times. This first prove (*pointage*) is an essential part of the leavening process and is largely designed to refine the final texture of the bread. During this stage, the yeast fungi are still relatively clumped together and will create large bubbles of gas (carbon dioxide), resulting in an irregular bread studded with large holes. The process of knocking the dough down is largely aimed at spreading the fungi around the dough, resulting in a bread with a denser and more refined texture.

Dividing and balling the dough

All breads need to be divided into the appropriate size and 'balled', a process aimed at tightening the dough prior to the final shaping of each individual product. (Doughs for flat breads such as pizza and fougasse do not need 'balling', as this will develop the gluten, making it difficult to roll the dough out flat.) Although it is difficult to accurately describe the balling technique used by professional bakers, as long as you know that the aim of the process is to stretch the gluten rather than make a nice round ball, your technique will develop with experience.

Place the dough on a lightly floured work surface and shape it into an even log *(photo 1)* — it doesn't matter what size, this is just to help you cut even portions of dough. Use a plastic scraper or small knife to cut the dough into the size needed *(2)*. If you are making one single loaf, skip this cutting step.

Remove any excess flour from the work surface. Take a portion of dough in the cupped palm of your hand and flatten slightly, then bring the outside edges into the middle and pinch to seal *(3)*. Turn the ball over and drag the base over the work surface several times *(4)* — this will ensure any air bubbles trapped in the middle are released and you don't end up with a big hole in the middle of the bread.

If you are making a full loaf, apply the same balling technique as above, but use the whole amount of dough. Use both your hands to run the dough ball over the work surface, to stretch the dough and tighten up your loaf.

Place the balls, seam side down, on a lightly floured tray, cover with a cloth and set aside to rest for 15 minutes.

more on yeast :

To understand the correlation between the dosage of yeast and flavour, you need to understand how dough ferments. Yeasted doughs rely mainly on fungus to metabolise sugars into gases (carbon dioxide and ethanol), which are then trapped by the gluten during baking. These gases, along with steam, help the dough to rise.

The sourness and depth of flavour are the result of a slow bacterial process that turns sugar into lactic acid and a small amount of carbon dioxide and ethanol. The less yeast you add to a dough, the longer the dough will take to prove, and therefore the more time for lactic acid to build up. This will result in a bread with a more complex flavour and creamier flesh. So, if you prefer a bread with slight undertones of sourness (but are not yet confident with the process of pre-fermentation needed for semi- or sourdough breads) and have a lot more time on your hands, simply reduce the initial amount of yeast. As an approximate guideline, every 1 g (^{1}/32 oz) reduction in yeast will increase the proving time by an hour.

proving times :

flour	yeast	first prove
500 g (1 lb 2 oz)	8 g	1 hour
500 g (1 lb 2 oz)	7 g	2 hours
500 g (1 lb 2 oz)	6 g	3 hours
500 g (1 lb 2 oz)	5 g	4 hours

1

2

3

4

Dividing and balling the dough

Pain sur poolish

(Semi-sourdough bread)

As I mentioned earlier, this is my favourite method of making bread. *Pains sur poolish* are breads that rely on a combination of yeast and pre-ferment for their fermentation process. The difference is that unlike the pure sour ferment, the poolish itself contains a small amount of yeast, which will not only give you a buttery and light crumb, a crisp crust and a beautiful subtle sourness, but also a faster and more consistent fermentation process.

Makes 500 g (1 lb 2 oz)

note : This method is done in two stages: first the poolish, which will need to ferment overnight, and then the final dough.

Poolish

1 g ($^1/_{32}$ oz) dried yeast
100 ml (3$^1/_2$ fl oz) cold water (20°C/70°F)
100 g (3$^1/_2$ oz) plain (all-purpose) flour ('0'/T55 or '1'/T65)

Dough

200 g (7 oz) plain (all-purpose) flour ('0'/T55 or '1'/T65)
100 ml (3$^1/_2$ fl oz) cold water (20°C/70°F)
6 g ($^1/_5$ oz) fine salt
3 g ($^1/_{10}$ oz) dried yeast

Making the poolish and dough

To make the poolish, put the yeast and cold water in a medium bowl and stir until fully dissolved. Add the flour and whisk gently until a soft, sticky paste forms. This process is extremely simple and as long as the flour is wet and the yeast has dissolved, it is always going to work. Cover with a cloth or plastic wrap and refrigerate overnight. Alternatively, if you are in a hurry, leave the poolish at room temperature for 3 hours, or until it triples in volume. The following day, remove the poolish from the fridge. By now it should have tripled in size *(photo 1)*.

To make the dough, put the flour, cold water, salt and yeast in the bowl of an electric mixer fitted with a dough hook attachment *(2)* and mix on low speed for 10 minutes.

Add the poolish *(3)*, increase the speed to medium and knead for another 5–6 minutes, or until the dough comes away from the side of the bowl *(4)*.

Windowpane test

To check whether the dough is kneaded properly, use the 'windowpane' test. Hold a small piece of dough in your hands and stretch the dough until it is almost thin enough to see through (see page 195, photo 4). If not, continue kneading for another 2 minutes.

Proving the dough

Remove the dough hook and dust a little flour over the dough, then cover with a cloth and set aside in a warm place to prove for 45 minutes. When the dough has risen, knock it down by using your hand to push the middle of the dough down, then fold the sides towards the centre to remove as much gas as possible.

Cover and set aside for another 45 minutes, or until doubled in size, then knock the dough down again. The dough is now ready to be divided and balled (see page 218).

1

2

3

4

Pain sur poolish

This is a great recipe to start with. This basic method is ideal if you haven't prepared a poolish the day before and want to bake a loaf or small bread rolls for dinner or a picnic at short notice. In a few hours you will have a beautifully crusty loaf with a soft, airy crumb that is just as delicious toasted with butter and jam as it is served with cheeses or liver parfaits.

Miche traditionnelle aux noix et aux raisins

(Traditional walnut and raisin loaf)

Makes 1 loaf

800 g (1 lb 12 oz) Bread Dough, direct method (page 214)
100 g (3¹/₂ oz) walnuts, lightly roasted
100 g (3¹/₂ oz) raisins or sultanas (golden raisins)
spray bottle filled with warm water

scoring the loaves

Traditionally bread is baked directly on the bricks on the base of the oven and the intense heat generated from the bottom forms a thick skin, forcing the steam upwards through the thinner skin on the top (there is less heat in the top of the oven). In convection (fan-forced) and static ovens the heat is dispersed evenly around the oven, so the skin thickens uniformly around the loaf, trapping the steam and turning it into the shape of a football. Scoring the loaf prior to baking weakens the skin and allows the steam to escape so the bread retains its shape during baking.

~ Prepare the dough following the method on page 214, to the end of the 'windowpane' test. With the dough still in the bowl of the electric mixer (fitted with a dough hook attachment), add the walnuts and raisins and mix on low speed for 2 minutes, or until evenly dispersed. Follow the method on page 218, to the end of the first prove.

~ Transfer the dough to a lightly floured work surface and proceed with the balling process, as described on page 218. Line a large bowl, about 25 cm (10 in) in diameter, with a lightly floured cloth. Gently tip the dough upside down into the lined bowl so that the bottom of the loaf faces up. Cover with another lightly floured cloth and set aside in a warm place to prove for 1–1¹/₂ hours, or until doubled in size. To check if the dough is ready, gently push it with the palm of your hand; it should feel soft but the dough should still spring back to its original shape. If the dough feels hard and dense, it is not ready.

~ Preheat the oven to 240°C (465°F) at least 30 minutes before baking the bread. Hold the bowl with one hand and rest the other hand gently on top of the dough with your fingers spread apart, then carefully tip the dough onto a lightly floured baking tray. Dust a little flour over the top of the dough. Using a sharp paring knife, cut a cross in the top of the loaf.

~ Place on the bottom shelf of the oven and spray water into the oven for 5 seconds (see tip, page 225), then quickly close the oven door. Bake for 20–25 minutes. To check if the bread is ready, open the oven door and tap the crust with your index finger. The bread is ready when the crust feels hard and the loaf sounds hollow and dry. Remove from the oven and set aside for at least 5 minutes before slicing, or the steam that is trapped inside the loaf may burn you.

The *pain de campagne* is the icon of rural baking, and while this rustic bread has enjoyed a trendy resurgence in the last few years, it is still best enjoyed with a hearty soup or stew during those long winter nights, deep in the countryside.

Pain de campagne
(Country bread)

Makes 1 loaf

Poolish
1 g (¹/₃₂ oz) dried yeast
100 ml (3¹/₂ fl oz) cold water (20°C/70°F)
50 g (1³/₄ oz) plain (all-purpose) flour ('0'/T55 or '1'/T65)
50 g (1³/₄ oz) rye flour

Dough
150 g (5¹/₂ oz) plain (all-purpose) flour ('0'/T55 or '1'/T65)
50 g (1³/₄ oz) rye flour
100 ml (3¹/₂ fl oz) cold water (20°C/70°F)
6 g (¹/₅ oz) fine salt
2 g (¹/₁₆ oz) dried yeast
spray bottle filled with warm water

~ To make the poolish, follow the method on page 220, adding in the rye flour with the plain flour. Cover and set aside at room temperature for 3 hours, or until the poolish triples in volume. To make the dough, follow the method on page 220, to the end of the first prove.

~ Transfer the dough to a lightly floured work surface and proceed with the balling process as described on page 218. Line a large bowl, about 25 cm (10 in) in diameter, with a lightly floured cloth. Gently tip the dough upside down into the lined bowl so that the bottom of the loaf faces up. Cover with another lightly floured cloth and set aside in a warm place to prove for 1 hour, or until doubled in size. To check if the dough is ready, gently push it with the palm of your hand; it should feel soft but the dough should still spring back to its original shape. If the dough feels hard and dense it is not ready.

~ Preheat the oven to 230°C (445°F) at least 30 minutes before baking. Hold the bowl with one hand and rest the other hand gently on top of the dough with your fingers spread apart, then carefully tip the dough onto a lightly floured baking tray. Dust a little flour over the top of the dough. Using a sharp paring knife, cut a cross in the top of the loaf.

~ Place on the bottom shelf of the oven and spray water into the oven for 5 seconds (see tip, page 225), then quickly close the oven door. Bake for 20–25 minutes. To check if the bread is ready, open the oven door and tap the crust with your index finger. The bread is ready when the crust feels hard and the loaf sounds hollow and dry. Remove from the oven and set aside for at least 5 minutes before slicing, or the steam that is trapped inside the loaf may burn you.

Why rye?
Rye flour was used extensively in the past due to its relatively low cost of processing and strong resilience to winter conditions. Nowadays, rye flour is added to semi-sour or sourdough breads for two main reasons. Firstly, it contains less gluten than wheat and is therefore less proficient at retaining the gas created during the fermentation process, which gives the bread a denser flesh with smaller holes, thus helping extend its shelf life. Secondly, it contains more soluble sugars than wheat and therefore ferments faster.

Whilst *fougasse aux olives* is commonly found in Provence today in its distinctive wheat kernel shape, very much like the fabled *pompe à l'huile*, similar breads are found all around the Mediterranean basin, from Italy (focaccia) to the Balkans (*pogaca*). Fougasse is a very simple bread made using the direct method, with added oil, sugar or butter. Traditionally it was topped with vegetables or fruits and was made at the start of the night and thrown into the oven to assess the accuracy of the temperature of the oven.

Fougasse aux olives

(Provençal olive bread)

Makes 1 loaf

50 ml (1³/4 fl oz) full-cream milk
2 teaspoons fleur de sel, or other salt flakes (do not use fine salt)
2 thyme sprigs, leaves picked
spray bottle filled with warm water

Dough

350 g (12 oz) plain (all-purpose) flour ('0'/T55)
150 ml (5 fl oz) cold water (20°C/70°F)
70 ml (2¹/4 fl oz) virgin olive oil
6 g (¹/5 oz) fine salt
3 g (¹/10 oz) dried yeast
100 g (3¹/2 oz) pitted black or green olives,
    coarsely chopped

~ To make the dough, put the flour, water, olive oil, salt and yeast in the bowl of an electric mixer fitted with a dough hook attachment and mix on low speed for 2–3 minutes, or until the dough comes together. Increase the speed to medium and knead for 8–10 minutes, or until the dough comes away from the side of the bowl. During the kneading stage, scrape the dough from the hook and the side of the bowl two or three times. Remove the dough hook, cover the bowl with a cloth and set aside in a warm place to prove for 1 hour, or until the dough has increased by two-thirds. Add the chopped olives and knead gently with one hand until the olives are evenly dispersed through the dough.

~ Place the dough on a lightly floured work surface, then sprinkle a little extra flour over the top. Using your palms, flatten the dough into a 2 cm (³/4 in) thick rectangle. Don't worry about making it too even, as this bread is supposed to look rustic. Transfer to a lightly floured baking tray, cover with a cloth and set aside in a warm place to prove for 1 hour, or until doubled in size.

~ Preheat the oven to 200°C (400°F) for at least 30 minutes before baking the bread. Using a small, sharp knife, cut four diagonal incisions on both sides of the dough to resemble a wheat kernel. Brush the top with the milk, then sprinkle with the salt and thyme leaves.

~ Place on the bottom shelf of the oven and spray water into the oven for 5 seconds (see tip), then quickly close the oven door. Bake for 15 minutes, or until the top of the fougasse begins to brown. Unlike other loaves or rolls that are made using the same dough, the thin shape of the fougasse means it cooks a lot faster, so keep an eye on it — one of the main characteristics of fougasse is its light colour. Remove from the oven and set aside until cool.

adding steam

Adding steam to the oven is beneficial for two reasons. Firstly, humidity delays the drying up of the dough's skin and this helps the bread develop properly. Secondly, the water in the oven (as steam) will gelatinise the starch in the flour, which gives the finished bread a glossy crust.

Pissaladière is an iconic fougasse from Nice, in the south of France. Often mistakenly called a pizza, it is actually made on a thick bread or a fougasse base — unlike pizzas which are traditionally baked on a thin and crispy dough — and then topped with a small amount of anchovy paste and a thick layer of confit onions. Even if, like me, you're not a fan of anchovies, this will take you by surprise. It's light, just sweet and just salty enough, it tastes like the earth and the sea all at once, and it will leave you with a nose full of nutty and fruity aromas. Nothing tastes quite as good as eating a pissaladière with a glass of red wine, lounging in a long chair under a shady tree, just before taking a nap.

Pissaladière

(Onion and anchovy focaccia)

Serves 4-6

50 ml (1³/4 fl oz) virgin olive oil
1 kg (2 lb 4 oz) brown onions, thinly sliced
1 teaspoon ground black pepper
salt, to taste
100 g (3¹/2 oz) anchovy paste (sold in jars or tubes)
100 g (3¹/2 oz) small black olives, pitted
6–8 anchovy fillets
6 thyme sprigs, leaves picked

Dough

350 g (12 oz) plain (all-purpose) flour ('0'/T55)
190 ml (6¹/2 fl oz) full-cream milk
30 g (1 oz) caster (superfine) sugar
40 g (1¹/2 oz) unsalted butter
3 g (¹/10 oz) dried yeast
6 g (¹/5 oz) fine salt

⌐ To make the dough, put the flour and milk in the bowl of an electric mixer fitted with a dough hook attachment. Mix on low speed for about 5 minutes, or until the dough comes together. Cover the bowl with a clean damp cloth and set aside to rest for 40 minutes.

⌐ Add the sugar, butter, yeast and salt to the hydrated dough and mix on low speed until well combined, then increase the speed to medium and knead for about 10 minutes, or until the dough begins to bind around the dough hook and starts to come away from the side of the bowl. During the kneading stage, scrape the dough from the hook and the side of the bowl two or three times. To check whether the dough is ready, use the 'windowpane' test. Cover the bowl with a floured cloth and set aside in a warm place to prove for 1 hour, or until the dough has increased by two-thirds. Knock the dough down, then cover with plastic wrap and refrigerate for at least 2 hours, or until firm to the touch.

⌐ Roll out the dough on a lightly floured work surface into a 5 mm (¹/4 in) thick rectangle measuring about 20 x 30 cm (8 x 12 in). Feel free to use your hands to stretch the dough into shape. Place on a baking tray lined with baking paper and freeze for 1 hour, or until firm.

⌐ Meanwhile, heat the olive oil in a large heavy-based saucepan over high heat for 1 minute. Add the onions and pepper and combine well. Reduce the heat to medium, then cover and cook, stirring occasionally, for 20–25 minutes, or until the onions are golden and softened almost to a purée. Remove from the heat, season with just a little salt, remembering the anchovy paste is already quite salty, and set aside until cool.

⌐ Preheat the oven to 220°C (430°F) at least 30 minutes before baking the bread. Remove the dough from the freezer and spread the anchovy paste evenly over the top. The anchovy paste balances out the sweetness of the onions, but can very quickly overpower the rest of the flavours, so make sure it is applied very thinly. Scatter over the caramelised onions and the olives, then arrange the anchovies evenly across the top.

⌐ Set aside in a warm place to prove for 30 minutes, or until the dough begins to rise again. Bake for 20 minutes, or until the bottom of the pissaladière begins to brown. Remove from the oven, scatter with thyme and cool to room temperature, then cut into squares and serve.

Baking, at least for me, is not so much about how intricate a certain pastry is or how rustic a loaf of bread looks — it goes far beyond the surface of what we can see. Cherished moments from our childhood, long since faded, can often be brought back with startling clarity just by the simple act of biting into a certain biscuit or the aroma of a cake baking in the oven. Even today, whenever I smell a fougasse, I'm taken back to the times when my sister and I stayed at my grandparents' house in a small village in Provence. Every Sunday morning we liked to laze in our beds, listening out for the sound of the baker's horn as he stopped his truck in the village square. We knew that when we eventually got up there would be two slices of crunchy, buttery fougasse waiting for us on the kitchen table. We would noisily devour our fougasse with a bowl of *chocolat chaud*, while my grandfather silently read his paper and my grandmother pored over the crossword, just as they did every Sunday morning.

Fougasse au sucre
(Sugar fougasse)

Makes 2 loaves

100 g (3¹/2 oz) unsalted butter
100 g (3¹/2 oz) caster (superfine) sugar
100 ml (3¹/2 oz) whipping cream (35% fat)

Dough

350 g (12 oz) plain (all-purpose) flour ('0'/T55)
190 ml (6¹/2 fl oz) cold water (20°C/70°F)
70 g (2¹/2 oz) caster (superfine) sugar
30 ml (1 fl oz) virgin olive oil
6 g (¹/5 oz) fine salt
3 g (¹/10 oz) dried yeast
40 g (1¹/2 oz) unsalted butter, at room temperature

⌣ To make the dough, put the flour, water, sugar, olive oil, salt and yeast in the bowl of an electric mixer fitted with a dough hook attachment. Mix on low speed for 2–3 minutes, or until the dough comes together. Increase the speed to medium and knead for 8–10 minutes, or until the dough comes away from the side of the bowl. During the kneading stage, scrape the dough from the hook and the side of the bowl two or three times. Add the 40 g (1¹/2 oz) of butter and knead for another 2–3 minutes, or until the butter has been absorbed into the dough. Remove the dough hook, cover the bowl with a floured cloth and set aside in a warm place to prove for 1 hour, or until the dough has increased by two-thirds.

⌣ Divide the dough in half. Place one portion on a lightly floured work surface, then sprinkle a little extra flour over the top. Using your palms, flatten the dough into a round about 2 cm (³/4 in) thick. Don't worry about making it too even, as this bread is supposed to look rustic. Repeat with the remaining dough. Transfer to two lightly floured baking trays and freeze for 20 minutes, or until the dough hardens slightly.

⌣ Meanwhile, put the butter and sugar in a small saucepan and stir over low heat until melted. Don't boil the mixture as this dissolves the sugar into the butter and, as a result, the bread will lose its crunchy top. Remove from the heat and set aside until cool to the touch. Remove the dough from the freezer and spread half the sugar and butter mixture evenly across the top of each, then cover with a cloth and set aside in a warm place to prove for 1 hour, or until doubled in size.

⌣ Preheat the oven to 200°C (400°F) at least 30 minutes before baking the loaf. When the dough has proved, use your fingertips to make small craters all over the fougasse, about 5 cm (2 in) apart; this prevents the cream from running off the sides of the bread during the final stage of baking. Bake for 10 minutes, then open the oven door and pour the cream evenly over the top of each hot fougasse. Bake for another 10 minutes, or until the sides of the bread begin to turn golden. Cool to room temperature before serving.

This most famous of pizza has withstood the test of time and the futilities of fads to remain the pizza of choice the world over for more than 100 years. Its history is well known. Made in honour of Queen Margherita of Savoy during one of her visits to the Italian city of Naples, it was topped with tomatoes, basil and mozzarella to emulate the colours of the national flag. Whether by coincidence of pure genius or not, this combination of flavours, textures and colours has come to illustrate how restraint and humility, when used properly, are far better than any long list of ingredients or methodology — two simple attributes that sometimes require a lifetime of learning, a fact poignantly captured by the Spanish painter Picasso when he said, 'It took me four years to paint like Raphael, but a lifetime to paint like a child'.

Pizza Margherita
(Margherita pizza)
Makes three 30 cm (12 in) pizzas

Dough

100 ml (3 1/2 fl oz) virgin olive oil
500 ml (17 fl oz) cold water (20°C/70°F)
1 kg (2 lb 4 oz) plain (all-purpose) flour ('0'/T55)
5 g (1/8 oz) dried yeast
20 g (3/4 oz) fine salt

Toppings

400 g (14 oz) fresh buffalo mozzarella, cut into 5 mm (1/4 in) slices
30 basil leaves

Sauce

2 tablespoons virgin olive oil, plus extra, for drizzling
2 brown onions, halved and thinly sliced
2 garlic cloves, thinly sliced
800 g (1 lb 12 oz) truss tomatoes, coarsely chopped
2 teaspoons dried oregano
3 thyme sprigs, leaves picked
fine salt and ground black pepper, to taste
10 basil leaves, finely chopped

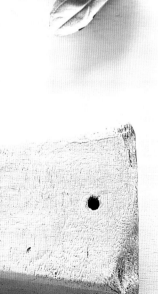

⁓   Prepare the dough following the method on page 214, to the end of the 'windowpane' test. Note that while this recipe is slightly different, the process remains the same. Simply add the oil to the water, then mix with the flour, yeast and salt.

⁓   Place the dough in a lightly floured bowl and cover with a cloth. Set aside in a warm place to prove for 1 hour, or until risen by one-third. When the dough has risen, knock it down with your fist. Following the dividing and balling method on page 218, divide the dough into three equal portions, then shape the dough. Cover and set aside in a warm place to prove for 15 minutes.

⁓   Meanwhile, to make the sauce, heat the olive oil in a large frying pan over medium heat. Add the onions and garlic and cook, stirring continuously, for 5–8 minutes, or until golden. Add the chopped tomatoes, oregano and thyme, and season to taste with salt and pepper. Remember that the sauce will lose volume as the water evaporates, so always hold back a little on the seasoning until the sauce has finished cooking. Reduce the heat to low, then cover and simmer for 10 minutes. Remove the lid, increase the heat to medium and simmer, stirring continuously until a thick paste forms. Stir in the basil and check the seasoning, then transfer to a bowl and leave to cool. Refrigerate until cold.

⁓   Preheat the oven to 240°C (465°F). Ideally, place a pizza stone or heavy-based baking tray on the bottom shelf of the oven to preheat at the same time. This helps the pizza base to cook quickly, which means it remains crisp after baking.

⁓   Roll out the three dough portions on a lightly floured work surface into 3 mm (1/8 in) thick rounds. Use a little extra flour when necessary to stop the dough from sticking. Place the rolled dough on three 30 cm (12 in) pizza trays, then use your hands to stretch the dough back into shape. Cover with a cloth and set aside in a warm place to prove for 30 minutes, or until increased in size by half.

⁓   Unless your oven is big enough to cook all three pizzas at the same time, it's best to cook one pizza at a time, then prepare another one while it is cooking. Using the back of a spoon, spread the sauce over the pizza base, leaving a 2 cm (3/4 in) border around the edge (the dark, crunchy crust is actually the tastiest part of a pizza!). Top with mozzarella but don't get carried away, because too much cheese will not only overpower the sharpness of the tomato sauce, but it will also make it difficult for the pizzas to cook properly.

⁓   Place on the hot pizza stone or baking tray on the bottom shelf of the oven and bake for 12–15 minutes, or until the base is golden. Remove from the oven, scatter with basil leaves and drizzle with a little olive oil, then eat piping hot, straight out of the oven.

Recently, people seem to be switching from white sliced breads to the more complex textures and flavours of traditional or sourdough breads. It's one of the few trends that I absolutely understand, however there are occasions when nothing beats a soft and fluffy white bread roll or sandwich bread. As the title of the recipe suggests, this bread is made with yoghurt, giving it a creamy sour flesh that is slightly denser than white bread, and a thin, velvety crust. It's the perfect alternative to traditional breads with their hard crusts and sometimes pungent sourness that can be a little overwhelming for some.

Pain de mie au yaourt
(Yoghurt bread)

Makes 1 loaf

Poolish
1 g ($^1/_{32}$ oz) dried yeast
100 ml (3$^1/_2$ fl oz) cold water (20°C/70°F)
100 g (3$^1/_2$ oz) plain (all-purpose) flour ('0'/T55)

Dough
100 g (3$^1/_2$ oz) plain (all-purpose) flour ('0'/T55)
2 tablespoons honey
50 g (1$^3/_4$ oz) Greek-style yoghurt
4 g ($^1/_8$ oz) fine salt
2 g ($^1/_{16}$ oz) dried yeast
10 g ($^1/_4$ oz) unsalted butter, at room temperature

Egg wash (for buns)
2 eggs
pinch of fine salt

~ To make the poolish, follow the method on page 220. Once prepared, cover and set aside at room temperature for 3 hours, or until the poolish triples in volume.

~ To make the dough, put the flour, honey, yoghurt and poolish in the bowl of an electric mixer fitted with a dough hook attachment and knead on low speed for 5 minutes, or until the dough comes together. Cover the bowl with a cloth and set aside for 20 minutes.

~ Add the salt, yeast and butter to the dough and knead for 10 minutes on low speed until well combined, then increase the speed to medium and knead for 2–3 minutes, or until the dough comes away from the side of the bowl. To check whether the dough is ready, use the 'windowpane' test. Remove the dough hook, cover the bowl with a cloth and set aside in a warm place to prove for 1 hour, or until doubled in size. Using your fist, punch the dough down to remove the gas bubbles.

~ This dough can be baked as a single loaf or divided into balls for hamburgers or hot dog buns. If making a loaf, lightly grease a 15 x 25 cm (6 x 10 in) bread tin. Shape the dough using the balling method described on page 218. Put the balled dough into the tin and set aside in a warm place to prove for 1–2 hours, or until approximately tripled in size. If making buns, divide the dough into 120 g (4¼ oz) portions for long buns (for hot dogs); 80 g (2¾ oz) portions for hamburger buns; and 40 g (1½ oz) portions for small slider buns. Once shaped, place the buns on a baking tray lined with baking paper, cover with a cloth and set aside in a warm place to prove for 1 hour, or until doubled in size.

~ If cooking the loaf, preheat the oven to 180°C (350°F). Cover the tin with a flat tray, then weight it down with a cast-iron pan or similar (the heavier the better). Bake for 40 minutes, then remove the top tray and weight, tip the loaf over and remove the tin and bake for another 15 minutes, or until golden. Leave to cool for 1 hour before slicing.

~ If cooking the buns, preheat the oven to 190°C (375°F). Meanwhile, to make an egg wash, lightly beat the eggs and salt together in a small bowl. When the buns are ready, brush them all over with the egg wash. Bake for 10–12 minutes for the larger rolls and 7–8 minutes for the small slider buns, or until golden. Unlike layered doughs used for croissant or puff pastry, brioches and breads cook quickly and have a tendency to dry up, so if you respect the temperatures, the colour is actually a very reliable way of deciding if your bread is ready.

tip

The main characteristic of *pain de mie* is its dense, white flesh, which is achieved by adding a fat to a traditional bread dough. As always, I recommend that you experiment with the recipes I have listed in this book. For a different result, why not try replacing the butter (fat) in this recipe with the same amount of soft blue cheese or creamy mascarpone.

Pain de mie au yaourt (Yoghurt bread)

Pompe à l'huile d'olive et à la fleur d'oranger
(Olive oil and orange-blossom sweet bread)

This is going to be an exception to the rule: a sweet bread made with a poolish method, the very thing I said I disliked to begin with. While I did mention that the distinctive characteristics of the poolish method were not to my taste for rich, buttery and subtle *viennoiseries* such as brioche or croissants, those very attributes are intrinsic to some of the most traditional sweet breads, and when it comes to traditional recipes, the *pompe à l'huile* is one not to be messed with.

This humble fougasse is actually one of the compulsory offerings of the thirteen desserts traditionally served during Christmas festivities in Provence, the number thirteen being representative of Christ and his twelve apostles at the Last Supper. Four desserts represent the *mendiants* (the four orders of monks) in the form of dried fruits and nuts (figs, hazelnuts, almonds and raisins); four confectioneries are used to represent good and evil (*pompe*, dark nougat, white nougat and jams); four fresh fruits; and a special dessert, which according to local custom could vary from candied fruits to elaborate confectioneries, to represent Christ. Even though the religious significance of this custom is now often forgotten, you will be hard-pressed to find a Christmas meal anywhere in the south of France that doesn't include some elements of this age-old tradition, which certainly always includes a *pompe à l'huile*.

Pompe à l'huile d'olive et à la fleur d'oranger

(Olive oil and orange-blossom sweet bread)

Makes 2

200 ml (7 fl oz) full-cream milk
1 egg yolk

Poolish

1 g (¹/₃₂ oz) dried yeast
100 ml (3¹/₂ fl oz) cold water (20°C/70°F)
100 g (3¹/₂ oz) plain (all-purpose) flour ('0'/T55 or '1'/T65)

Dough

300 g (10¹/₂ oz) plain (all-purpose) flour ('0'/T55 or '1'/T65)
150 g (5¹/₂ oz) caster (superfine) sugar
2 tablespoons orange blossom water
120 ml (4¹/₄ fl oz) virgin olive oil
6 g (¹/₅ oz) fine salt
8 g (¹/₄ oz) dried yeast

⁓ To make the poolish, follow the method on page 220. Once prepared, cover and set aside at room temperature for 3 hours, or until the poolish triples in volume.

⁓ To make the dough, put the poolish and all the ingredients for the dough in the bowl of an electric mixer fitted with a dough hook attachment. Knead on low speed for 10 minutes, then increase the speed to medium and knead for 2–3 minutes, or until the dough comes away from the side of the bowl. To check whether the dough is ready, use the 'windowpane' test. Remove the dough hook and dust a little flour over the dough, then cover the bowl with a cloth and set aside in a warm place to prove for 45 minutes, or until doubled in size.

⁓ Divide the dough in half, then shape the dough using the balling method described on page 218. Place the balls on a tray lightly dusted with flour, cover with a cloth and set aside to rest for 15 minutes.

⁓ Roll out each ball on a lightly floured work surface into a 20 cm (8 in) round about 2.5 cm (1 in) thick. These breads are meant to be quite rustic, so don't stress too much about making a perfect circle. Concentrate instead on making sure the dough is an even thickness, as any thinner areas may burn. Place the rounds on baking trays lined with baking paper. Cover with a cloth and set aside in a warm place to prove for 1–2 hours, or until doubled in size.

⁓ Preheat the oven to 190°C (375°F) at least 30 minutes before baking. Lightly beat the milk and egg yolk in a small bowl, then brush all over the breads. Using a paring knife dipped in the egg wash, cut patterns straight through the dough (use the photograph on page 235 as a guide). I usually cut a hole in the middle, then make four long cuts opposite each other, similar to the numbers on a clock face. Feel free to be creative with your design — the cuts in the bread only serve to improve the overall look of the *pompe* after baking, nothing more. Bake on the bottom shelf of the oven for 15 minutes, or until golden. Remove from the oven and cool to room temperature before serving.

I don't mean to scare you or anything, but superstition dictates that you should never cut the *pompe* with a knife or you will risk a year of bad luck. Instead, you should always 'break' the bread with your hands. You can never be too careful!

This recipe is very similar to the earlier one for olive fougasse, but this is made with a more complex poolish dough. My main intention of including it here is to illustrate that, irrespective of the traditional methods and flavours used in the recipe, it's the type of recipe that will suit most flavours and toppings — it's entirely a matter of personal preference. Serve this soft, aromatic flat bread as a quick lunch or cut it into bite-sized pieces and serve as an appetiser.

For this recipe, I am sticking with my favourites: potatoes, thyme, rosemary and olives. For me, this is Provence on a plate — humble, resourceful and intoxicating all at once.

Fougasse aux herbes, à la pomme de terre et aux olives noires

(Potato, black olive and herb fougasse)

Makes 1 loaf

500 g (1 lb 2 oz) Pain sur Poolish (page 220)
500 g (1 lb 2 oz) all-purpose potatoes, such as desiree
olive oil, for drizzling
3 rosemary sprigs, leaves picked
80 g (2³⁄4 oz) thyme (about ¹⁄2 bunch), leaves picked
   (reserve a few sprigs)
salt and ground black pepper, to taste
200 g (7 oz) black olives, pitted

~ Prepare the dough following the method on page 220, to the end of the first prove.

~ Roll out the dough on a lightly floured surface into a 20 x 40 cm (8 x 16 in) rectangle, about 5 mm (¹⁄4 in) thick. As with most doughs for pizzas and focaccia, don't spend too much time trying to get a perfect rectangle. Not only are they meant to be rustic, but the dough will become too soft and will begin to prove if you spend too much time fiddling about. Place the rolled dough onto a lightly greased or lined baking tray, cover with a cloth and set aside in a warm place to prove for 1 hour, or until doubled in size.

~ Meanwhile, peel the potatoes and keep them in a bowl of cold water as you go, to stop them from browning. Using the slicing attachment on the food processor or a mandolin, cut the potatoes into 2 mm (¹⁄16) thin slices. The potato has to cook quickly before the bread burns, so it is important that all the potato slices are cut into thin, even slices. You can use a large knife to do this, but you will have to make sure the potatoes are thinly sliced — there is nothing worse than raw potato! As you slice the potatoes, place them into a bowl full of cold water to prevent them from browning, and refrigerate until needed.

~ Preheat the oven to 220°C (430°F) at least 30 minutes before baking. Brush the fougasse generously with olive oil, sprinkle half the rosemary and thyme leaves over the top and push them into the dough using your fingertips. Drain the potatoes and pat dry on paper towel, then place them in slightly overlapping layers over the herbs. Spend a bit of time organising your potatoes slices in a nice pattern, starting from one corner of the dough and working your way to the opposite side. Drizzle with oil, season with a generous amount of salt and pepper, then scatter with the olives and remaining rosemary and thyme leaves and sprigs. Bake for 12–15 minutes, or until the edges of the potatoes begin to turn brown. Serve straight out of the oven or at room temperature.

tip

These toppings are typically Provençal, but you can use whatever suits your own taste. As one idea: spread a thin layer of thick (double/heavy) cream directly onto the dough, top with thinly sliced pumpkin and season with nutmeg.

One of my all-time favourites, this *chausson* is a variation on the traditional *pompe* bread recipe (page 236). It's filled with sweet poached apricots, balanced with just the right amount of acidity from the yoghurt and a subtle floral earthiness from the saffron. This recipe is a perfect example of how complex flavours, when used correctly, can produce wholesome simplicity.

Chausson à l'abricot safrané et au yaourt

(Apricot, saffron and yoghurt pockets)

Makes 15

200 ml (7 fl oz) full-cream milk
2 egg yolks
250 g (9 oz) Greek-style yoghurt
200 g (7 oz) flaked almonds

Poolish

1 g (¹/₃₂ oz) dried yeast
100 ml (3¹/₂ fl oz) cold water (20°C/70°F)
100 g (3¹/₂ oz) plain (all-purpose) flour ('0'/T55 or '1'/T65)

Poached apricots

1.2 kg (2 lb 10 oz) caster (superfine) sugar
2 vanilla beans, halved lengthways
1 kg (2 lb 4 oz) fresh apricots, halved and pitted
¹/₂ teaspoon saffron threads

Dough

300 g (10¹/₂ oz) plain (all-purpose) flour ('0'/T55 or '1'/T65)
100 g (3¹/₂ oz) caster (superfine) sugar
120 ml (4¹/₄ fl oz) virgin olive oil
6 g (¹/₅ oz) fine salt
8 g (¹/₄ oz) dried yeast

⌒ To make the poolish, follow the method on page 220. Once prepared, cover and set aside at room temperature for 3 hours, or until the poolish triples in volume.

⌒ Meanwhile, to make the poached apricots, put the sugar, halved vanilla beans and 2 litres (70 fl oz) water in a large saucepan and bring to the boil over high heat. Remove from the heat, add the apricots and saffron, then cover with plastic wrap and set aside until cool. Refrigerate overnight. Strain the apricots and vanilla beans over a bowl, reserving the syrup for another use (it can be refrigerated for months and can be used for a variety of things, from cordial to cocktails or even as a syrup for pound cakes). Pat the apricots dry on paper towel and place them in a small food processor. Using a small knife, scrape the vanilla seeds into the food processor and discard the vanilla beans. Pulse the apricot mixture one or two times to break the apricots up a little. Alternatively, mash them a little with a fork.

⌒ To make the dough, put the poolish and all the ingredients for the dough in the bowl of an electric mixer fitted with a dough hook attachment. Knead on low speed for 10 minutes, then increase the speed to medium and knead for 2–3 minutes, or until the dough comes away from the side of the bowl. To check whether the dough is ready, use the 'windowpane' test. Remove the dough hook and dust a little flour over the dough, then cover the bowl with a cloth and set aside in a warm place to prove for 45 minutes, or until doubled in size.

⌒ Line a baking tray with baking paper. Roll out the dough on a lightly floured work surface until about 1 cm ($^{1}/_{2}$ in) thick. Using a 20 cm (8 in) round cutter, cut out 15 circles from the dough, carefully place on the lined tray and freeze for 1 hour. At this stage, the dough will be soft and the dough circles will lose their shape easily, but chilling them will help fix this, so don't worry too much about how regular the circles are.

⌒ To make an egg wash, lightly beat the milk and egg yolks together in a small bowl. Remove the dough circles from the freezer and roll them again until 3 mm ($^{1}/_{8}$ in) thick, then cut the excess dough with the cutter. At this stage they should be firm. Brush the egg wash around the outside edges of each circle — use just enough so that the dough is tacky enough to stick together when folded. Reserve the remaining egg wash for later.

⌒ Spoon 1$^{1}/_{2}$ tablespoons of apricots into the middle of each round, then cover the apricots with 2 teaspoons yoghurt. Fold one side of the dough over the filling to form a semicircle, then use your fingertips to press around the edge to seal. Use the cutter to trim and neaten any excess dough, then place on lined baking tray, cover with a cloth and set aside in a warm place to prove for 1$^{1}/_{2}$ hours, or until the dough has risen.

⌒ Preheat the oven to 180°C (350°F) at least 30 minutes before baking. Brush the *chausson* with the remaining egg wash and sprinkle with flaked almonds. Poke a small hole in each one with the tip of a knife, to allow the steam to escape. Bake for 15 minutes, or until golden. Remove from the oven and allow to cool on the tray. Serve warm or at room temperature.

Confitures, compotes, pâtes à tartiner et crèmes

'The rule is, jam tomorrow and jam
yesterday — but never jam today.'

THROUGH THE LOOKING GLASS, LEWIS CARROLL

Confitures, compotes, pâtes à tartiner et crèmes

(Jams, compotes, spreads and creams)

From salt to sugar, vinegar to alcohol, people have been experimenting with various ways of preserving seasonal fruits and vegetables for millenniums. Nowadays, with advances in methods of preserving foods, sterilisation and so on, concoctions such as jams and preserves of all forms are just another delicious way of enjoying our fruit and vegetables.

If you've ever been to France, you will have noticed how much the French love their spreads and jams — no breakfast table would be complete without an assortment of jams and a sliced baguette, to dip into your bowl of *café au lait*. When I was a child I was lucky enough to spend my time off school in the country, when picking fruits and berries to make jams and preserves was considered fun. We would spend days scavenging for berries, occasionally raiding a nearby fruit orchard, then go home with our buckets brimming. Our grandmother helped us mix all those fruits in large copper pots, and my job was to stay close to the stove, stirring the fragrant jams with a wooden spoon. When they turned translucent and shiny, we poured them into an assortment of jars that we'd saved up over the winter.

Confitures

(Jams)

The food industry in France, from production all the way to the retail shelf, is stringently controlled by governmental decrees, proprietary methods or regional brand names. As such, jams manufactured for retail need to contain at least 55 per cent sugar after cooking, and at least 35 per cent fruit before cooking, in order to be sold under the name of *confitures*.

While I am sure those rules and regulations are critical in maintaining the standards and consistency of products sold around the world, the recipes in this book don't meet those rules — I was actually more concerned with writing recipes that were tasty and easy to achieve. The sugar content and boiling time for the jams in the following recipes have been dramatically reduced to preserve the integrity of the flavour and taste of the fruits, and to preserve some of the vitamins and colour that all but die off during the traditionally lengthy cooking period.

storage instructions :

⌒ Due to their low sugar content, these jams must be kept in the fridge, even prior to opening, and labelled with the expiry dates suggested in the recipes.

Confiture de framboises
à la noix de coco

(Raspberry and coconut jam)

Makes about 800 ml (28 fl oz)

200 g (7 oz) caster (superfine) sugar
10 g (¼ oz) powdered pectin
100 ml (3½ fl oz) tinned coconut cream
500 g (1 lb 2 oz) fresh or frozen raspberries (see tip)

~ To sterilise the jars, place four 200 ml (7 fl oz) capacity jars and their lids in a large saucepan and cover with hot water. Bring to the boil over high heat, then reduce the heat to medium and simmer gently for 5 minutes. Remove the pan from the heat. Using a pair of kitchen tongs, carefully remove the jars and lids from the hot water and place them upside down on a clean cloth on your work surface. Take care as they will be extremely hot!

~ Put the sugar and pectin in a bowl and stir until very well combined — this avoids the formation of lumps later in the process.

~ Put the coconut cream and raspberries in a heavy-based saucepan over medium heat. Heavy-based pans are great at spreading the direct heat of the flame or heating element, which reduces the chance of burning the jam. Bring to the boil, stirring occasionally. At this point the berries should be breaking down. Add the sugar mixture and stir continuously until the sugar has completely dissolved. Reduce the heat to low and continue stirring gently for 10 minutes, or until translucent. It is hard to tell by sight if the jam is ready, as the jam has very little sugar and has to rely predominantly on the pectin (for its texture and thickness) to bloom overnight to set. As soon as the jam begins boiling, the pectin has been activated.

~ Pour the hot jam into the sterilised jars, making sure you don't spill any on the rims, then seal immediately. Label the jars and write the expiry date (3 months from the day they were made) on them. Set aside until cool, then store in the fridge.

tip

I always recommend using fresh berries for these recipes. That being said, you will get a very similar result using frozen fruits, providing you account for the fact that they contain a slightly higher water content, and will therefore need to simmer for an additional 5 minutes to allow for extra evaporation.

Confiture de fraises à la menthe et au citron vert

(Strawberry, mint and lime jam)

Makes about 800 ml (28 fl oz)

200 g (7 oz) caster (superfine) sugar
10 g (¹/₄ oz) powdered pectin
10 large mint leaves, chopped
550 g (1 lb 4 oz) strawberries, hulled
finely grated zest and juice of 1 lime

⌒ Sterilise four 200 ml (7 fl oz) capacity jars and their lids following the method described on page 247.

⌒ Put the sugar and pectin in a bowl and stir until very well combined — this avoids the formation of lumps later in the process. Wrap the chopped mint in a piece of muslin (cheesecloth) or a clean cloth and secure the top with string, to make a bag similar to a bouquet garni.

⌒ Put the strawberries, 1 tablespoon water and the mint parcel in a heavy-based saucepan over very low heat. Heavy-based pans are great at spreading the direct heat of the flame or heating element, which reduces the chance of burning the jam. Cover the pan and cook, stirring occasionally and making sure the mixture doesn't boil, until the berries start to break down. Add the sugar mixture and stir continuously until the sugar has completely dissolved. Then, continue stirring gently for 10 minutes, or until translucent. It is hard to tell by sight if the jam is ready, as the jam has very little sugar and has to rely predominantly on the pectin (for its texture and thickness) to bloom overnight to set. As soon as the jam begins boiling, the pectin has been activated.

⌒ Remove the mint parcel, then stir in the lime zest and juice. Pour the hot jam into the sterilised jars, making sure you don't spill any on the rims, then seal immediately. Label the jars and write the expiry date (3 months from the day they were made) on them. Set aside until cool, then store in the fridge.

Confiture de melon à la cannelle et au citron confit

(Rockmelon, cinnamon and confit lemon jam)

Makes about 800 ml (28 fl oz)

¹/2 lemon, preferably organic
200 g (7 oz) caster (superfine) sugar
¹/2 teaspoon ground cinnamon
15 g (¹/2 oz) powdered pectin
700 g (1 lb 9 oz) ripe rockmelon (about 1 large melon),
   peeled and cut into 2 cm (³/4 in) pieces
2 vanilla beans, halved lengthways

technical tip

Pectin is a colloid, a polysaccharide found in the skin and, to a lesser extent, the flesh of fruits and vegetables. It is widely used as a gelling agent and stabiliser in food (E440), but also in therapeutic medicines and the pharmaceutical industry. Now, getting back to our jam … As pectin needs an acid to activate fully, we can control the thickness or viscosity of the jam by adding or reducing both the amount of pectin and acid we add. In this recipe, I have increased the amount of pectin and added an acid (the lemon). This will help stabilise the high water/ low pectin content of the rockmelon.

~ Wash the lemon thoroughly under hot water to remove any wax. Remove the seeds, then finely chop the skin and flesh into a rough paste.

~ Put the sugar, cinnamon and pectin in a bowl and stir until very well combined — this avoids the formation of lumps later in the process. Add the lemon paste, chopped melon and vanilla beans and, using your hands, combine well. Cover the bowl with plastic wrap and set aside for 1 hour.

~ Meanwhile, sterilise four 200 ml (7 fl oz) capacity jars and their lids following the method described on page 247.

~ Transfer the fruit and sugar mixture to a heavy-based saucepan and place over medium heat. Heavy-based pans are great at spreading the direct heat of the flame or heating element, which reduces the chance of burning the jam. Bring to the boil, stirring continuously, then reduce the heat to low and continue stirring for another 15 minutes, or until the melon becomes translucent. It is hard to tell by sight if the jam is ready, as the jam has very little sugar and has to rely predominantly on the pectin (for its texture and thickness) to bloom overnight to set. As soon as the jam begins boiling, the pectin has been activated.

~ Using a pair of kitchen tongs, remove the vanilla beans and reserve. Pour the hot jam into the sterilised jars, making sure you don't spill any on the rims. Add one halved vanilla bean to each jar and seal immediately. Label the jars and write the expiry date (3 months from the day they were made) on them. Set aside until cool, then store in the fridge.

Confiture d'ananas poivrée

(Peppered pineapple jam)

Makes about 800 ml (28 fl oz)

¹/₂ lemon, preferably organic
500 g (1 lb 2 oz) ripe pineapple flesh (about 1 small pineapple),
    cut into 2 cm (³/₄ in) cubes
¹/₈ teaspoon finely ground black pepper
10 g (¹/₄ oz) powdered pectin
2 vanilla beans, halved lengthways
250 g (9 oz) caster (superfine) sugar

technical tips

Sugar, once dissolved in a liquid will have a propensity to return to its crystallised state, causing your hot syrup to *masse*, or crystallise into a lump of opaque, hard sugar. So, the goal is to stop any of the sugar crystallising during cooking. Here are a few tips to prevent this problem:

〜 Make sure your sugar does not contain any impurities (such as crumbs, small coffee grains or flour).

〜 When making heavy syrup (high in sugar) or cooked sugar, always dissolve the sugar slowly in the water (you can complete this stage even a few hours before you need it), and then cook the sugar quickly to avoid crystallisation.

〜 Always dissolve your sugar by adding at least 30 per cent of its weight in water.

〜 Use as small a pan as possible, to maintain consistent heat across the whole syrup.

〜 Use a small brush to remove any sugar crystals that form on the side of your pan during cooking.

〜 Don't stir the syrup once it has begun to boil.

〜 Sterilise four 200 ml (7 fl oz) capacity jars and their lids following the method described on page 247.

〜 Wash the lemon thoroughly under hot water to remove any wax. Remove the seeds, then finely chop the skin and flesh.

〜 Put the lemon, pineapple, pepper, pectin and vanilla beans in a bowl and combine well. Cover and set aside for 1 hour. Unlike the other jams in this book, the pectin is not added to the sugar, as it would burn during the caramelisation process. Consequently, it requires at least 1 hour to hydrate and soften up in the juices of the fruit prior to cooking.

〜 Put 80 ml (2¹/₂ fl oz) water in a heavy-based saucepan, then add the sugar and mix gently with your fingertips or a small spatula. Be careful not to splatter too much sugar around the side of the pan or you will increase the risk of crystallising the sugar (see tips). Bring to the boil over high heat, then reduce the heat to medium and cook, without stirring, until the sugar begins to caramelise. Stirring the syrup will increase the chances of the caramel crystallising, so gently tilt the pan until the caramel is an even, light brown colour throughout. As soon as you are happy with the colour of the caramel, increase the heat to high, then immediately add the pineapple mixture and stir continuously. Be very careful when adding a liquid (or fruit that contains a lot of liquid) to caramel as this creates a lot of very hot steam. Always keep your hands as far away from the mixture as possible when adding the fruit.

〜 Reduce the heat to low, then cover and simmer, without stirring, for 10 minutes. The steam and heat will force the water out of the pineapple and dissolve any pieces of hard caramel. Remove the lid, add 200 ml (7 fl oz) water, then increase the heat to medium and simmer, stirring continuously, for another 30 minutes. It is hard to tell by sight if the jam is ready, as the jam has very little sugar and has to rely predominantly on the pectin (for its texture and thickness) to bloom overnight to set. As soon as the jam begins boiling, the pectin has been activated.

〜 Using a pair of kitchen tongs, remove the vanilla beans and reserve. Pour the hot jam into the sterilised jars, making sure you don't spill any on the rims. Add one halved vanilla bean to each jar and seal immediately. Label the jars and write the expiry date (3 months from the day they were made) on them. Set aside until cool, then store in the fridge.

Compotes

(Compotes)

First described in a fifteenth-century cookbook as a 'spiced and sweetened apple purée', compotes now come in all manner of flavours. The basic requirements of compotes are that they should be made of chunks of fleshy fruit (such as apples, figs or pears), be cooked in a light, spiced syrup and rely entirely on the fruits' own pectin for their texture. This is unlike jams, which contain much more sugar and often the addition of pectin, to preserve the fruit.

Personally, I think compotes are a more refined and healthy alternative to classic jams. They are full of vitamins (unlike jams, which lose a lot of their nutrients during the boiling process), they contain a lot less sugar and can be served as a spread on a buttered baguette, a warm croissant or French toast. They also taste amazing as an accompaniment to a simple fruit salad, yoghurt and cheese, or as a substitute for ice cream on a warm chocolate cake or tarte tatin.

storage instructions

~ Due to their low sugar content, these compotes must be kept in the fridge, even prior to opening, and labelled with the expiry dates suggested in the recipes.

Compote de poires à l'orgeat

(Pear and orgeat syrup compote)

Makes about 800 ml (28 fl oz)

600 g (1 lb 5 oz) firm williams (bartlett) pears (about 4),
   or any buttery pear
juice of 2 lemons
100 g (3½ oz) caster (superfine) sugar
60 ml (2 fl oz) orgeat syrup (see page 40)
2 vanilla beans, halved lengthways

∼ Sterilise four 200 ml (7 fl oz) capacity jars and their lids following the method described on page 247.

∼ Peel, core and cut the pears into 2 cm (¾ in) cubes and place in a heavy-based saucepan. Add the remaining ingredients and use your hands to combine well. Cover the pan and cook over medium heat, stirring occasionally, for 10 minutes, or until the pears begin to break down into a coarse purée. The steam generated and trapped under the lid will provide the heat necessary to break down the fibres in the fruit and will release the water with little or no risk of burning the bottom of the pan.

∼ Using kitchen tongs, remove the vanilla beans, then scrape the seeds out of the beans into the compote. Stir the compote until the vanilla seeds are dispersed evenly throughout.

∼ Spoon the hot compote into the sterilised jars, making sure you don't spill any on the rims, then seal immediately. Label the jars and write the expiry date (1 month from the day they were made) on them. Set aside until cool, then store in the fridge.

Compote d'abricots à la verveine citronnelle

(Apricot and lemon verbena compote)

Makes about 800 ml (28 fl oz)

50 g (1³/4 oz) lemon verbena leaves, coarsely chopped (or 6 lemon verbena tea bags)
600 g (1 lb 5 oz) ripe apricots, halved and stones removed
150 g (5¹/2 oz) caster (superfine) sugar
2 vanilla beans, halved lengthways

~ Wrap the chopped lemon verbena leaves in a piece of muslin (cheesecloth) or a clean cloth and secure the top with string, to make a bag similar to a bouquet garni.

~ Put the apricots, sugar, vanilla beans and the lemon verbena parcel in a heavy-based saucepan and combine well. If you are using tea bags, don't add them yet as they are fragile and will break apart during the early stages of cooking. Cover the pan and cook over medium heat, stirring occasionally, for 15 minutes, or until the apricots begin to break down into a coarse purée. The steam generated and trapped under the lid will provide the heat necessary to break down the fibres in the fruit and will release the water with little or no risk of burning the bottom of the pan. If using the lemon verbena tea bags, reduce the heat to low and add them to the pan. Simmer for 5 minutes, stirring continuously.

~ Transfer the compote to a heat-resistant bowl. Cover and set aside until cool, then refrigerate overnight. Don't remove the muslin parcel (or tea bags) or the vanilla beans at this stage, as they will release the bulk of their flavour during the cooling-down period.

~ Meanwhile, sterilise four 200 ml (7 fl oz) capacity jars and their lids following the method described on page 247.

~ Remove the lemon verbena parcel or tea bags from the compote and squeeze them gently with your hands to extract as much flavour as possible — don't squeeze the tea bags too hard or they will burst. Scrape the seeds out of the vanilla beans into the compote and stir until the seeds are evenly dispersed throughout.

~ Spoon the compote into the sterilised jars, making sure you don't spill any on the rims, then seal immediately. Label the jars and write the expiry date (1 month from the day they were made) on them. Set aside until cool, then store in the fridge.

Compote de pommes et de rhubarbe

(Apple and rhubarb compote)

Makes about 1 litre (35 fl oz)

300 g (10½ oz) rhubarb stems (about 5 stems)
600 g (1 lb 5 oz) green apples (about 4), such as granny smiths
100 g (3½ oz) honey
100 g (3½ oz) caster (superfine) sugar
½ teaspoon ground cinnamon

technical tip

For this recipe, I have substituted some of the sugar with honey. Honey is an inverted sugar, high in fructose. This monosaccharide has two very beneficial properties in baking. Firstly, it is approximately 65 per cent sweeter than sucrose (sugar) and is therefore ideal to balance out acidic recipes, such as this apple and rhubarb compote, without dramatically needing to increase the ratio of refined sugar. Secondly, the honey slows down the crystallisation of sucrose in your mix, therefore increasing both the texture and shelf life.

〜 Sterilise five 200 ml (7 fl oz) capacity jars and their lids following the method described on page 247.

〜 Trim the rhubarb of any leaves and cut the stems into 1 cm (½ in) thick slices. Put 500 ml (17 fl oz) water in a large saucepan and bring to the boil over high heat. As soon as the water boils, add the rhubarb and cook for 5 minutes, or until tender, then drain well. Place on a clean cloth and pat dry.

〜 Peel and core the apples and cut into 2 cm (¾ in) cubes. Put the rhubarb, apples, honey, sugar and cinnamon in a heavy-based saucepan and combine well. Cover the pan and cook over medium heat, stirring occasionally, for 10–15 minutes, or until the apples begin to break down into a coarse purée. The steam generated and trapped under the lid will provide the heat necessary to break down the fibres in the fruit and will release the water with little or no risk of burning the bottom of the pan.

〜 Spoon the hot compote into the sterilised jars, making sure you don't spill any on the rims, then seal immediately. Label the jars and write the expiry date (1 month from the day they were made) on them. Set aside until cool, then store in the fridge.

Pâtes à tartiner

(Spreads)

Literally speaking, *pâtes à tartiner* can be translated as 'paste to spread on tartines', those being slices of bread usually eaten in the morning, dunked into a large bowl of hot chocolate or *café au lait*. Of course jams, marmalades, honeys, soft cheeses … all of those are indeed spreads, but the way I look at it is that they already have a specific name to categorise them and the recipes that follow don't — just like peanut butter, they are simply spreadable … and delicious.

storage instructions :

~ Due to their low sugar content, these spreads must be kept in the fridge, even prior to opening, and labelled with the expiry dates suggested in the recipes.

Pâte à tartiner choco-noisette

(Hazelnut and chocolate spread)

Makes about 800 ml (28 fl oz)

200 g (7 oz) caster (superfine) sugar
600 g (1 lb 5 oz) hazelnuts, roasted and skinned
  (see tip, page 151)
100 g (3½ oz) unsweetened cocoa powder
50 g (1¾ oz) full-cream milk powder
2 tablespoons vegetable oil
large pinch of salt flakes

tip.

The hazelnuts in this spread can be replaced with any other nut; however, you must adjust the levels of fat accordingly to achieve a similar texture. This recipe is designed for hazelnuts, which contain around 60 per cent oil, or 360 g (12¾ oz). If you were to use almonds, which contain 50 per cent oil (300 g/10½ oz for 600 g/1 lb 5 oz of almonds), or pistachios, you would have to add an additional 60 g (2¼ oz) of vegetable oil, bringing the total vegetable oil amount to 100 g (3½ oz).

~ Sterilise four 200 ml (7 fl oz) capacity jars and their lids following the method described on page 247. Place a 50 cm (20 in) long piece of baking paper or a large silicone mat on the work surface.

~ To make the praline, put 80 ml (2¾ fl oz) water in a heavy-based saucepan, then add the sugar and mix gently with a small spatula. Be careful not to splatter too much sugar around the side of the pan or you will increase the risk of crystallising the sugar. Bring to the boil over high heat, then reduce the heat to medium and cook, without stirring, until the sugar begins to caramelise. Stirring the syrup will increase the chance of the caramel crystallising, so gently tilt the pan until the caramel is an even light brown colour.

~ Reduce the heat to low, then stir in the hazelnuts and quickly tip the mixture over the paper or silicone mat, spreading it out as thinly as you can with a spatula. Leave to cool, then cover the praline with a cloth and use a rolling pin or saucepan to bash it into small pieces.

~ Put the praline pieces into a food processor with the cocoa powder, milk powder, oil and salt flakes. Using the pulse button, process until finely chopped, then process on high speed until a paste forms. Stop mixing as soon as you are happy with the texture of your spread. The longer you mix it, the smoother it will get.

~ Divide the paste among the sterilised jars and seal. Label the jars and write the expiry date (6 months from the day they were made) on them. Store in the fridge.

Confiture de lait

(Milk jam)

Makes about 600 ml (21 fl oz)

1 litre (35 fl oz) full-cream milk
300 g (10¹/₂ oz) caster (superfine) sugar
¹/₂ teaspoon salt flakes
3 vanilla beans, halved lengthways

~ Sterilise three 200 ml (7 fl oz) capacity jars and their lids following the method described on page 247.

~ Put all the ingredients in a heavy-based saucepan and combine well. Cook over high heat until the mixture comes to the boil, then reduce the heat to low. Using a slotted spoon, remove the foam from the top of the milk, then continue to simmer for 1¹/₂ hours, stirring every 10 minutes with a heat-resistant flat spatula (using a whisk will create foam, which you want to avoid). During the last 30 minutes of cooking, the mixture should begin to thicken and caramelise slowly, so pay close attention and stir continuously to make sure the mixture doesn't catch on the bottom of the pan and burn. It is important to note that the cooking times indicated are purely to be used as a guide. This jam is ready from the minute it thickens and caramelises; the longer you leave it, the thicker it will get and the less sweet it will become.

~ Using kitchen tongs, remove and discard the vanilla beans, then spoon the hot caramel into the sterilised jars, but do not seal them for at least 1 hour, or until the caramel reaches room temperature. Label the jars and write the expiry date (1 month from the day they were made) on them. Seal and store in the fridge.

Pâte de caramel au beurre salé

(Salted caramel spread)

Makes about 600 ml (21 fl oz)

150 ml (5 fl oz) whipping cream (35% fat)
300 g (10½ oz) caster (superfine) sugar
200 g (7 oz) unsalted butter, chopped
4 g (⅛ oz) salt flakes

~ Sterilise three 200 ml (7 fl oz) capacity jars and their lids following the method described on page 247.

~ Put the cream in a small saucepan and cook over low heat until just warm. Remove from the heat and set aside.

~ Put the sugar in a heavy-based saucepan over high heat and stir continuously with a flat, heat-resistant spatula. Always use a medium to large saucepan for these types of caramels, as introducing a cooler liquid to a very hot caramel creates a lot of steam and intensely hot bubbles, so the larger the pan, the better. As soon as the sugar begins to caramelise around the edges, reduce the heat to low and continue stirring. At this stage, you will notice large, crystallised lumps of sugar; this is actually part of the process of cooking a dry caramel. When the caramel begins to foam (at this stage, the colour should be turning brown/red and the lumps should be totally dissolved), increase the heat to high, and slowly incorporate the warm cream while mixing. Always keep your hands as far away from the caramel as you can during this process!

~ Cook the mixture, stirring occasionally, until it reaches 110°C (230°F) on a sugar thermometer. Remove from the heat and stir in the butter until well combined. Using a stick blender, process the caramel for 1–2 minutes, or until emulsified. Stir in the salt flakes.

~ Spoon the hot caramel into the sterilised jars, but do not seal them for at least 1 hour, or until the caramel reaches room temperature. Label the jars and write the expiry date (2 months from the day they were made) on them. Seal and store in the fridge.

What makes salted caramel so delicious?
To understand this, you need to understand a little about how tastes, in particular saltiness and bitterness, work together. Tastes are sensed by taste buds in our mouth. Each of those tastes are detected individually, so therefore any strong taste will reduce the perceived taste of others. For instance, an overly sweet curd will numb your tongue to any other taste or any subtle nuances in flavour. You can either increase or reduce the perceived effect of a particular taste (and overall flavour) by increasing or even introducing another taste. Salted caramel is a very good example of this. We overcook the caramel to reduce the inherent sweetness of the sugar. We then add a little salt to neutralise the bitterness borne out of overcooking the caramel, resulting in a harmonious balance of flavours, where no taste overpowers the other.

Crèmes

(Creams)

Crème d'amandes

(Almond cream)

Makes about 500 g (1 lb 2 oz)

note : To make pistachio cream, substitute 100 g (3¹/₂ oz) of the almond meal with pistachio meal and use kirsch instead of rum.

150 g (5¹/₂ oz) unsalted butter, soft but not melted

150 g (5¹/₂ oz) caster (superfine) sugar

1 egg

1 egg yolk

150 g (5¹/₂ oz) almond meal

25 g (1 oz) plain (all-purpose) flour

75 g (2³/₄ oz) Custard (opposite) (optional)

40 ml (1¹/₄ fl oz) rum

tip

Aerated batters, such as almond creams, will lose their creaminess and texture when they are refrigerated for more than a few hours. If you're not using them straight away, bring back to room temperature, then whisk in the bowl of an electric mixer fitted with the paddle attachment until smooth.

~ Using an electric mixer fitted with a paddle attachment, beat the butter and sugar on medium speed, scraping down the side of the bowl with a spatula, until creamy and smooth.

~ Reduce the speed to low, then add the egg and egg yolks one at a time, making sure each addition is fully absorbed before adding the next.

~ Add the almond meal and flour and beat until just combined, then increase the speed to medium and beat until light and fluffy. Add the custard, if using, and rum and beat until smooth and well combined. Transfer to a bowl, cover the surface with a piece of plastic wrap to prevent a skin forming, then refrigerate for up to 7 days.

Crème pâtissière

(Custard)

Makes about 700 g (1 lb 9 oz)

500 ml (17 fl oz) full-cream milk

1 vanilla bean, halved lengthways, seeds scraped

25 g (1 oz) plain (all-purpose) flour

35 g (1¼ oz) maize cornflour (cornstarch)

100 g (3½ oz) caster (superfine) sugar

1 egg

1 egg yolk

50 g (1¾ oz) unsalted butter, at room temperature

~ Bring the milk, vanilla bean and seeds to the boil in a saucepan over medium heat.

~ Meanwhile, put the flour, cornflour and sugar in a heatproof bowl and combine well. Add the egg and egg yolk and, using a hand-held whisk, beat until well combined and creamy.

~ When the milk reaches boiling point, remove the vanilla beans. Whisking continuously, gradually add half of the milk to the sugar and egg mixture and combine well, then transfer to the pan with the remaining milk. Whisk continuously over medium heat until the custard comes to the boil, then continue whisking for another 2 minutes.

~ Remove from the heat and transfer the custard to the bowl of an electric mixer fitted with a paddle attachment. Add the butter and beat on low speed for 10 minutes, or until warm to the touch. Transfer to a bowl, cover the surface with a piece of plastic wrap to prevent a skin forming, then refrigerate for up to 2 days.

~ Before using, lightly whisk in the bowl of an electric mixer fitted with a paddle attachment until smooth.

Glossary

abaisse A laminated or flattened block of pastry.

ameliorated A term describing the addition of ingredients to a base dough to improve its texture or flavour. Examples of ameliorated bread doughs are brioches and fougasses.

autolyse Also known as the 'delayed salt method', this is a bread-making technique where the flour and water are mixed together prior to introducing the yeast and salt. The dough is then left to rest, improving water absorption and subsequent gluten development. Autolysing ultimately reduces the kneading time and improves the texture of the dough. Salt inhibits this process, so is added afterwards.

bain-marie Used to slowly and gently warm, melt or cook ingredients in a vessel suspended over a saucepan of hot or warm water; a double boiler; a water bath.

balling After the first prove, the dough needs to be balled, a process designed to stretch the gluten and increase elasticity so the dough retains its shape during the proving stage.

beurre noisette Butter cooked until the water has evaporated and the fat has gone through the Maillard reaction (non-enzymatic browning). This process adds the subtle flavour of hazelnuts (*noisettes*) to your butter. Most commonly called 'brown butter' in English.

blanch (*blanchir*) Literally translated as 'whitening', this refers to a process where food is briefly cooked in boiling water to deactivate the enzymes that cause oxidation (enzymatic browning). The food is then plunged into iced or cold water to stop the cooking process.

caramelisation A non-enzymatic browning process that occurs when sucrose (sugar) is exposed to extreme heat.

colloid A substance made of microscopic particles that are suspended in a liquid (or solid), altering its texture.

corps Means 'body'; refers to the elasticity of a dough. The more *corps* a dough has, the tougher it will be to roll out or shape.

deglaze To add a liquid to remove the cooked browned bits of residue from the bottom of a pan, or to a hot caramel or sauce to liquefy it.

demould To carefully remove a cake or tart from its mould or tin.

denaturation A process that causes proteins to lose their structure by applying an external stress such as heat, an acid (such as lemon juice) or alcohol.

détrempe The dough for puff or croissant pastry, prior to adding the butter for turning.

direct method One method of making bread, where the dough relies exclusively on the addition of yeast for fermentation.

egg wash A mixture of egg and salt (and sometimes milk or water) brushed over pastries prior to baking, to add colour and shine.

emulsion A process whereby two liquids – usually a fat and water – are bound together to create a foam or cream, adding texture and reducing the perceived effect (the overall sensation) of the fat.

enzymatic browning *see* oxidation

feuilleté A general type of pastry, savoury or sweet, made with puff pastry.

fraiser/fraisage A method of using your fingertips and the heel of your hand to incorporate eggs and butter into flour, without kneading. This technique minimises the length of the strands of gluten and is used for shortcrust or any dough where elasticity is undesirable.

ganache An emulsified cream made with chocolate and a liquid. Although the most common ganaches are made using cream (18–35% fat), ganaches can also be made using fruit juices, purées and even water.

knocking down Using the palm of your hands or your fist to push down (deflate) a yeasted dough, following the first prove, to remove the carbon dioxide (gas) that has formed.

laminating The incremental thinning or flattening of a dough with a rolling pin or dough breaker (used commercially to roll out large quantities of dough).

levain A mixture of flour and a liquid left to ferment over time. Levain, the 'starter', is the building block of any sourdough and the only leavening (rising) agent used during the proving process.

lining The process of applying a thin layer of dough to a cake tin or tart tin.

long dough A dough, such as that used for *viennoiserie* or breads, where the strands of gluten have been lengthened during the mixing or kneading process, which increases the elasticity of the dough necessary to trap the gases released during the proving and baking stage, a process essential to the development of any yeasted dough.

Maillard reaction A non-enzymatic browning process that occurs between amino acids and reducing sugars when exposed to heat, producing a desirable flavour and colour. Examples of Maillard reaction browning are bread crusts, seared meat or fish and roasted coffee beans.

masse/masser A process by which sucrose crystallises within a syrup.

non-enzymatic browning *see* Maillard reaction; caramelisation

oxidation A biochemical process whereby enzymes brown when exposed to oxygen; also called enzymatic browning.

pasteurisation A process, particularly applied to milks and creams, where ingredients are heated from 72°C–88°C (162°F–190°F) — depending on the fat content and use of the product — to kill harmful germs, and then cooled rapidly to 4°C (39°F).

pâtisserie A type of sweet concoction and the shop that sells them.

pâtissier/pâtissière A professional baker (male/female).

pâton A block of dough that has been folded around the block of butter.

pectin A substance (see colloid) primarily used as a gelling agent and preservative in jams that occurs naturally in many fruits (especially in the skin and seeds).

pointage The first stage of proving of any yeasted dough.

poolish A pre-ferment, or 'starter', made of equal parts water and flour with the addition of a small amount of yeast. Breads and fougasses made with poolish will have a strong flavour due to the build-up of lactic acid in the poolish, and will also have a buttery, light crumb and a crisp crust.

proving The development of a dough under the action of yeast, poolish or levain; the process of allowing the bread dough to rise.

roux A thickening agent, used often in sauces, made by cooking together flour and a fat (usually butter).

sablage To mix butter and flour together before adding the liquids in the preparation of certain types of shortcrust pastry.

short dough A dough, such as *pâte sablée* and most shortcrust pastry, where the strands of gluten are not lengthened during the mixing process. Short doughs are crumbly and can be difficult to handle.

viennoiserie A type of leavened pastry. Examples of *viennoiseries* are croissants, brioche and roulades.

French recipe list

Page numbers in *italics* refer to photographs.

Index

Page numbers in *italics* refer to photographs.

Acknowledgments

~ My most humble thank you to my first chef, Robert Schicchi, for not only teaching me the skills but, more importantly, for opening my eyes to an almost never-ending world of learning and discovery.

~ My absolute thanks to Julia Taylor for your help during those long nights of baking, and for your unwavering support.

~ Maximum respect and thanks to my great team of pastry chefs at La Renaissance Pâtisserie and Baroque Bistro, past and present, you rock!

~ A very big thank you to the Charkos family for all your support.

~ Paris Cutler, thank you so much for making it all possible to begin with.

~ And, of course, all the amazingly patient, talented and supportive people at Murdoch Books: Diana Hill and Sue Hines for actually entrusting me with this book from the start ... *merci beaucoup.*

~ The team of editors: Barbara McClenahan, Kim Rowney and Christine Osmond — I literally have no idea how you put up with me and my convoluted manuscript, thank you.

~ Vivien Valk, what can I say, your design makes me look a lot better than I am ... the book is just beautiful.

~ Steve Brown, for your incredible pictures, strong coffees and fine tunes, and Jane Hann, who can, quite literally, make anything look stunning.

Published in 2015 by Murdoch Books, an imprint of Allen & Unwin

Murdoch Books Australia
83 Alexander Street
Crows Nest NSW 2065
Phone: +61 (0) 2 8425 0100
Fax: +61 (0) 2 9906 2218
murdochbooks.com.au
info@murdochbooks.com.au

Murdoch Books UK
Erico House, 6th Floor
93–99 Upper Richmond Road
Putney, London SW15 2TG
Phone: +44 (0) 20 8785 5995
murdochbooks.co.uk
info@murdochbooks.co.uk

For Corporate Orders & Custom Publishing contact
Noel Hammond, National Business Development Manager, Murdoch Books Australia

Publisher: Diana Hill
Editorial Manager: Barbara McClenahan
Designer: Vivien Valk
Project Editor: Kim Rowney
Photographer: Steve Brown
Stylist: Jane Hann
Food Editor: Christine Osmond
Production Manager: Mary Bjelobrk

A cataloguing-in-publication entry is available from the catalogue of the National Library
of Australia at nla.gov.au.

ISBN 978 1 74336 334 8 Australia
ISBN 978 1 74336 354 6 UK

A catalogue record for this book is available from the British Library.

Colour reproduction by Splitting Image Colour Studio Pty Ltd, Clayton, Victoria
Printed by 1010 Printing International Limited, China

IMPORTANT: Those who might be at risk from the effects of salmonella poisoning
(the elderly, pregnant women, young children and those suffering from immune deficiency
diseases) should consult their doctor with any concerns about eating raw eggs.

OVEN GUIDE: You may find cooking times vary depending on the oven you are using.
For fan-forced ovens, as a general rule, set the oven temperature to 20°C (35°F) lower than
indicated in the recipe.

MEASURES GUIDE: We have used 20 ml (4 teaspoon) tablespoon measures. If you are
using a 15 ml (3 teaspoon) tablespoon add an extra teaspoon of the ingredient for each
tablespoon specified.